Giving and Taking Voice in Learning Disabled Theatre

Giving and Taking Voice in Learning Disabled Theatre offers unique insight into the question of 'voice' in learning disabled theatre and what is gained and lost in making performance. It is grounded in the author's 18 years of making theatre with Different Light Theatre company in Christchurch, New Zealand, and includes contributions from the artists themselves.

This book draws on an extensive archive of performer interviews, recordings of rehearsal processes, and informal logs of travelling together and sharing experience. These accounts engage with the practical aesthetics of theatre-making as well as their much wider ethical and political implications, relevant to any collaborative process seeking to represent the under- or un-represented. *Giving and Taking Voice in Learning Disabled Theatre* asks how care and support can be tempered with artistic challenge and rigour and presents a case for how listening learning disabled artists to speech encourages attunement to indigenous knowledge and the cries of the planet in the current socio-ecological crisis.

This is a vital and valuable book for anyone interested in learning disabled theatre, either as a performer, director, dramaturg, critic, or spectator.

Tony McCaffrey is a Senior Lecturer at the National Academy of Singing and Dramatic Art, Ara Institute, Christchurch, New Zealand. He has been Artistic Director of Different Light Theatre since 2004 and is the Co-convenor of the Performance and Disability Working Group of the International Federation for Theatre Research.

Giving and Taking Voice in Learning Disabled Theatre

Tony McCaffrey

Routledge
Taylor & Francis Group
LONDON AND NEW YORK

Designed cover image: Paul McCaffrey for Different Light Theatre.
Different Light performer Josie Noble.

First published 2023
by Routledge
4 Park Square, Milton Park, Abingdon, Oxon OX14 4RN

and by Routledge
605 Third Avenue, New York, NY 10158

Routledge is an imprint of the Taylor & Francis Group, an informa business

© 2023 Tony McCaffrey

The right of Tony McCaffrey to be identified as author of this work has been asserted in accordance with sections 77 and 78 of the Copyright, Designs and Patents Act 1988.

All rights reserved. No part of this book may be reprinted or reproduced or utilised in any form or by any electronic, mechanical, or other means, now known or hereafter invented, including photocopying and recording, or in any information storage or retrieval system, without permission in writing from the publishers.

Trademark notice: Product or corporate names may be trademarks or registered trademarks, and are used only for identification and explanation without intent to infringe.

British Library Cataloguing-in-Publication Data
A catalogue record for this book is available from the British Library

Library of Congress Cataloging-in-Publication Data
Names: McCaffrey, Tony, author.
Title: Giving and taking voice in learning disabled theatre / Tony McCaffrey.
Description: Abingdon, Oxon ; New York : Routledge, 2023. | Includes bibliographical references and index.
Identifiers: LCCN 2022049562 (print) | LCCN 2022049563 (ebook) | ISBN 9780367539009 (hardback) | ISBN 9780367538972 (paperback) | ISBN 9781003083658 (ebook)
Subjects: LCSH: Actors with disabilities. | People with mental disabilities in the theater. | People with disabilities and the performing arts.
Classification: LCC PN1590.H36 M325 2019 (print) | LCC PN1590.H36 (ebook) | DDC 792.02/8087--dc23
LC record available at https://lccn.loc.gov/2022049562
LC ebook record available at https://lccn.loc.gov/2022049563

ISBN: 9780367539009 (hbk)
ISBN: 9780367538972 (pbk)
ISBN: 9781003083658 (ebk)

DOI: 10.4324/9781003083658

Typeset in Sabon LT Std
by KnowledgeWorks Global Ltd.

This book is dedicated to all the performers
and supporters of Different Light Theatre.

Contents

Acknowledgements   viii

Introduction: Giving and Taking Voice   1

1   Setting the Scene: *The Shadow Whose Prey the Hunter Becomes*   42

2   Community Theatre and Myths of Community   51

3   Dramatic Theatre and the Temporality of Learning Disabled Theatre   84

4   Intertextuality and Intermediality: Performing Responses to the Disabling of the City   114

5   Learning Disabled Performance Research: Ecologies, Histories, Philosophies   152

6   From the Theatre to the After Party   179

Appendix: Chronology of Different Light Theatre Performances, Presentations, and Participants   193
Index   197

Acknowledgements

I wish to thank Kelsie Acton, ADSA, Margaret Ames, Cloé Anngow, Andrés Aparicio, Simon Atkinson, Awakenings Festival, Meli Bach, Back to Back Theatre, Alan Barnes, Adam Benjamin, Sara Brodie, Damian Bumman, Glen Burrows, Dave Calvert, Marla Carlson, Marvin Carlson, Danielle Carter, Verity Carter, Merrin Cavell, Felipe Cervera, Beth Cherne, Kyle Chuen, Colette Conroy, Stuart Craig, Creative New Zealand, Christiane Czymoch, Andrew Dever, Angelia Douglas, Janette Dovey, Ben Ellenbroek, Peter Falkenberg, Rebecca Flint, Terry Fogarty, Free Theatre, Christchurch, Katrine Gabb, Kim TePairi Garrett, Janet Gibson, Bruce Gladwin, Vibeke Glørstad, Richard Gough, Sara Granath, Amiria Grenell, Inez Grim, Julia Guthrey, Sarah H., Bree Hadley, Steph Hines, Theodore Hoffman, Nick Hollamby, Hohepa Canterbury, Hemi Hoskins, International Federation for Theatre Research Working Group on Disability and Performance, Tatiana Josz, Amber Kennedy, Theresa King, Esa Kirkkopelto, Petra Kuppers, Roslen Langton, John Lambie, Demarnia Lloyd, Stuart Lloyd-Harris, Kate Maguire-Rosier, Alison Mahoney, Nanaia Mahuta, Neil Marcus, Claire Margerison, Sofie Martinsdotter, Yayoi Mashimo, Mojo Mathers, Marian McCurdy, Drew McLean, Ben Morris, Missy Morton, Rachel Mullins, NASDA, Ara Institute, Alice Nash, Josie Noble, David O'Donnell, Shawn O'Rourke, Andrew Oswin, George Parker, Louise Payne, Per. Arts, Performance Philosophy, Performance Studies international, Ben Piggott, Yoni Prior, Caroline Quick, Paul Rae, Peter Rees, Nicholas Ridout, Salamanda Tandem, Yvonne Schmidt, Theron Schmidt, Michael Shone, Elizabeth Sinclair, Tony Smith, Andrew Snell, Michael Stanley, Biddy Steffens, Matthew Swaffield, Isaac Tait, Theater HORA, Catriona Toop, Trisha Ventom, Mick Wallis, Natalie Walton, Jessica Watkin, Benjamin Wihstutz, Moira Williams, Emma Willis, Carrington Wilson. Special thanks to Marie, Mary, and Paul, and to Greta Bond, for her intelligence, consideration, and generosity.

Introduction: Giving and Taking Voice

The learning disabled artists are present

In contemporary theatrical performance, learning disabled people are increasingly present *as artists*. They are no longer the voiceless to whom voice must be given, neither are they required merely to be the 'authentic' voice of learning disabled experience. This presence is, however, still subject to negotiation between non-disabled and disabled participants and is dependent upon networks of support, care, and collaboration. It is also caught up in the complexities, ironies, and ambivalence that the role of the artist implies. Learning disabled artists are finding and raising their voices in theatre and performance, but questions remain that will be considered throughout this book. How are learning disabled artists invited into, or included, in theatre? How are they given voice, how do they give voice, and to what do they give voice? What might be gained in understanding theatre, ability, and disability by attending to the emergence of these voices?

This book focuses on *voice*, a very loose term that is capable of various interpretations. I have chosen it for its very imprecision and fluidity. The ubiquity, inadequacy, and instability of the term align with the complexity of the shifting and slippery ideas of presence, identity, selfhood, autonomy, and power that are in play in an analysis of learning disabled theatre. Voice and presence have meanings that are specific to theatre training and performance, but these are inextricably linked to representation in its political meaning. Any consideration of voice in learning disabled theatre involves far-reaching questions of agency, identity, representation, presence, self-expression, personhood, and selfhood. My experience is that there is a complex interrelationship between disabled and non-disabled participants in the making and reception of such theatre. Considering this interrelationship can teach us much about the possibilities of co-creation, collaboration, and mutual care. There is currently an urgent need to understand and develop practices of interdependence in the face of ever-increasing social inequities and injustices and the related cries of the planet: what Moten and Harney in *All Incomplete* call 'The Socioecological Disaster' (45).

DOI: 10.4324/9781003083658-1

Introduction

This book emerges from 18 years of messy, error-laden, but the vivid experience of making theatre with Different Light Theatre, an ensemble of learning disabled artists, in Christchurch, New Zealand. It is written, for the most part, in my voice. I need, therefore, to give an account of my 'positionality'. This is an awkward account by an unreliable narrator. It is an unreliable analysis by a para-academic, a theatre practitioner, and practitioner-researcher. I cannot hope to offer a 'definitive' account of work in which I have been so heavily involved. This work, moreover, has been done with learning disabled co-researchers, whom I count as friends, and with whom I have undergone shared experiences that extend into our personal lives and are far beyond the conventional meanings of research. Work in theatre with learning disabled artists has an undeniable affective dimension. Any analysis of this work needs to consider affect, empathy, sympathy, support, and care. In short, it needs to consider love. This is a four-letter word that sits uncomfortably in an academic context. It needs to be acknowledged in any account of making learning disabled theatre. There exists a core tension in such work between care and rigour: the care needed to support and accommodate learning disabled artists, and the rigour of artistic challenge. Writing of rigour in dance practice, Sarah Whatley offers the following:

> The principle of rigour relates to the depth of investigation and creative enquiry which develops through immersion in a practice and is evident in how dance works take shape but which resists hierarchies of knowledge and techniques in dance …. Rigour is ensured through the mechanism of critical judgment applied in the creative process.
> (Whatley et al 3728)

I continue to think about this tension in relation to learning disabled theatre. My experience of making theatre with learning disabled artists aligns with the resistance to hierarchies of knowledge and technique, but questions remain over who applies the mechanism of critical judgment. Rigour needs to be applied carefully in learning disabled theatre. In the Oxford English Dictionary, the first few definitions of the word have negative connotations: rigidity, harsh inflexibility, hardness of heart, hostility, hardship, but then there is the following: 'austere quality, state, or condition; duties, observances, etc., of an austere or exacting character'. This reminds me of the famous closing lines of *Those Winter Sundays* by Robert Hayden:

> What did I know, what did I know of love's austere and lonely offices?

Hayden refers to the silent love of his hard-working but uncommunicative father who gets up every cold winter Sunday morning to light the fires in the house and to polish his son's shoes for church: love in action, love as action, as difficult, demanding, and repeated action.

Care and rigour in the offices and duties of disability theatre means to be rigorous about care, to be exacting, to acknowledge and act on principles of access and inclusion. These offices of care also require rigour and commitment over time and a constant and reiterative awareness of the need for adjustment in attending to, or attuning to, the needs and rights of others.

In this account, the presence and voice of the learning disabled artists with whom I have worked are far too often filtered through my perceptions and judgments. Whilst the prevalence of my voice is part of the problem, it can also, I hope, make a minor contribution towards finding different ways of giving voice to collaborative practice and research that engages people subjected to 'epistemic injustice' (Fricker). It is my firm belief that the voices of learning disabled artists in theatre only emerge in a polyvocal mix, in an account of the imprecise and messy assemblage of living and working together. My intention is to offer an account that, whilst incomplete and partial, stands as one turn amongst others in a continuing conversation on learning disabled arts.

By offering an account of work in which I have been extensively involved I am trying to 'show my hand'. This is an attempt to show the process in which I have been substantially engaged. It will also reveal underlying bias, privilege, and structures of power, the times when my involvement as director and creative enabler has been heavy-handed. I draw at times on Geertz's 'thick description' (1973) as a methodology to try to stay close to the performers about whom I am writing. Proximity, of course, does not equal understanding. I am also aware that I am in danger of creating even more stories at the expense of the lived experience of disadvantaged access to social inclusion that is far too often a lot of learning disabled artists. Part of the purpose of this book, though, is to question the reductive approach to understanding learning disabled theatre as offering an unmediated or unproblematic access to 'learning disabled experience', whatever that might be. In my experience, the really interesting, subversive, and challenging features of learning disabled theatre emerge in the encounter between learning disabled artists and various assumptions about, or expectations of 'theatre'. This includes questioning theatre as a transparent or unambiguous instrument for the mediation of experience. It also includes deconstructing the epistemic injustice in the disciplinary formations and hierarchies of theatre and representation. This awkward encounter between learning disabled artists and 'theatre' often results in a kind of collapse that itself becomes, paradoxically and interestingly, theatrical. Theatre is created out of learning disabled artists' 'issues with theatre' in Bruce Gladwin's useful phrase (2010). The focus of this book will be on learning disabled theatre that has 'issues with theatre', that challenges rather than accepts the aesthetic, social, and economic conventions and hierarchies of producing theatre. I will draw heavily on my 18 years of work with Different Light Theatre but seek to connect this with the experimentation, performance research, and commercial success of other learning disabled companies. I will make particular connections with the work of Geelong's Back to Back Theatre, Zurich's Theater HORA, and Per.Arts from Novi Sad as these are the companies with whose work I and my learning disabled co-researchers are most familiar and with whom we feel a kinship. This is a highly selective choice as learning disabled theatre is becoming increasingly rich, diverse, and sophisticated in many parts of the globe.

Listening different voices to speech

The emergence of voice in learning disabled theatre resonates with an emphasis in contemporary theory and politics that might be termed a turn to *listening* that includes Ratcliffe (2005), Couldry (2010), and Lacey (2013); Dobson (2014), Stauffer (2015), and Bassel (2017).

This turn has been taken up in performance and theatre studies by, amongst others, Kochar-Lindgren (2006), Home-Cook (2015), Eckersall, Grehan, and Scheer (2017), Kendrick (2017), Voegelin (2018), and Bennett (2019). Within this turn to listening I am drawing specifically on the work of Lisbeth Lipari and how it might be applied to learning disabled theatre, in particular, her notion of 'listening others to speech' an arresting phrase taken from her essay 'Ethics, Kairos, and Akroasis' and one of the characteristics of which she defines as:

> … a listening others to speech that can reverse authoritative normative social arrangements that either silence others and refuse to listen. (95)

For the voices of learning disabled theatre to emerge it takes a great deal of time, attention, and attunement on the part of non-disabled allies, collaborators, or co-researchers. Lipari develops this formulation from Nelle Morton's feminist ethics; 'we empower one another by hearing the other to speech. We empower the disinherited, the outsider'(60). She categorizes this listening to speech as 'the empowerment of *kairos* as *akroasis*' (95), defining these terms as follows:

> *kairos*—most superficially understood as right timing or the opportune moment—and *akroasis*—translated as listening and invoking the idea of secret, esoteric teachings.

Kairos is a concept that is likewise utilized and reconfigured in Yergeau's consideration of autistic rhetoric (2017) and in Margaret Price's use of 'kairotic space' (2014). I find their reconfiguration of kairos useful in terms of how good or right timing is reconfigured in a kind of 'crip time'[1] in learning disabled theatre. Lipari's formulation of kairos as akroasis generates a way of thinking that enables the potential:

> to relinquish linear spatial and mechanical models of communicative interaction in favor of nonlinear, musical, and embodied models wherein temporality and communication ethics are enacted and perhaps even accomplished by speakers and listeners in concert. (–)

This reconfiguration of the relationship of what is active and passive in listening and speaking opens up the possibilities for interdependence in the processes of making learning disabled theatre. Rather than a model in which knowledge, skills, and techniques are transmitted from non-disabled creative enablers to disabled artists, this offers a more reflexive model in which participants co-create and in which non-disabled participants learn from learning disabled artists and listen others to speech. This equally has implications for the interrelationship between performers and audience in the performance event. The event becomes an expression of a mutual musical engagement (akroasis) that is not the linear model of the transmission of performance in which disabled performers perform *for* or *at* or *to* an audience assumed to be non-disabled. Such an event becomes more an experience of being together or *being-with* in the performance event, or of conviviality. I am indebted here to the work of Dave Calvert on conviviality in learning disabled theatre (2019) who draws on meanings of conviviality from Illich, Gilroy, and Puar and on Kittay on care and to the dialogues I have had with Calvert, Kate Maguire-Rosier, and Janet Gibson in constructing with members of Different Light Theatre 'Care Collaboration and Conviviality' a Key Group presentation at the Performance Philosophy Problems Conference at the University of the Arts, Helsinki in June 2022, referred to in Chapter 6.

Fugitivity and study

My experience of co-creating and learning from learning disabled artists, and how different voices emerge from this practice, resonates deeply with the writings of Fred Moten and Stefano Harney, in particular their concept of 'fugitivity'. In *The Undercommons* (2013) they refer to 'Fugitivity'... '(as) being separate from settling'(11) or escaping the 'call to order' (125). This book is quite simply an account of how my various attempts to *call to order* the learning disabled artists with whom I have worked have repeatedly met with the benevolent and generous fugitivity of their resistance to settling. This fugitivity, this creative and generative resistance, has driven us to keep trying to make theatre together and to find new and different ways of being together.

Moten's own writing in *Consent not to be a Single Being: Black and Blur* (2017), *Stolen Life* (2018), and *The Universal Machine* (2018) is composed of involved and beautiful cadences of sentences, the interweaving of citations and rhythms of thought that embodies the improvised variations and togetherness of a jazz ensemble. His thinking and writing is replete with ideas of anoriginality, attunement, apposition, and the play of performance and non-performance that speaks to my experience of co-creating learning disabled theatre. In this mixconventional hierarchies of knowledge are overturned. I am constantly challenged to check the fundamentals of what I regard as my 'understanding'. I am likewise checked in my assumptions of the temporalities of process, made aware of my tendency to rush to meaning, narrative, and clichéd notions of characterization, and of how much I am driven by an economically-based momentum of theatrical production as product or output. The learning disabled artists with whom I have worked are much more at ease in an ecological model of process, where time is taken and space is given to each and every one. At the same time, it needs to be acknowledged that without going through the push, the rush, and the momentum of producing a theatrical product we might not have come upon these interesting resistances and fugitivities.

This book is about voices. It is an attempt to celebrate, to critique, but, above all, *to listen to* the voices of learning disabled artists in contemporary theatre. I have so far spent 18 years in the study of learning disabled theatre. This has involved academic study and writing but, more importantly, the 'study' that is the making of theatre alongside learning disabled artists. This has become a 'study' of ways of being together, as Fred Moten defines the term in *The Undercommons*:

> ... It's talking and walking around with other people, working, dancing, suffering, some irreducible convergence of all three, held under the name of speculative practice. The notion of a rehearsal—being in a kind of workshop, playing in a band, in a jam session, or old men sitting on a porch, or people working together in a factory.... (110)

This is a very loose but useful definition of 'study' as it acknowledges that meaningful study takes place outside the confines of academic systems. It is particularly useful in my account of the work with Different Light. The company's methodology that has emerged over the years is one in which meaningful connections are made and ideas and texts generated not necessarily in the call to order of rehearsal and devising sessions but in the spillout times and places of cafe breaks and of travelling together. These are times and spaces that are 'in the break' from the call to order of theatre-making discipline. Trying to make theatre with artists who have 'issues with theatre' in terms of cognitive processing, rememoration, and physical and mental stamina is 'speculative' practice. Developing and reconfiguring methodologies of creation and performance that afford accessibility make the process even more speculative. In her latest book,

EcoSoma: Pain and Joy in Speculative Performance Encounters disabled artist and scholar Petra Kuppers indicates how disabled people's tracing of pathways in their encounter with an ableist world are so many speculative ventures. Methodologies of working alongside learning disabled artists need to be flexible, particularly with regard to orientation towards 'goals'. In this respect, here and elsewhere in this book, I am reminded of the work of Fernand Deligny in his speculative engagement with 'autistics' in the anti-concentration camp in the Cevennes in which he and other (anti) therapists lived alongside autistic young people, merely tracing the maps and lines of their movement around the camp, responding to the different qualities and patterns of movement and eschewing the need to direct the communal activities in terms of le projet pensé or the thought through project. It has taken me 18 years of such study or speculative practice alongside learning disabled artists to learn to stop and take the time to listen to them.

Polylogues: a diversity of voices

One strategy adopted in performance and theatre studies engaged with learning disabled theatre is to present a mix of voices that the voices of the learning disabled artists might emerge. *'We're People Who Do Shows': Back to Back Theatre: Performance, Politics, Visibility* (2013) edited by Helena Grehan and Peter Eckersall gives an account of the work and influence of this leading learning disabled theatre company by curating an assemblage of voices, a polylogue composed of academic criticism, interviews with the performers, archive documentation, and drafts of scripts in an attempt to let different voices speak with, alongside, and across each other. This strategy is taken in a very different direction in 'A proper actor? The politics of training for learning disabled actors' in which Emma Gee and Matt Hargrave (2011) take a polyvocal approach in a more radical direction by using a montage technique or 'collage of voices'(34) in which they offer 101 numbered contributions in which 'rather than a singular authorial voice the reader listens in on many voices'(35). In their strategy, these different voices are cited or identified only in footnotes in order to provide 'an uncanny reading experience, one which troubles notions of precision or accountability, originality or appropriation' (35). This is a bold choice that attempts both to stage and de-stabilize the act of reading and understand different voices in learning disabled theatre.

Different Light Theatre, an introduction

I will refer throughout this book to Different Light Theatre or Different Light, but the company was formed in 2004 as A Different Light: to align with the notion of viewing learning disabled people 'in a different light'. A charitable trust was formed in this name but over the years the indefinite article was dropped and at times the word 'theatre' as the activities of the company became more diverse and moved away from the designated buildings and practices of the theatre, if not necessarily from theatre's shadow. The company's first performance was with nine learning disabled performers but the loosely constituted 'company' has varied in number at different times between five and 20 learning disabled performers. There is no qualification or audition process for membership. Many members are people with Down's Syndrome, diagnoses of autism, cerebral palsy, some with visual or physical impairments, and some who have had experience of the psychiatric system. The non-disabled component of the company has likewise included a fluctuating number of people. I am the only person who has been present throughout the company's existence. The company has had a precarious relationship with money throughout its existence. Sometimes we have received funding and box office that has allowed us to remunerate participants, sometimes not. Major contributions and supports have been made by Kim TePairi Garrett as assistant director, Stuart Lloyd-Harris as creative designer of sound, video, and light, and Paul McCaffrey as photographer, designer, and co-deviser, several National Academy of Singing and Dramatic Art (NASDA) students listed in the Appendix, and a number of visiting artists and scholars mentioned in the rest of the book. An account of the changing methodologies of making and performing theatre, in particular the negotiation of the relationship of non-disabled and disabled participants, forms the substance of this book.

The minor voice and the an/archive

It is my intention to find different ways to include the voices and contributions of the learning disabled artists with whom I have worked. There are certain strategies that I have prioritized over others. I have hours of audio and video recordings upon which I will draw: radio and television interviews, devising workshops, rehearsals, discussions formal and informal, recordings of Zoom meetings and rehearsals, sketches for projects that never eventuated in performance, interviews undertaken by me and other non-disabled participants, interviews undertaken by the performers, and the equivalent of video diaries of touring, 'home movies' often filled with private jokes and references. I have records of text messages, Facebook Messenger communications, and other written texts submitted by the performers, at times in response to requests from me, at times unsolicited. These comprise the archive around the scripted public theatrical performances of the group. These consist of the traces of speech: conversations and interactions in rehearsal rooms, in cafes during the break from rehearsals, in the liminal spaces of travelling and touring nationally and internationally, in the hybridity of private and public spaces of the disabled performers' residences and accommodation on tour, and the online spaces prompted by the pandemic. They are the traces of the gestures, proxemics, and interactions of the group in collaboration and conviviality, the sharing of time, of laughter and difficulties, of a range of struggles and emotions. This archive is also an 'anarchive' in Erin Manning's term (2019, 75) – an anarchic anti-archive devised to ask fundamental questions of the giving of an account of processes of collaboration: 'How to reconcile the freshness ... of processes underway with the weight of experience captured? How to reconcile force and form?' (Ibid). The anarchive of Different Light is not just the context of the traces of speech, gesture, and action around the performances of the group. It consists of what is held in the singular and collective memories of Different Light, an entity that started out as a community theatre project and that has continued over 18 years as a multi-modal and shifting site of performance and performance research. Different Light has also become, quite simply, a way of being together. This includes being 'un-together' – at times allowing incoherence, inchoateness, and inconclusiveness to emerge as wayward and elusive forces that drive us on or drive us hither and thither. It also encompasses the bonds of love and care that when company members die, or move on, or in other ways disappear, reconfigure around and within us.

The processes of making, performing, and positioning such theatre are implicated with the politics of learning disability and disability itself, of communication and representation, of visibility and performance, of inclusion and identity, and of systems of power and the construction of the subject that intersect in particular ways with the politics of gender, of racial capital, and of posthumanism. An argument that this book is trying to make is that the emergent form of learning disabled theatre has the potential to go beyond inter-relationships based on an economy of giving and taking, to generate different ecological approaches to thinking, making, and being together.

The politics of communication

This book contains many voices of the people with whom I have worked, some of which are very different, and it takes time and effort to listen to them. In this my experience aligns precisely with that of Joshua Saint Pierre in 'Fluency Machines' (2018) in encountering:

> a vast range of "voices": from the non-linguistic voices of those severely cognitively disabled or autistic, to the dysfluent speech of stutterers and those with cleft palate, the vocal tics induced by Tourette's, or the opaque speech present in some forms of cerebral palsy. (13)

A voice with a speech impediment or stutter or using an assistive device requires the taking of time and care on the part of the listener. The process of listening to such voices becomes a kind of micro-political act in that it disrupts the expected free flow of free speech that contemporary capitalism demands, to cite Saint Pierre:

> ... crip voices that are unclear and produce uncomfortable aporia and silence, that stretch and break temporal norms and perceptible worlds point towards not simply an ethic but a politic. (77)

The giving and taking of voice is also political in that it subverts the neoliberal autonomy of the subject, as Eva Feder Kittay has articulated:

> liberalism invokes a notion of political participation in which one *makes* one's voice heard. It depends on a conception of the person as independent, rational, and capable of self-sufficiency. And it holds to a conception of society as an association of such independent equals. (258)

The 'disabled' voice is a spanner in the works of not only the legal and economic fiction of autonomous personhood but also of society as a collection of autonomous beings engaged in the free exchange of communication, testifying to Dolar's astute understatement that 'the voice and hearing are at the core of politics' (189). The radically different temporality of the 'crip time' (McRuer, 2018) required for interaction with disabled voices opens up other possibilities of interaction, makes time for interdependence and mutual consideration. This has profound and interesting implications not only for the temporal dimension of theatre and the relationship between performer and audience, but also for relationships that begin in theatre-making and go beyond the theatre.

My own lived experience of studying alongside learning disabled artists, tells me that 'voice' is not a clear, untroubled process of the transmission of some pre-linguistic lived experience into verbal or even theatrical expression. There is, however, an expectation of self-devised learning disabled theatre, as with other forms of theatre seeking to give voice to marginalized sectors of the population, that just 'giving voice' will somehow solve everything and include the excluded. This ignores epistemic injustice, the reality of exclusion from, or marginalized access to, language and symbolic systems of those who are expected to give voice to their experience. It also ignores the fact that experience is mediated through language and that a speaker's 'voice' is never entirely authentic. It is always already determined by language and may well be channeling the 'voices' of others. In the case of a marginalized speaker these may include the voices of authority or the voice of 'common sense' adopted as a coping strategy or way of passing as belonging to a community that excludes them. The marginalized speaker may be attempting to assimilate to the tone, register, or discourse of their interlocutor, particularly if that interlocutor appears to have more power or social capital than the speaker themselves.

Any discussion of 'voice' in learning disabled theatre needs to take account of the othering that takes place even in speaking one's mother tongue. Derrida refers to this in *Monolingualism of the Other*: 'I only have one language, yet it is not mine'(1). I intend to show in very specific ways how the voices of learning disabled artists speak as much *in spite of* the language in which they are framed as *through* it and the ways in which the 'minor voice' of such theatre emerges. This is a phrase I am adapting from Erin Manning's conception of the *Minor Gesture*:

> A minor key is always interlaced with major keys – the minor works the major from within. What must be remembered is this: neither the minor nor the major is fixed in advance. The major is a structural value that organizes itself according to predetermined definitions of value. The minor is a force that courses through it,

Her description is useful in giving an account of how the voices of learning disabled theatre have the potential to operate both within, and in resistance to, Western mimetic theatre and the social and economic hierarchies and relations it both embodies and represents.

Voice can mean something as all-encompassing as Giorgio Agamben's definition: 'The search for the voice in language, this is what is called thought' as cited by Mladen Dolar in *A Voice and Nothing More*, who interprets this to mean 'the search for what exceeds language and meaning' (11), in Lacanian terms the *objet petit a*, the unattainable object of desire. The weight and depth of the elusive concept of voice is also of central concern to Derrida from *Voice and Phenomenon* onwards, as he delineates voice as the privileged side of the binary in the relationship with writing, in terms of the metaphysics of presence that haunts so many social and symbolic systems and is exposed as différance in the process of deconstruction. In terms of learning disabled theatre, I would argue that some funders, practitioners, and spectators of learning disabled theatre continue to engage in the pursuit of the *objet petit a* of the authentic voice or presence of learning disability. In a similar way, the metaphysics of presence hangs over or haunts the practice and reception of this theatre in terms of the perception of learning disabled actors as *others* who are human only more so, or touched by God, in some of the charity or 'spiritual' models of learning disabled theatre. That this is not entirely my own fancy is perhaps borne out in the choice of title of Back to Back Theatre's *The Shadow Whose Prey The Hunter Becomes*. This title is not only taken from the writings of Lacan on the mirror-stage and the construction of the subject (Gladwin in Mordue 2019) but the piece itself is a kind of extended deconstruction of différance in voice, presence, selfhood, and identity devised and presented in a totally engaged and engaging performance by five learning disabled actors.

12 *Introduction*

In the investigation of the giving and taking of voice in learning disabled theatre that is the focus of this book I intend to show:

a   how non-disabled facilitators both *give* but also *take* the 'voices' of the artists in learning disabled theatre due to an inequity fundamental in the idea of 'giving' deconstructed by Derrida in his paradox of hospitality and hostility.
b   how learning disabled performers both give voice as expression of themselves *and* have voice taken in that (i) there is no original of voice or self that has not already been constructed by social and cultural formations; (ii) the 'self' cannot exist outside of a matrix of interdependence, and 'giving voice' cannot exist without an environment of listening.
c   how ideas such as liberating the 'authentic' voice of a marginalized group of people, or 'giving voice to the voiceless' is a kind of (neo)liberal chimera that posits 'voice' or representation as a marker of fixed, static identity when such concepts as self and identity are context-dependent, fluid, and fugitive.
d   how the imperative to conduct 'social sciences' type interviews or to demand an account of experience and subjectivity is itself fraught with oppressive dynamics of power manifest in interpellation, the kairotic time of the interview itself, and the tendency of the interviewee to assimilate to, appease, or please the interviewer.
e   how the disciplinary formations of theatre and performance are inflected with a kind of ableism at the level of the voice, the body, character/persona, object, light, sound, dramaturgy, scenography, space, and time.

The interview effect

To give a specific example of what has motivated this approach, I will refer to some video interviews undertaken with members of the company by Paul McCaffrey at a relatively early stage in the group's development. The performers were given the prompt to tell us why they liked drama and in doing so they could stay in front of the camera as much or as little as they liked. We as non-disabled members of Different Light were seeking to learn what the performers understood by performance and what they got from performance by asking them the question 'Why do you like drama?' The following is a selection of the responses received:

ANDREW OSWIN: I like drama because it involves doing role-plays, and making up stories, and I also like being involved in being with a group, doing teamwork, being very supportive. And I also like drama because I'm an actor and I really enjoy doing it because drama is my thing. It's my ability to get along with all people, to be a role model to all of the actors in drama, and to show what is expected of them, how to behave, and how to co-operate well in the public.

REBECCA FLINT: I can't do much with a camera on me!
PAUL MCCAFFREY: You can tell me why you like drama, though.
REBECCA FLINT: I like drama because it's different all the time and I like being with my friends and hanging out with them. (She looks to the side, makes some non-verbal sounds and walks away from the camera.)
DAMIAN BUMMAN: I was very close being in a production at primary school but I didn't get a part in it. One day I might become an actor and be the director. (long pause) And also, and also writing, you know, and stuff.
PETER REES: I have developed a passion for drama through my dad's side of the family. I've done drama through school when I was in Years 11, 12 and 13. And I'm still doing drama not at SkillWise but at CPIT[2] every Sunday morning. I can, I can use emotions in the performances. I can go from sadness into pathos, happiness into sadness and and it goes on and on and on And so I like doing drama here because I can really connect with my audience. Thank you. (Walks away)
MICHAEL STANLEY: I'll be doing drama on Sunday and also doing recording on my Flip HD and also we were doing exercises and also drama acting and also we have a break at the café.
ANDREW DEVER: The reason drama is fun is that I get to learn new things ehm see all the see all my friends they're all gorgeous and beautiful (Rebecca laughs) ehm and I'm just loving it. And in my experience with Tony I've done Irish dancing and and and sing some songs like 'O Danny Boy' and I also invented cry-singing.
MATTHEW PHELAN: One day I might be the second Chris Burke. Cos I used to like him on an old television series called *Life Goes On* hopefully some day one day I'd like to do it be on a television series just like him on a show just like him yeah and just live my life as an actor on stage.
THERESA KING: I loved it. Being here as drama. Like (she moves her body from side to side with her arms out) fitness and exercise. (She smiles broadly.)
JOSIE NOBLE: That's a hard question.
INTERVIEWER: It is a hard question. What's fun about it?
JOSIE NOBLE: The improv, the games ehm and getting to meet new friends. (Long pause. Looks to the interviewer.) And having a break.
INTERVIEWER: (Laughing) Is it time for a break now?
JOSIE NOBLE: (Looks at watch) Break time (She smiles.)
('Why I like drama': 2012)

It is possible to interpret these responses as the performers coming to terms with or accommodating a number of different determinants on their 'voices'. These would include:

a   The performance element of the interview itself as a determining factor: the fact that it takes place under the scrutiny of a video camera. The implicit expectations of the question that manifest an interview bias within which interviewees are likely to produce the answers that they think are expected in this context. Would it have been possible for the interviewees to have introduced what they didn't like? Rebecca Flint's response does make explicit reference to the limitations of the video interview format. Perhaps references to the 'break' are a way of signalling that there is more taking place than theatre-making. For some this process may have been a by-product of spending time with friends and making new friends

b   Many of the performers give answers that could easily be influenced by discourses they have experienced of justifying 'drama' as an activity that is worthy of support or funding. The performers refer to many of the supposedly key attributes of socially engaged community theatre: that it increases confidence and encourages personal development, collaboration, and sociality.

At the same time, the answers suggest that each performer does seem to get 'something' that is distinctive to them from the activity. The individual predilections and preferences of particular performers are apparent from their answers. The question of how the performers' 'voices' are constituted, influenced, and constructed from contextual and social determinants is complex. How the performers answer the question of what they like about drama is influenced by a number of factors. These include their own perceptions of the demands of the question in the context of the interview, their experience of what constitutes drama for them, and their desire to choose activities that will be approved by the communities and organizations to which they belong.

A note on transcription

The 'voices' of the learning disabled artists, as with anybody's voice, are not adequately translated by transcription, however much this takes account of stops and starts, pauses, mis-speaking and correction, tangents and ellipses. Transcription cannot be adequate for subtle changes in tone, non-verbal cues, shifting eye contact, and related or unrelated body movements or gesture. This non-verbal rhetoric or slippage between character, persona, and person or the various performances of the self is a particularly crucial element when considering learning disabled theatre but the perception of these features of communication are also of course determined by the eye of the beholder. Transcription takes, as in takes away, so many of the live and holistic elements of 'voice' as much as it gives it. In this book, it is one amongst other unreliable instruments of translation as the traducing or betrayal of the idealistic notion of 'original' or 'authentic' voice and thought.

Learning disabled theatre and the entitled self?

There is undoubtedly the potential for learning disabled performance to contribute towards a different sensorium, to adapt Rancière's term, a different 'distribution of the sensible' (2004), in the experience of theatre. Learning disabled theatre has the potential to challenge at ontological, phenomenological, and epistemological levels the normative conceptions of the self, the subject, and the state, in the sense of the political state of things and the status quo. This is what constitutes the political potential of learning disabled theatre in the current moment. In *All Incomplete* Moten and Harney offer the following provocation:

> Modernity's constitution in the trans-Atlantic slave trade, settler colonialism and capital's emergence in and with the self, the state and all the other apparatuses of sovereignty, is The Socioecological Disaster. (45)

For Moten and Harney, modernity, the Enlightenment, and the construction of the bourgeois subject, homo economicus, are built upon the Atlantic slave trade. Saidiya Hartman in *Scenes of Subjection* offers a related, extensive critique of 'the fashioning of the self-possessed individual'(4). The bourgeois 'self' of the Enlightenment in possession of themselves, as much as they are in possession of land and capital, and in possession of slaves, is the basis for the normative self upon which, and for which, knowledge is assumed. This is the progenitor of the neoliberal self, the entitled self of the current socio-ecological disaster. This is the entitled self we need to go beyond to have any hope of addressing the climate crisis, the pandemic, and the deep inequities of racism, ableism, and misogyny, and the host of other hatreds and exclusions needed to affirm the ego of this entitled self.

I seek to connect how Moten and Harney and Hartman's critique of this conception and practice of the self aligns with Erin Manning's critique in *For a Pragmatics of the Useless* and *The Minor Gesture* of the neurotypical subject and the 'volitional intentionality agency triad'(64) and with Joshua Saint Pierre's critique in 'Fluency Machines' of the fluent subject who produces transparent accountable communication, communication as information only, the self that data and algorithms both want and call into being – and 'the political possibilities of disabled voices to "de-face" the power of speech that has now become entwined with capital' (255).

I would also seek to connect these critiques with the turn in Theatre and Performance Studies exemplified by the online cross-disciplinary project *Performance, Possession, and Automation* involving Nicholas Ridout, Orlagh Woods, Joe Kelleher, Rebecca Schneider, Dhanveer Singh Brah, and others. This project poses questions of how performance critiques, or contributes to, capitalism's construction of the myth of self-possession, the legal fiction of the self, the construction of an ongoing accountable self and, if indeed the fantasy of a modern agential self is a fantasy of white supremacy. These critiques are part of much wider contemporary investigations into how the construction of the bourgeois subject at the time of the Enlightenment was built economically and epistemologically upon the erasure of personhood and commodification of black bodies as objects in the Atlantic slave trade. Possession is at the crux of both sides of the colonialist, racial capitalist coin: in the construction of the self-possessed citizen and their entitlement to possess land, objects, and enslaved people on the one hand, and, on the other, in the dispossession of enslaved people and the phenomenon of their resistance through states of the body possessed by the Other. This constellation of meanings of action and acting around possession and automation (derived from the plantation as the prototype of the factory) then continue to haunt the acting subject in contemporary theatre and performance. This haunting plays out in particularly complex and interesting ways in the case of learning disabled theatre.

Learning disabled people have been and continue to be routinely denied access to selfhood in juridical, educational, medical, and social contexts. The 'self-possession' or autonomy that Moten and others critique is for many learning disabled people something of which they can only dream. This is a desire for self-determination that is so often denied to them. The question is, though, is the only option of inclusion for learning disabled people the acquisition of the entitled self of a neoliberal late capitalist economy? Saint Pierre articulates the crux of this problem:

> Communication has been thoroughly co-opted by capital. How might disabled speakers reclaim agency under these conditions? (91)

Manning offers a set of questions that challenge any attempt to view learning disabled theatre as offering a critique of neoliberal self-possession when many learning disabled people would welcome any form of inclusion in social life, whether on neoliberal terms or not:

> How to problematize identity while remaining sensitive to the fact that for some the loss of a sense of stable identity may feel like the very same gesture as the colonial act of exclusion from the category of the human? How not to engage in re-disenfranchising those very bodies that have historically been denied subjectivity? How to create an affirmative politics of a production of subjectivity ...? (51)

For many learning disabled people inclusion in terms of economic self-sufficiency and meaningful employment is still an unachievable dream. Learning disabled theatre is the performance and form of expression of a dispossessed, discounted minority. Is it possible for learning disabled theatre to find a way to challenge the dominant concept and practice of self-possession? Is it possible for learning disabled theatre to raise its own voice and state its own presence without succumbing to the dominant, neurotypical, supremacist forms of selfhood, self-possession, and entitlement? How can the subaltern voice of learning disabled people speak?

In learning disabled theatre, presence and voice are doubly ambiguous. Firstly, this presence and voice takes place in an actual and conceptual space, the theatre, that bespeaks uncertainty, and that for thousands of years has invited, simultaneously, both belief and disbelief. Secondly, learning disabled performers offer challenges to dominant concepts of selfhood that underpin conventional meanings of political and artistic representation.

Learning disabled theatre: the critical context

Matt Hargrave in one of the first full-length studies of this area of performance, *Theatres of Learning Disability*, expresses this as a challenge to 'a cherished ideal of Western liberal ideology: that of the individual rhetor producing speech acts, which in turn confirm the existence of a fixed core self' He goes on to say that the 'presence' or 'voice' conventionally associated with the personhood of the actor is configured as 'the product of a deeply inter-subjective collaborative process' (135–6).

Much critical discussion and analysis has been generated around *Disabled Theater*, the collaboration between the anti-choreographer Jerome Bel and the Zurich-based company Theater HORA that toured internationally in 2013. In the course of the highly atomized and simplified dramaturgy and choreography of *Disabled Theater,* at one point each of the performers responds to one of Bel's six directorial demands to give their profession by speaking into a microphone on a stand on a bare stage and stating: 'and I am an actor'. Much critical discourse has been generated about this simple affirmative statement, including in Umathum and Wihstutz's 2015 book, *Disabled Theater*. It has been interpreted variously as a) an affirmation of emancipation, b) a statement of pride, c) a performative utterance, d) a statement designed to shock the assumptions of a non-disabled audience that learning disabled people might be employed as actors, e) a response shaded with criticism of Bel's project and direction that required trained actors to present themselves as objects of scrutiny with no sense of objective, to choreograph themselves in dances when they were actors[3] and not choreographers and dancers.

It must of course also be acknowledged that theatrical performance does not operate only at the hermeneutic level, there is a powerful affective charge associated with a learning disabled performer occupying the stage (still an uncommon sight) and speaking their right to be there. The meaning or effect of the presence of learning disabled actors on stage is to a large extent created in the reception of their presence by an audience. That reception is likely to be different for those in the audience unfamiliar or familiar with learning disabled people in the public sphere or onstage, whether the audience member has auditory or visual impairments, or whether that audience member has been diagnosed with a learning disability. Does the very presence of the learning disabled actor onstage open up more of a mutual awareness of disability within the audience? Does the artistry or the resistant presence of the learning disabled artist encourage a radical reassessment of what constitutes learning disability and artistry?

In 'Towards a new directional turn?: Directors with cognitive disabilities' Yvonne Schmidt, who has been an embedded researcher with Theater HORA for many years, focuses on HORA's more recent research into facilitating the authorship, autonomy, and creativity of learning disabled artists. This included an investigation into the power dynamics of the relationship between non-disabled and disabled participants. She reveals how HORA's intention of handing over power from non-disabled to disabled participants was complicated by the need for various forms of *support* for learning disabled performers. In conventional dramatic theatre support for actors is expected to be hidden labour. This expectation of concealment is amplified in learning disabled theatre, especially given the questioning of the actors' agency and autonomy that still seems to accompany such performance. As an example of the issues at stake in the question of support, does an audience feel cheated if the script is placed somewhere in the performance space or the learning disabled actors are assisted by loop microphones of text or music played into their ears to guide the narrative? Schmidt responds to this concern by citing Kittay's perspective on the necessity of care and support for disabled people: '[t]he need for care, or as many would rather say "assistance," is viewed not as a sign of dependence but as a sort of prosthesis that permits one to be independent' (2011, 50)

Drawing on the earlier work of Graeae Theatre and Michael Achtman's characterization of the role of 'creative enabler' as a kind of support worker helping to facilitate the artistic expression of disabled artists, Schmidt comes up with what she terms a 'spectrum of collaboration' in empowering learning disabled artists. Her categories include Organizer/Framer/Coach/Artistic Collaborator/Filter (450). Each role, or at times combination of roles, negotiates in different ways the complex relationship between non-disabled and learning disabled participants. A paradox revealed by HORA's research is that adopting those roles that seem to offer the greatest emancipation often creates their own constraints for the performers, and adopting those roles that seem to constrain the development of the performers often leads to more creative outcomes.

When Schmidt applies this spectrum to an actual account of the work and processes of Theater HORA on the 'multi-step experiment' of *Freie Republik HORA* the complexity of the division of labour and power became increasingly apparent. She gives an honest account of how non-disabled facilitators who are seeking 'merely' to frame the work of learning disabled artists end up having an inordinate influence over the subsequent development of the project. She relates how at a certain stage in the project a learning disabled artist wished to focus on sexuality and violence in their individually focussed experimentation. At that point the non-disabled facilitators felt forced to step in to avoid the possibility of danger or harm to the participants, although on reflection their actions subsequently gave them pause: 'Is the prohibition of violence on stage an intervention, or is it a normative projection of a non-disabled director?' (454)

Her account also highlights a crucial tension between the notion of 'crip time' and the teleological time of a rehearsal process that leads to a performance. Schmidt draws on Matzke's division of the rehearsal process into two phases: the 'open investigation' and the 'target-oriented work, which is focused on the premiere' (2010, 165). As Schmidt articulates this division: 'The first one is 'research driven' and characterized by breaks, cracks, and interruptions. The second is linear and aimed at the premiere'(455). In the context of learning disabled performance, crip time might refer both to different *durations* needed by disabled artists to explore or accomplish tasks and to a different sense of *kairos* or the 'good timing', rhetorically apposite timing within a performance.

In 'Convivial theatre: care and debility in collaborations between non-disabled and learning disabled theatre makers', Dave Calvert pays attention to specific moments in *Contained* by Mind the Gap Theatre and Theater HORA's *Disabled Theater* to reveal how the participation of learning disabled artists allows different meanings of care to emerge, and what implications this has for being and making together. Calvert draws attention to some specific moments in *Contained* that centre around the presence of Charli Ward, the non-disabled academy director of the company who is acting as a kind of onstage support for some of the learning disabled actors. On the surface, this feels like the kind of presence that might go some way to invalidating the participation of the learning disabled performers as 'proper actors'. One of the fundamental principles of Western mimetic theatre is that the audience does not see the hidden labour of line learning and rehearsal, backstage support crew, and the relationship between director and performers. Ward's presence in *Contained* flouts this principle. She participates with the other learning disabled actors in movement routines and onstage manipulation of technology. She is there when each performer tells stories specific to them. She prompts one of the performers 'whose impairment prevents him from fixing the story sequentially' with questions 'to guide his narrative and negotiate a route through to the completed story'. She is 'visibly alert' when another performer who struggles with memory difficulties is telling their story. In terms of the expectations of conventional mimetic theatre, this might seem like cheating, to those concerned with the development of learning disabled theatre from its origins in institutional settings and a 'charitable' model of community performance this might seem like a backward step. Calvert in his analysis goes into some depth and detail to observe the 'kindly and encouraging' presence of

Ward and her ability to improvise strategies to gently guide the performers along the paths of their narratives. Calvert characterizes the interactions of Ward and the performers as combining personal care: 'Ward's epistemic responsibility at an intimate level, understanding the individual nuances and dependencies of these particular performers,' and professional care in her attention to 'the well being of the actors and the maintenance of the performance'. What is crucial in Calvert's analysis of the dynamics of care and conviviality in *Contained* is that this attention is reciprocated later in the performance when the learning disabled actors become 'caregivers rather than dependents'. Ward is given the opportunity to tell a story of her own and gives an account of a recent painful relationship breakup: 'Ward could not contain the rawness of her own emotion, often breaking down as she tried to complete the story. Invariably the performers around her responded with care' (96), offering care to their usual caregiver. The nature and manner of the care varied from night to night during the season, in response to the words and the emotions of Ward's account. She herself has recorded how the responses did not feel like the actors were performing but allowing themselves to respond to her emotional account in a kind of deep and caring engagement.

The emergence of these moments of care and mutual dependence then affords Calvert the opportunity to re-read some specific aspects of *Disabled Theater* in which the learning disabled performers open up similar dynamics of care and 'traces of conviviality' in the face of the deliberately atomized and formal dramaturgy established by Jerome Bel's choreography and direction. Calvert details the occurrence of an accident that occurred in Julia Hausermann's performance of the dance she herself choreographed to Michael Jackson's 'They Don't Care About Us' in which she banged her head on the stage. In the performance season, the translator Simone Truong normally sat at the side of the stage as a kind of director-surrogate giving the instructions and asking the questions that were Bel's original directorial input and that then became the framing of the performance and translating the Swiss German of the performers. When Hausermann had an accident, Truong rushed onstage to comfort her and organize an icepack. In subsequent performances, at the end of her individual dance sequence, Hausermann would conclude by saying 'Merci Simone' to Truong who would then smile and nod her appreciation. Calvert analyzes how this breakdown in the performance conventions imposed by Bel – to investigate how theatre and performance itself is 'disabled' – takes the performance somewhere else, disabling conventions to allow mutual care to emerge: 'shattering the demarcation of individual roles set up by the task structure to acknowledge the relationship between the performers'. He connects these moments of mutual care with another moment in the production where the performers are asked to give their opinion of the Bel-directed performance and two of the performers Gianni Blumer and Matthias Brücker 'present negative criticisms of the show, but choose to soften their critiques'

(99). He cites Blumer's words in performance: 'I didn't dare to complain to Jérôme Bel. Because actually he is very nice'. Much of the criticism of *Disabled Theater* has centred around how Bel's formal structure that of an 'anti-choreographic' dance performance, a post-modern social experiment in how theatre disables performers, audience, and itself, and disavows the agency and autonomy of the learning disabled performers. Calvert brings to this critique an interesting perspective: the perspective of a different form of participation by the learning disabled actors: 'the aesthetics of *Disabled Theater* may be ... shaped as much by the performers responding to the perceived needs of the other (Truong, Bel, other performers) as by the pursuit of a conceptual discourse' (100). This is an observation that I feel is grounded in the depth of Calvert's years of experience working with learning disabled artists in Mind the Gap and Dark Horse Theatre Companies. It opens up an extremely significant and interesting perspective: how the presence of learning disabled artists emerges *in spite of* as well as *through* the conventions of performance with which they have been presented by non-disabled directors, choreographers, and facilitators. If we assume a very mechanistic and reductive exchange in which non-disabled facilitators give theatre and performance as they know it to learning disabled artists, what we do not know yet, and are only just beginning to discover, is what learning disabled artists might be able to do with this 'gift'.

Margaret Ames has spent many years working alongside learning disabled research colleagues and choreographers at the dance company Cyrff Ystwyth in Aberystwyth, Wales. In 'Learning Disability, Thought and Theatre' she argues, not unreasonably, that even a severe learning disability does not preclude a person from thinking. She then draws on Maike Bleeker's observations in 'Thinking no-one's thought' that 'thought becomes apparent through the process of devising theatre ...' and framing of 'dramaturgy as a relational process of thought that is distributed between people in the process of creating performance' to formulate her conclusion that performance provides a channel of expression for 'learning disabled thought' (293). She characterizes the collaborative research project of Cyrff Ystywth as an exploration of 'the aesthetic possibilities that emerge when following the lead of colleagues with learning disabilities' (293). She also, crucially, seeks to address concerns expressed by Gorman (2017) about the ethics of non-disabled people theorizing about work by disabled people. Ames is at pains to point out how such work not only offers a critique of ableism but 'reveals new choreographic and aesthetic possibilities that sidestep constructions of bodies and abilities and gives the lie to the notion that people with learning disabilities cannot think and therefore must always represent, in some way, the abject other' (294).

Ames poses the question: 'If theatre thinks, what thoughts do practitioners with learning disabilities reveal through their chosen themes and embodied responses?' (295). If thought generated by performance research and practice is a potential 'thinking in-between', then for disability performance this in-between avoids the 'need to exclude the Other that is learning disability, or to suggest inclusion into an assumed desirable community of the competent'. Ames reconciles the tensions of the differences non-disabled and disabled artists bring to collaboration by reference to Esposito's concept of 'community' as the opposite of the fullness often described as essential to the experience of belonging, but rather as a community that is 'impossible and yet essential' (Ames, Calvert et al 91) and that comes about only through obligation, *munus*, the 'giving that assigns one to the other in an obligation' (91) and that this mutual giving and mutual obligation elides boundaries of ability and disability.

I would also like to consider briefly how voice and presence is negotiated and expressed by the performers of Per.Arts in the dance theatre performance *Dis_Sylphide* (2018). This performance by the ensemble from Novi Sad, Serbia engages with, and cites – after a fashion – three canonical performances of 20th-century avant-garde dance: Mary Wigman's *Hexentanz* (1928), Pina Bausch's *Kontakthof* (1978), and Xavier Le Roy's *Self Unfinished* (1998). The performance itself operates on several levels. The performers cite, hack, and reinhabit extracts from the three works. They place themselves into these avant-garde explorations of otherness predicated in the original works on assumptions of virtuosity, on demands made of and only certain, very particular bodies. These three dis-citations are interspersed with the performers themselves talking about their processes, their difficulties, the problems they have with certain demands of the movement sequences, and some account of their relationships to the company, to the other performers, and to the director of the company, Saša Asentiç. If the performance consisted of only these two modes of performance, then it would exemplify two of the prevalent strands of learning disabled performance. The first is the citational model: the parody or pastiche of certain canonical texts, literary, dramatic, or choreographic. The second is the testimonial model in which the voices of the performers are called to testify or bear witness to the lived experience of learning disability. *Dis_Sylphide* is something more than a combination of these two modes because of the ease with which the performers switch between them and the traces that are left of one mode in the other. It is in going between the dance performance and the improvised talking that the particular virtuosity of the learning disabled performers emerges. This is a virtuosity that includes technical facility and expressive capability in inhabiting the choreography and the ability to extemporize about the performance, the process and the history of the company but above all the ease or facility to go between the two that speaks to the time spent together in rehearsal and performance. This emerges as not just a goal-oriented time but something closer to what Moten and Harney characterize in *The Undercommons* as 'study' a place for 'the crafting of problems' a non-qualification-oriented activity, a 'speculative practice' (110). In Per.Art's processes in making *Dis_Sylphide* learning disabled artists, it becomes clear in the performer discussions that alternate with the dance sequences it becomes clear that Natalija Vladisljević is crafting a problem around the sequence in *Kontakthof* in which she is literally manhandled by a group of men, some of whom, in the Per.Arts version, have been called onstage from the audience. It is clear from her performance in the Kontakthof sequence that she has agency, but that it is a problematic agency. It is also clear from Vladisljević's contribution to the spoken discourse that this sequence disturbs her. Her participation needs to be appreciated in the context of the whole performance. This opens with Vladisljević's version of the powerful and empowering *Hexentanz* in which she conjures up power and agency, such is the intensity of her performance that one might almost say she channels powers and agencies other than herself. This sequence provides an affirmation of female power that resonates to underscore the manhandling sequence. Vladisljević herself has a commanding presence in conventional theatrical terms. The performance does not seek to smooth over the contradictions and risks inherent in Vladisljevic's participation in the *Kontakthof* sequence. Contemporary dance verges on the punitive in its disciplinary and virtuosic requirements of the dancer, Pina Bausch's dance theatre exacerbates this challenge by requiring the female dancer's commitment and submission to emotional and sexual provocation. Should the audience be *more* outraged if that dancer is learning disabled? This opens up a debate around agency, sexuality, autonomy, and exploitation that is deeply nuanced and complex. In Per.Art's *Dis_Sylphide*, Natalija Vladisljevic's voice, presence, and performance are the most prominent in this debate. Her 'voice' is, however, so much more than just her spoken contribution to the testimonial sequence. It includes her embodied presence in and re-presentation of *Hexentanz* and *Kontakthof,* it is informed by the seeming-possessed trance-like quality of aspects of her performance, and by her facility and engagement with study in her wider role within the company as a choreographer and a published author.

Different Light Theatre: the voice of Isaac Tait

As a way of introducing how voice and presence is in continual exploration and negotiation in the work of Different Light Theatre Company, I wish to offer an analysis of a transcript of a brief, one and a half minute, extract from the beginning of an interview with one of the performers, Isaac Tait. This was undertaken with Katy Gosset from Radio New Zealand in the rehearsal period for *Still Lives* in 2011. I am including this firstly because the radio interview is the medium of voice, and secondly, because *Still Lives* is a play all about the different voices that are at play in and around the three performers.

>   COMPUTERIZED VOICE (US accent): Isaac is intellectually disabled. He doesn't look it, but he is. This confuses people.

Brief excerpt from a gentle, dreamy version of *My Favourite Things,* xylophone and female voice: Raindrops on roses … FADES OUT/CROSS FADES TO ISAAC.

ISAAC (rehearsal voice, slight echo in studio space): Once upon a time there was a quiet time for stillness and silence. And Isaac listened. And he listens now. And he hears nothing. Only not nothing. FADES OUT

INTERVIEWER: Rehearsing for A Different Light's latest production, *Still Lives,* Isaac Tait is in some ways telling his own story.

ISAAC (rehearsal voice): The boys in school kicked me up the butt. And every day take the lunch out of my hand. Swimming pool. Someone did a floater. And blamed me. And held my head underneath the water. And he listens now. And he hears nothing. The thoughts. The feelings … FADES OUT/CROSS FADES TO INTERVIEWER.

INTERVIEWER: The actors brainstorm ideas and create their own material.

ISAAC (interview voice, quieter, closer to microphone): We usually write it together. We talk about stuff and then write as a group sometimes. But then we go away and think about things, write things.

INTERVIEWER: So then the … the Isaac in your piece in the soliloquy we heard before is that you, effectively, is that your experience?

ISAAC (interview voice) Yeah cos like every Sunday we get together with Glen that's in the wheelchair and Ben an' er And we jot things down. And I think it is about Isaac himself … yeah. Yeah. ('One in Five' 2012)

It is apparent even from this brief extract that both Tait and Gosset, whilst acknowledging the presence of Tait's voice in the creation and performance of *Still Lives,* are also aware of the othering that occurs in giving voice: Interviewer; *in some ways* telling his own story … *the Isaac* in your piece …. Isaac: I think it is about *Isaac himself.* This othering occurs in theatre, particularly in that mode of learning disabled theatre that is self-devised. My experience is that this othering occurs on a number of levels. In this case, my closeness to the performer and to the material puts me in a compromised position but also affords me the opportunity to offer some observations at close quarters of the levels of othering in giving voice. In the first instance, this occurs at the level of a speaker entering into language, a language that has always already been pre-formed, acquired over years as a (m)other tongue, experienced in hearing the myriad voices of others that inform the mentalese and spoken utterances that then echo and resonate in their 'own' speech. The speaker is continually confronted with the force of Derrida's assertion in *Monolingualism of the Other*: 'I only have one language, yet it is not mine' (1). For Tait to 'come up with' the material he has devised he is to some extent letting the voices of others and the otherness of his own voice go through him. To take some specific examples, 'Once upon a time' is obviously an attempt to give presence to the mother tongue of storytelling. In the devising process for *Still Lives* each of the three performers was given this simple prompt to initiate narrative. Different versions of how they continued this prompt are interspersed throughout the play. The stillness and silence that Tait repeatedly mentions was in part an attempt to facilitate his quieter voice, his thoughtful presence, it was also a strategy devised between us to attempt to calm down his performance anxiety, to bring him back to the quietness that was on offer by going within himself in any given moment when he became anxious because of the scrutiny of public performance. Tait's swimming pool reference contains within it what sounds very like the voice of one of the groups that bullied him: 'Someone did a floater'. In the interview extract, it is not only Tait's voice that is inhabited by, or channeling, the voices of others. The interviewer's job is in a way to channel the thoughts and questions of 'the listener', presumably some normative concept of the listener. It is possible to interpret her tuning in to the expectations or expected voice of the interview in her pauses and periphrasis: So then the ... the Isaac in your piece in the soliloquy we heard before *is that you, effectively, is that your experience?* (emphasis mine). It is then possible to witness in the course of the interview Tait himself quickly taking on board the expected assumptions of the interview about devised performance or disability performance. This is something that he does within the relatively short time of speaking: We just talk about *like er ... our life experiences you could say. Yeah.* He uses the filler 'like,' he pauses, he qualifies: 'you could say' and then it is almost as if he checks himself that he is aligning with the expected narrative of 'devising from life experience': *Yeah.* Tait is also showing sensitivity in the response to the interviewer's line of thought. Which 'voices' are where in this exchange? There are fundamental gaps that emerge between what is termed lived experience and what is termed vocal expression. That the speaker might give unmediated and transparent vocal expression of their lived experience is an ideal or a chimera akin to 'the individual rhetor producing speech acts, which in turn confirm the existence of a fixed core self' This ideal of communication elides how experience is mediated to the speaker through language. It also does not allow for the possibility of other voices speaking through any given speaker's speech. Derrida poses this possibility as a question in *Cinders*: 'Who will decide whether this voice was lent, returned, or given? And to whom?' (7). Each of these examples leads us to a consideration that underpins this book: in what ways, in what locations, and as a result of what negotiations are the voices of learning disabled artists present or absent in contemporary theatre, and what emerges when such movements towards presence and absence are traced?

Learning disabled artists: the wider cultural context

A cursory glance at the practice of learning disabled theatre in the first two decades of the 21st century appears to reveal that learning disabled theatre companies are not merely increasingly present but flourishing in a number of countries. Companies such as Back to Back, Theater HORA, and Mind the Gap continue to produce innovative and challenging theatre, and, more recently, film, that has achieved great commercial success and critical acclaim. These and other companies are also significantly involved in the future development of the art form and the continuing viability of employment for learning disabled artists. In 2017, the inaugural Crossing the Line Festival took place in Roubaix, France 'a pan-European festival celebrating artists with intellectual disabilities'. This was part of a two-year European Union funded small-scale co-operation project leading to three days of presenting performances, sharing practice, and screenings and workshops between members of Mind the Gap, Compagnie de l'Oiseau Mouche, and Moomsteatern. The next iteration was due in 2020, but deferred, due to the pandemic, to 2021 and online, including Blue Teapot Theatre from Galway, Theater Babbel, from Rotterdam, and Teatr 21 from Warsaw.

Back to Back Theatre continues to tour internationally with company-devised productions and were touring *The Shadow Whose Prey the Hunter Becomes* in the United States in 2019 when pandemic travel restrictions came into effect. Prior to that they had been artists in residence at London's Victoria and Albert Museum, produced an original film *Oddlands,* as well as a film version of the theatre production *Ganesh versus the Third Reich* whilst continuing to engage in community outreach programmes and collaborations. Theater HORA in Zurich has been in existence since 1993 during that time offering a two year actor training course. The company came to prominence more recently with the contentious collaboration with Jérôme Bel on *Disabled Theater* that toured extensively internationally. Since that collaboration, the company has been working on *Freie Republik HORA* an ongoing performance research project to facilitate the development of learning disabled directors. They continue to develop a number of other creative collaborations with other companies as well as film production, combining commercial performance with experimentation and performance research. In Eastern Europe, Per.Art from Novi Sad and Teatr 21 from Warsaw in addition to developing and touring dance theatre and theatre performance have created *Dis_Lecture*, 'a series of lecture performances by artists with learning disabilities … in which the artists are invited to appropriate the format of the lecture performance and challenge its ableism thereby 'entering a field from which they are historically excluded: the field of discourse on dance and performance'(Dis_Lecture website).

In the United Kingdom, Mind the Gap has produced a series of groundbreaking performances including *ZARA*, a large-scale, site-specific, immersive performance about a learning disabled mother featuring 'more than 100 performers, tanks, and a puppet of a baby bigger than a double-decker bus' that has played in outdoor venues and been streamed online.

Access All Areas, a London-based group, set *Madhouse:re exit* a large scale fantasy work in a former hospital that had previously confined and institutionalized learning disabled people. It was performed at Shoreditch Town Hall and Manchester's Barton Arcade. They have also collaborated with the Royal Central School of Speech and Drama to offer a two-year Performance Making Diploma for Learning Disabled and Autistic Adults to be delivered at RCSSD that includes tuition by practitioners from leading UK theatre companies such as Punchdrunk, Told by an Idiot, and Frantic Assembly. They also operate a Transforming Leadership programme 'a programme and coaching culture for emerging learning disabled leaders'.

In Canada, prominent learning disabled companies include Entr'Actes in Quebec who have been developing learning disabled performance and theatre and arts training since 1994, and Theatre Terrific in Vancouver, an award-winning company creating professional productions and developing learning disabled performance training since 1985. In the USA, established companies include Phamaly Theatre Company in Denver, who have been including physically and learning disabled performers in making commercially focused theatre since 1989, Sound Theatre Company in Seattle, Mixed Blood Theatre Company in Minneapolis, Open Circle Theatre Company in Washington DC, and Outside Voices Theatre Company in New York City. In 2018, Mickey Rowe, the first autistic actor to play the role of Christopher Boone in *Curious Incident of the Dog in the Night-Time* helped establish the National Disability Theatre as an organization to promote the development of 'professional inclusive theatre'. Operating from a more activist perspective Sins Invalid collective 'a disability justice-based performance project that incubates and celebrates artists with disabilities, centralizing artists of color and LGBTQ/gender-variant artists as communities who have been historically marginalized' have produced *Skin, Tooth, and Bone,* a disability justice primer.

Learning disabled actors are becoming increasingly visible in television and film. In the UK, Liam Bairstow an artist with Mind the Gap Theatre, became a core cast member of long-running soap *Coronation Street*. Tommy Jessop from Blue Apple has appeared in *Coming Down the Mountain* and taken a leading role in *Line of Duty* season 6. Sarah Gordy, who has received an Honorary Doctorate and MBE for services to acting, has appeared in *Strike: the Silkworm, Upstairs Downstairs, The A Word*, and *Call the Midwife* and in the spin-off of *The A Word, Ralph and Katie.* Male actors with Down's Syndrome appeared in significant roles alongside Gordy: Daniel Laurie in *Call the Midwife* and Lauren Harrop in *The A Word* and *Ralph and Katie*. In 2021 George Webster, a performer in training with Mind the Gap, became the first presenter with Down's Syndrome on the BBC children's channel, CBeebies. In an interesting development, his first appearance on the programme made no mention of his learning disability. In the USA, Zack Gottsagen's recent starring role in *The Peanut Butter Falcon* (2019) points to a recent genealogy of actors with Down's Syndrome that goes back to Jason Kingsley as a baby on *Sesame Street* in 1975 and subsequently on *The Fall Guy* and *Touched by an Angel*, Chris Burke on *Life Goes On* in 1989, Pascal Duquenne as the lead in the 1996 film *Le Huitième Jour*, Paula Sage in *AfterLife* (2003), Alejandro Manza in *Anita* (2009), Pablo Pineda in *Yo Tambien* (2009), Jamie Brewer's recurring role in *American Horror Story*, Becky Potter in *Glee* and Evan Sneider in the 2010 film *Girlfriend* (Shanley 2019). Brazilian film *Colegas* (2012) has about three people with Down's Syndrome.

In 2020, Zack Gottsagen became the first learning disabled actor to present an award at the Oscars ceremony, or at least to co-present with Shia LeBoeuf. In the same year in the UK Tommy Jessop presented an award at the BAFTA TV ceremony. In 2015, the punk band Pertti Kurikan Nimipäivät, whose members have Down's Syndrome, represented Finland at the Eurovision Song Contest. Drag Syndrome 'a drag collective featuring highly addictive queens & kings with Down's Syndrome' has taken learning disabled performance into a different direction with their Radical Beauty project, Instagram presence, and performance tours to clubs and queer festivals in Malmö, Sao Paulo, Berlin, and Montreal.

Screen, print, and online media are almost obsessively concerned with presenting learning disabled people (over)achieving, and promoting the success stories of people with Down's Syndrome. To take but a few recent examples: 'Models with Down Syndrome Are Killing It in the Fashion Industry' (Kirkland 2021). "Damn It, That's Huge": Actors With Down Syndrome Are Finding More Work in Hollywood' (Shanley 2019). '13 people with Down syndrome who are breaking barriers in entertainment, athletics, fashion, and more' (Ettinger). There is a ubiquitous journalistic trope that combines a narrative of overcoming adversity with the appearance of commitment to inclusion and diversity contributing to a teleological account of continuous progress and improvement. Whilst it is important to acknowledge that visual and mediatized representation *matters* in how learning disabled people see themselves and how others see them, it is also important to question the terms of this representation. As Peggy Phelan pointed out in 1996 in *Unmarked: The Politics of Performance*: 'If visibility equals power, then almost-naked young white women should be running Western culture' (10). This has been reinforced in more recent disability and community activism, Tania Cañas in 'Ethics and Self-Determination' in *The Relationship is the Project*: 'Just because a community is visible (or even hyper-visible like refugees) doesn't automatically mean they have equal representation or power' (32). Moten and Harney in *All Incomplete* (2021) cite Hortense Spillers on 'the ruse, or the lure of personality' (143) in accepting the institutional gift of tokenism that offers representation, visibility, and a place at the table to a chosen few individuals, which Moten and Harney recognize makes an illusory switch from presence to representation: 'mere presence in the institution …' that appears to afford the participant 'a model of heroic representation' (143). Drawing on Snyder and Mitchell's *Biopolitics of Disability* we might characterize the valorization and commodification of a select few disabled people as 'ablenationalism': 'Both "the able-disabled" and "ablenationalism" develop as late twentieth-century neoliberal strategies for the tightly regulated entrance of people with disabilities into neoliberal economies ....' (12)

The situation is of course highly nuanced. Entrance or subsumption into neoliberal economies may be a strategy that is subject to vehement criticism by those of us seeking to analyze or theorize about the representation of disabled people. It may be something else entirely for a learning disabled actor trying to make a living. Tim Wheeler, former Artistic Director of Mind the Gap, puts this somewhat more bluntly in 'A proper actor?: The politics of training for learning disabled actors': 'It should not be an academic sitting there and saying 'it's wrong to be in the mainstream' it's about the choice of the individual performer' (Hargrave and Gee, 45). This statement has a rhetorical and pragmatic force that should not be ignored. It hinges, however, on a contentious idea of 'the choice of the individual'. How is 'the individual' expected to make choices in a society in which consumer capitalism has co-opted most 'choice'? This is especially the case for learning disabled individuals, who may have been given only disadvantaged and 'special' access to education.

The media narratives of progress and inclusion for 'exceptional' learning disabled people need to be taken in the context of the extremely precarious existence of learning disabled people. The abortion rate of foetuses with Down's Syndrome at 67% in the USA, 100% in Denmark, and 90% in the Netherlands. There is a continuing litany of abuse meted out to learning disabled people in institutions. The abuse exposed at Whorlton Hall in the UK in 2020, is but one example in a line that can be traced back 50 years to the exposé of Willowbrook State School in the USA in 1972 to the origins of institutionalization in the 19th century. During the peaks of the COVID pandemic from 2020 onwards Do Not Resuscitate Notices were given out to learning disabled people without seeking their consent, leading to many avoidable deaths. This amongst a section of the population in the UK amongst whom, even in pre-COVID times life expectancy is so much lower than for the rest of the population: only two out of five learning disable people live until 65. The recurring invisibility and discounting of learning disabled people that shadows the shining mediatized exemplification of a select few emerged again with a particular brutality in the rush to necropolitical eugenics that occurred in some supposedly developed countries as a reaction to the pandemic. The question remains how the invisibility of lives that do not matter relates to the visibility of learning disabled actors: is it the context, the background? Is the visibility of learning disabled artists somehow informed by the wider and deeper invisibility of learning disabled people? Are the voices of learning disabled theatre informed by a historical and still prevalent silence?

Notes on terminology

I choose to use the term 'learning disability' and 'learning disabled' because these terms suggest that the disabling is systemic. They suggest that there might in fact be a deficiency in systems of learning and teaching, that learning disability is in part due to educational disadvantage, and that one is disabled by and through learning. A medical diagnosis, legal pronouncement, or educational assessment of learning disability is profoundly performative as they are all likely to augment the learning disability of the people on the receiving end. It is a self-fulfilling prophesy of impaired access to selfhood.

Learning entails coming up against the experience and in response to that experience changing, adapting, and developing strategies for better coping with the subsequent experience. It is premised upon continuous improvement over time. Primary, secondary, and tertiary education seeks to mark this continuous improvement through degrees and qualifications. It is interesting to compare this imperative to continuous improvement with Moten and Harney's notion of study in *The Undercommons* and developed in *All Incomplete*:

> 'In study we are engaged consciously and unconsciously. We revise, and then again. This is not just about distinguishing improvement as capitalist efficiency.' ... 'Study emerges as the collective practice of revision in which those who study do not improve but improvise, do not develop but regenerate and degenerate .... Study is the (im)permanently unformed, insistently informal, underperforming commitment to each other not to graduate but instead indefinitely to accumulate an invaluable debt to each other rather than submit to their infinitely fungible line of credit'. (68)

This account of study resonates with my experience of working with learning disabled artists. Such theatre, however, requires of the performers a high degree of what is measured in conventional educational learning in the processes of devising, rehearsing, and performing before an audience. This might include the rote learning of lines of spoken text, the build-up of stamina and muscle memory to execute the movement, the ability to improvise and devise, to extemporize in performance in response to environments, audience, and the contingencies of live performance. In many contemporary learning disabled theatres, these switches and shifts might be required within a single performance that is then repeated over a season. In fact, the actor is required not merely to repeat but consistently to refresh and recreate vocal, physical, and holistic elements of performance. In much contemporary learning disabled theatre, such as that of Back to Back and Per.Art, mimetic acting is only one level of representation. The actor is also engaged in modes of (re)presentation more associated with post-dramatic or post-humanist theatre drawing on the poiesis and praxis of performance art. Learning disabled artists often slip between the boundaries of representational acting, presentational acting, and acting as persona. They switch between deploying their disability as performance and the presentation of disability clichés. In any estimation of acting or performance, this is a highly complex nexus requiring literacies, sensitivities, and mental and physical intelligence not conventionally associated with learning disabled people.

I have chosen not to use the terms intellectual or cognitive disability as I feel that these terms tend to emphasize that the disability is the result of a lack or deficiency within an individual person. What is more, the terms 'intellectual' and 'cognitive' disability reinforce a Cartesian split between mind and body that disability scholars, artists, and activists have questioned as not tallying with the complex interrelationship of 'body' and 'mind' in human lived experience, and particularly in the lived experience of disability. Eli Clare, Margaret Price, Sami Schalk and others have developed the formulation 'bodyminds'(Schalk 2018) as a way of reconfiguring thinking in terms of the braiding, intertwining, or intra-action (Barad 2007) of the physical and the mental that is crucial in understanding the operations, sites, and implications of disablement.

I choose to use *learning disabled people* rather than people with learning disabilities to foreground disability and to honour the activism of disabled people who developed the #*saytheword* movement in order to counter the continuing neglect of disability in the wider discourses and practices of inclusion and diversity, to encourage solidarity across different disabilities and to reject terms such as 'physically challenged', 'differently abled' that act as euphemisms that gloss over the need for disability rights and justice. Other 'people with disabilities' choose to identify themselves with 'people first' language and that is their right.

Learning disabled is a placeholder term. To put it simply and practically, when I engage in work or discussion with the performers of Different Light Theatre such a term does not often enter the room. It only does so if somebody is having a problem with being interpellated in that way or needs to disclose the diagnostic term to access funds or support that will afford them disability justice. The term comes and goes as needed.

'Learning disabled' as a marker of identity is also deeply unsatisfactory. It is unlikely that the stigma of the term is ever likely to be flipped and reappropriated as an affirmative badge of identity as has occurred with the terms 'queer' and 'crip'. Alternative and overlapping terms such as 'autistic' and 'neurodiverse' may well achieve this flipping of the script of stigmatization and exclusion but learning disabled is likely to remain a placeholder until other terms take its place. This may be to its advantage in terms of a deferral of the closure of identity as a static category and what Fred Moten has termed 'the consent not to be a single being'.

Learning disabled is not a homogeneous term. It is messy. It does not describe a consistent set of characteristics and is always in danger of spilling out and over boundaries. Should dementia, Alzheimer's, and Attention Deficit/Hyper-Activity Disorder (ADHD) be classed as learning disabilities, and what are the implications if they are? It is a categorization that is imposed variously at the level of the juridical, educational, and medical formations of power that has profound implications at the social and personal levels. Because of this deep-rootedness and prevalence, it is difficult to build solidarity and resistance across a multiplicity of people who are in effect, individualized and disempowered by being categorized as learning disabled from birth or early childhood and subsequently excluded and marginalized through puberty and beyond. Learning disabled subjects are constituted in the strange mixture of, on the one hand, atomized prescription and, on the other, erased as bodies that do not matter, deprived of personhood at the level of ontology. It is, however, in this contradiction in the formation of a learning disabled subjectivity that there might emerge the potential for fugitive and generative aesthetics and politics. In its fugitive 'refusal to settle' (Moten and Harney 2013, 11) between therapy, aesthetics and politics, community and subjecthood, learning disabled theatre often blurs lines: between the professional and the amateur, the healing of the social bond and the exposure of inequities in the movement towards and away from disability rights and justice. To lean on the work of Ashon Crawley in *Black Pentecostal Breath* there is an *otherwiseness* to learning disabled theatre, it is potentially both other and wise, comprising other kinds of wiseness, and certainly an 'aesthetics of possibility' (2). Both intersectionality and the 'diversity in diversity' need to be respected. Disability artist and activist Moira Williams puts this quite simply in her Access Guide: 'We recognize and center those who know most about the systems that affect our lives: queer, trans, Black, Indigenous, disabled people' (2021). This is a direct and simple recognition and acknowledgement that those who are most subjected to marginalization and exclusion are likely to 'know,' in the sense of experiential knowledge, more about the systems that have thus (mis)treated them. This knowledge, however, may not necessarily exist solely within language, reason, and logic due to the epistemic injustice of the historical marginalization and exclusion of learning disabled people from these systems of expression, knowledge, and power. The question then becomes how to let this experiential knowledge inform how we might think, make, and be together.

I am using the term artist because my experience in the co-creation and spectatorship of learning disabled theatre leads me to this term. The learning disabled members of Different Light Theatre, Back to Back Theatre, Theater HORA, and other companies, are more than just performers or devisers they are some combination of artiste, artisan, and artist, performing to a standard that commands respect, crafting their own access to theatre, and living the artful life that is so often required of disabled people navigating an ableist world.

The greatest learning I have experienced, the most profound research in which I have participated, has occurred in the process of recognizing and respecting the *mana* of learning disabled artists. Mana is a concept from Te Ao Māori (The Māori world) that denotes a way of being that induces awe and respect. Respecting the mana of learning disabled artists involves affording their human right to voices that are contradictory, ambiguous, humorous, and caught up in the dialectics of desire that can never be fulfilled.

Structure of the book

Prior to the account of the work of Different Light Theatre that constitutes the main body of the book there is a brief Chapter 1 that presents an analysis of Back to Back Theatre's 2019 production *The Shadow Whose Prey the Hunter Becomes* as a way of introducing some of the key concepts of voice, presence, and performance in the book. These are introduced and explored in the specific context of a learning disabled theatrical production that occurred at a crucial time, just prior to the lockdowns of the global pandemic, and that has influenced the turn to self-examination of Different Light Theatre in recent performance practice and in this book. Chapter 2 gives a detailed account of the first three public performances by Different Light Theatre after the company had been founded after initial theatre workshops conducted at the Hohepa residential community in 2004. These performances were devised around the narrative framework of myths and European canonical literature using methodologies based on the movement improvisation of Lecoq and Boal and verbal improvisation from Johnstone and Spolin. They were attempts to find common ground between the learning disabled actors and an assumed non-disabled audience. The theatre practice in these early performances was a 'mixed ability' model with both disabled and non-disabled performers on stage. The chapter intends to show how these first attempts at giving theatre to the participants or welcoming them into the theatre were inflected with Derrida's paradox of hospitality and hostility and the inequity in the relationship between giving and receiving. This operated at a deep level in the establishment of a company ethos and in terms of the imposition of an ableist drama school model on the participants. All of these top-down initiatives then came into an interesting encounter with the contributions of the learning disabled participants.

The chapter introduces the learning disabled actors and how they came to adopt or to be perceived as adopting, particular performance personae based on observations of their participation in the improvising and devising process by non-disabled facilitators. Devising methodologies, narrative frameworks, and dramatic characterizations were all in the service of exploring community, or that ephemeral community of theatre that both enacts and explores the myth of commonality. It also charts some of the early 'issues with theatre' or problems with performance that the performers experience, an important strand of anti-theatricality or what is 'taken away' in the giving of voice in learning disabled theatre that is developed throughout the book. The early performances were attempts at performing community through community theatre. This was based on the premise that the learning disabled performers would explore what they had in common with characters from European canonical drama and literature and with the mediatized culture of what was assumed to be a mainstream Christchurch theatre audience.

Chapter 3 attempts to show how the company then proceeded on different paths of development. These included touring a production overseas to a disability arts festival, the shift to including only disabled performers on stage, and the further shift to giving the performers more creative autonomy in the creative processes of making theatre. The chapter gives an account of how successive attempts to empower the performers or to afford them autonomy were still caught up in the inequitable dynamic of giving and taking from non-disabled to disabled participants. The attempted negotiation of a more democratic politics and interdependent ethics of the group was in continual tension with the hierarchical processes and disciplinary formations of dramatic theatre still being imposed by non-disabled facilitators.

The problems inherent in the broadly emancipatory urge to 'give voice' or representation within the group were playing out in the performances. At times this was a conscious staging of the struggles within the group. At times the performances 'spoke back' to these tensions. In *Ship of Fools*, a group of settlers 'discover' a country and indigenous inhabitants who are, of course, already there. In *Frankenstein's Children*, repeated attempts are made to create perfect replicants who all emerge as failed experiments. In *The Poor Dears*, a learning disabled theatre group attempts to gain entry into another country under the name 'We are not the Poor Dears' but the Byzantine algorithms and systems of admission reduce them to 'The Poor Dears'. All of these dramatic narratives might have served as metaphors for the negotiation of the processes of making theatre between non-disabled and learning disabled participants at this stage in the group's development.

Chapter 4 charts the shifting aesthetics and politics of the group in and around the Christchurch earthquakes of 2010–11 and the progress of the 'recovery'. It gives an account of *The Wizard of Oz* that explored different ways of working with material chosen by the performers and different possibilities of creating performance that shifted between character, persona and the lived experience of the performers. Experiences of the group travelling and presenting at a conference at the Powerhouse Museum in Sydney were incorporated into this performance and a deeper questioning by means of intertextual and intermedial performance of what constitutes the presence of learning disabled performers was initiated. The first Christchurch earthquake had an impact on this performance and the second, more destructive and more deadly, informed the company's subsequent work.

This included the *Still Lives* project that had three iterations at the Society for Disability Studies conference in San Jose in 2011, back in Christchurch in 2012, and in a more developed form at the Ludus Festival and Performance Studies international conference in Leeds in 2012. This extended performance project focused on only three performers and was the company's most intensive experiment in presenting the giving and taking of voice in learning disabled theatre. It used a combination of computerized voices of authority, the voices in the head of the three young men, ironic narrative voices, the voices of electronic devices, captions, signing, and an intermedial mix of pre-recorded and live-feed video to assemble a polylogue or polyphony that required the audience to listen to the voices of the learning disabled young men into speech.

This also included *The Earthquake in Chile* and *Canterbury Tales*, two attempts at collaboration with non-disabled artists and companies in site-specific and immersive performances presented whilst Christchurch was still shaking with thousands of aftershocks. These performances sought to build on the sense of community experienced in the immediate aftermath of the quakes when people shared food, accommodation, and resources. These impromptu community initiatives, which led to Gap Filler, Life in Vacant Spaces, and Greening the Rubble, were soon co-opted into the neoliberal 'recovery' of the National government. The segregated and 'special' participation of Different Light Theatre at these events, exposing inequities of access, intimated that, unlike the earthquakes, the recovery would not be inclusive. The final project at this period was the Different Light Soap Opera project *The Lonely and the Lovely*. An extract from this was first presented at the Concourse in Chatswood, Sydney accompanying a parodic Powerpoint about Rebuilding Christchurch. The soap opera format presented the heroes and villains of the recovery, the cliffhangers, the plot twists and turns, and the concerns of the learning disabled artists that they would be 'written out' of the recovery. It also exposed tensions over the use of personal experience in the shifting between character, persona, and person that came to dominate the group's work at this stage.

Chapter 5 details another shift in the praxis of the company away from paid public performance in theatres and towards performance research. This included performances at the Performance Studies international conference at the University of Melbourne in 2016 and the Australasian Association for Theatre, Drama and Performance Studies (ADSA) conference in Auckland, 2017. It also included performance research in the interstices of the company's 'host' drama school, NASDA, performance experiments in street actions, derives, and ecological performance with Petra Kuppers and other international collaborators. Finally, it also included a return to public performance, the company's last 'live' performance to date, and the self-examination by means of performance of *The History of Different Light* presented in the Christchurch Arts Festival, 2019. The account of this performance presents some of the most marked tensions between what is given and what is taken in learning disabled theatre, between theatricality and anti-theatricality and the complexities of presentations of the self supposedly drawing on lived experience.

Chapter 6 opens with a brief anecdote that epitomizes the problematic pathway from learning disabled theatre to social inclusion. It then traces the response of the company to the Human Pause of the pandemic. There is a brief analysis of the potential opportunities this offers for greater inclusion, as well as the reiteration of old exclusions, and the development of newer forms of exclusion. It considers how Different Light Theatre attempted to hold onto the idea and the practice of theatre in a global environment in which many theatre lights went dark. The chapter goes on to offer some analysis of how theatre and learning disabled theatre made a shift online and the continuing implications of that shift. The final section of the chapter gives an account of the learning disabled artists of Different Light participation at international academic conferences finding a place as uneasy guests at the symposium or after party of academic discussion. It ends with how the company is learning to listen to the voices of indigenous knowledge and the cries of the planet as the collective continues its journey.

Notes

1. 'A concept arising from disabled experience that addresses the ways that disabled/chronically ill and neurodivergent people experience time (and space) differently than able-bodyminded folk' (https://cdsc.umn.edu/cds/terms). See Samuels (2017) and Kuppers (2022) 153–197.
2. Christchurch Polytechnic Institute of Technology which has subsequently become Ara Institute, and in 2022 Te Pukenga, the New Zealand Institute of Skills and Technology.

References

AfterLife. Directed by Alison Peebles. Gabriel Films Ltd, 2005.
American Horror Story. TV series. FX. 11 seasons, October 5, 2011- present.
Ames, Margaret. "Learning disability, thought, and theatre." *Contemporary Theatre Review*, vol. 29, no. 3, 2019, pp. 290–304.
Ames, Margaret, Calvert, Dave, Glørstad, Vibeke, Maguire-Rosier, Kate, McCaffrey, Tony, and Schmidt, Yvonne. "Responding to Per.Art's Dis_Sylphide: Six voices from IFTR's performance and disability working group." *Theatre Research International*, vol. 44, no. 1, 1 March, 2019, pp. 82–101.
"An angel by any other name." *Touched by an Angel* Season 3, Episode 28. CBS, May 10, 1997.
Anita. Directed by Marcos Carnevale. Instituto Nacional de Cine y Artes Audiovisuales, 2009.
Barad, Karen. *Meeting the Universe Halfway: Quantum Physics and the Entanglement of Matter and Meaning.* Duke University Press, 2007.
Bassel, Leah. *The Politics of Listening: Possibilities and Challenges for Democratic Life.* Palgrave Macmillan, 2017.
Bennett, Susan. *Theory for Theatre Studies: Sound.* Methuen, 2019.
Boal, Augusto. *Games for Actors and Non-Actors.* Translated by Adrian Jackson. Routledge, 1992.

Calvert, Dave. "Convivial theatre: care and debility in collaborations between non-disabled and learning disabled theatre makers." In *Performing Care: New Perspectives on Socially Engaged Performance*. Edited by Amanda Stuart Fisher and James Thompson. Manchester University Press, 2020.

Cañas, Tania. "Ethics and self-determination." In *The Relationship Is the Project: Working With Communities*. Brow Books, 2020.

Canterbury Tales. Directed by Peter Falkenberg, Free Theatre Christchurch FESTA Festival of Transitional Architecture, Central city and Cathedral Square, Christchurch. 25–28 October, 2013.

Carlson, Licia. *The Faces of Intellectual Disability: Philosophical Reflections*. Indiana University Press, 2010.

Colegas. Directed by Marcelo Galvão. Gatacine, 2012.

Couldry, Nick. *Why Voice Matters: Culture and Politics After Neoliberalism*. Sage Publications, 2010.

Crawley, Ashon T. *Black Pentecostal Breath: The Aesthetics of Possibility*. Fordham University Press, 2017.

Crossing the Line Festival, 2021. http://www.crossingtheline.eu/the-festival/

Deligny, Fernand. *Cartes Et Lignes d'Erre/Maps and Wander Lines: Traces Du Réseau De Fernand Deligny 1969-1979*. Edited by Sandra Alvarez de Toledo, Translated by Cyril Le Roy and John Angell. L'Arachnéen, 2013.

Derrida, Jacques. *Cinders*. Translated by Ned Lukacher. University of Nebraska Press, 1991.

———. *Monolingualism of the Other or the Prosthesis of Origin*. Translated by Patrick Mensah. Stanford University Press, 1998.

———. *Voice and Phenomenon: Introduction to the Problem of the Sign in Husserl's Phenomenology*. Edited by Leonard Lawlor. Northwestern University Press, 2011.

Different Light Theatre. "Why I like drama." Video interviews, 10 May, 2012. Different Light video archive.

Disabled Theater. Directed by Jérôme Bel. Vimeo file. Password provided by Theater HORA. Recording of performance at Hebbel Am Ufer, HAU1, 11 March, 2012. Web.

Dis_Lecture. Online lecture series. https://sophiensaele.com/en/archiv/stueck/sasa-asentic-collaborators-dis-lecture. Accessed 8 October, 2021.

Dobson, Andrew. *Listening for Democracy: Recognition, Representation, Reconciliation*. Oxford University Press, 2014.

Dolar, Mladen. *A Voice and Nothing More*. MIT Press, 2006.

Eckersall, Peter, Grehan, Helen, Scheer, Edward *New Media Dramaturgy: Performance, Media, and New-Materialism*. Palgrave Macmillan, 2017.

Ettinger, Zoe. "13 people with Down syndrome who are breaking barriers in entertainment, athletics, fashion, and more." *Insider*, 11 March, 2020.

Frankenstein's Children. Devised by the ensemble. Directed by Tony McCaffrey. Different Light Theatre. NASDA Theatre Body Festival 9–12 October 2008 NRID Conference, Christchurch Town Hall. 8–10 July 2009.

Fricker, Miranda. *Epistemic Injustice: Power and the Ethics of Knowing*. Oxford University Press, 2017.

Ganesh versus the Third Reich. Devised by the ensemble. Directed by Bruce Gladwin. Back to Back Theatre. Malthouse Theatre, Melbourne, September 29–October 9, 2011.

Gee, Emma and Hargrave, Matt. "A proper actor? The politics of training for learning disabled actors." *Theatre, Dance, and Performance Training*, vol. 2, no. 1, 2011, pp. 34–53.

Geertz, Clifford. "Thick description: toward an interpretive theory of Culture." *The Interpretation of Cultures: Selected Essays*, Basic Books, 1973, pp. 3–30.

Girlfriend. Directed by Justin Lerner. Wayne/Lauren Film Company, 2010.

Gladwin, Bruce. "Searchlight Pitch Session for Ganesh versus the Third Reich." Australian Performing Arts Market, Adelaide Festival Centre. February 24, 2010. Presentation.

Glee. TV series. Fox. May 19, 2009-March 20, 2015.

Gopal, Priyamvada. "On decolonization and the university." *Textual Practice*, vol. 35, no. 6, 2021, pp. 873–899.

Gorman, Sarah. "Performing Failure? Anomalous Amateurs in Jérôme Bel's DIsabled Theater and The Show Must Go On 2015'" *Contemporary Theatre Review*. Taylor and Francis, 2017.

Gosset, Katy Radio interview with Isaac Tait, Ben Morris, and Tony McCaffrey. "One in Five." *Radio New Zealand National Radio*, 18 April, 2012.

Grehan, Helena and Eckersall, Peter, eds. *'We're People Who Do Shows': Back to Back Theatre: Performance, Politics, Visibility*. Performance Research Books, 2013.

Hargrave, Matt. *Theatres of Learning Disability: Good, Bad or Plain Ugly?* Palgrave Macmillan, 2015.

Hartman, Saidiya V. *Scenes of Subjection: Terror, Slavery, and Self-Making in Nineteenth-Century America*. Oxford University Press, 1997.

Hexentanz II. (Witch Dance) Wigman, Mary. Film: *Mary Wigman Tanzt* Bundesarchive-Filmarchiv, Berlin, 1928.

Home-Cook, George. *Theatre and Aural Attention: Stretching Ourselves*. Palgrave Macmillan, 2015.

I belong in the past and the future and the very now ... Different Light Theatre. Devised by the ensemble. Directed by Tony McCaffrey. ADSA Conference, Auckland University of Technology. 27–30 June, 2017.

Johnstone, Keith. *Impro: Improvisation for the Theatre*. Methuen, 1990.

Kendrick, Lynne. *Theatre Aurality*. Palgrave Macmillan, 2017.

Kirkland, Colin. "Models with Down Syndrome are killing it in the fashion industry." www.boppermusic.com. Accessed 8 October, 2021.

Kittay, Eva Feder. "When caring is just and justice is caring: justice and mental retardation." In *The Subject of Care: Feminist Perspectives on Dependency*. Edited by Eva Feder Kittay. Rowman and Littlefield, 2002, pp. 257–276.

Kittay, Eva Feder and Carlson, Licia, eds. *Cognitive Disability and Its Challenge to Moral Philosophy*. Wiley-Blackwell, 2010.

Kochar-Lindgren, Kanta. *Hearing Difference: The Third Ear in Experimental, Deaf, and Multicultural Theater*. Gallaudet University Press, 2006.

Kontakthof Pina Bausch. Opernhaus Wuppertal, September 12, 1978.

Kuppers, Petra. *Eco Soma: Pain and Joy in Speculative Performance Encounters*. University of Minnesota Press, 2022.

Lacey, Kate. *Listening Publics: The Politics and Experience of Listening in the Media Age*. Wiley, 2013.

Lecoq, Jacques. *The Moving Body: Teaching Creative Theatre*. Translated by David Bradby. Methuen, 2000.

Le Huitième Jour. Directed by Jaco Van Dormael. Pan-Européenne Productions, 1996.
Life Goes On. TV series. ABC, Sept 12, 1989 – May 23, 1993.
Lipari, Lisbeth. "Ethics, kairos, and akroasis: an essay on time and relation." In *Philosophy of Ethics, Alterity and the Other.* Edited by Ronald C. Arnett and Arneson. Patricia. Fairleigh Dickinson University Press, 2014, pp. 87–106.
Manning, Erin. *For a Pragmatics of the Useless.* Duke University Press, 2020.
———. *The Minor Gesture.* Duke University Press, 2016.
McRuer, Robert. *Crip Times: Disability, Globalisation, and Resistance.* New York University Press, 2018.
Mitchell, David T. and Snyder, Sharon L. *The Biopolitics of Disability: Neoliberalism, Ablenationalism, and Peripheral Embodiment.* University of Michigan Press, 2015.
Mordue, Mark. *Ghosts in the Machine: Back to Back Theatre and 'The Shadow Whose Prey the Hunter Becomes'.* Back to Back website <https://backtoback-theatre.com>. Accessed 28 October, 2019.
Moten, Fred. *Black and Blur.* Duke University Press, 2017.
———. *Stolen Life.* Duke University Press, 2018.
———. *The Universal Machine.* Duke University Press, 2018.
Moten, Fred and Harney, Stefano. *The Undercommons: Fugitive Planning and Black Study.* Minor Compositions, 2013.
———. *All Incomplete.* Minor Compositions, 2020.
Oliver, Michael. *The Politics of Disablement.* Macmillan, 1990.
"Oscar the grouch shows a home movie", *Sesame Street.* Episode 2, Season 8. PBS Kids, 1975.
Phelan, Peggy. *Unmarked: The Politics of Performance.* Routledge, 1993.
Price, Margaret. "Ways to move: presence, participation, and resistance in kairotic space." *Mad at School: Rhetorics of Mental Disability and Academic Life,* University of Michigan Press, 2014, p. 60.
Puar, Jasbir K. *The Right to Maim: Debility, Capacity, Disability.* Duke University Press, 2017.
Ratcliffe, Krista. *Rhetorical Listening: Identification, Gender, Whiteness.* Southern Illinois Press, 2005.
Read, Alan. *The Dark Theatre: A Book about Loss.* Routledge, 2020.
Ridout, Nicholas. *Scenes from Bourgeois Life.* University of Michigan Press, 2020.
Ridout, Nicholas and Woods, Orlagh. *Performance, Possession and Automation.* https://possessionautomation.co.uk. Online research project and collaboration, 2020.
Saint Pierre, Joshua. "Fluency Machines: Semiocapitalism, Disability and Action." PhD thesis, University of Alberta, 2018.
Samuels, Ellen. "Six ways of looking at crip time." *Disability Studies Quarterly.* Vol 37, No. 3 Summer, 2017.
Schalk, Sami. *Bodyminds Reimagined: (Dis)ability, Race, and Gender in Black Women's Speculative Fiction.* Duke University Press, 2018.
Schmidt, Yvonne. "Towards a new directional turn? Directors with cognitive disabilities." *Research in Drama Education: The Journal of Applied Theatre and Performance*, vol. 22, no. 3, 2017, pp. 446–459.
———. "After disabled theater: authorship, creative responsibility and autonomy in *freie republik HORA*." in S. Umathum and B. Wihstutz, eds. *Disabled Theater.* Diaphanes, 2015, pp. 227–240.

Self Unfinished. LeRoy Xavier. Substanz-Cottbus, TIF Staatsschauspiel Dresden, 1998.

Shanley, Patrick. "'Damn it, That's Huge!' Actors With Down Syndrome Are Finding More Work in Hollywood." *The Hollywood Reporter*, 25 October, 2019.

Ship of Fools. Devised by the ensemble. Directed by Tony McCaffrey. Different Light Theatre. Awakenings Festival, Horsham, Victoria, Australia, 13–15 October 2007.

Sins Invalid. *Skin, Tooth, and Bone: The Basis of Our Movement Is Our People: A Disability Justice Primer*. Second Edition. Sins Invalid, 2019.

Spolin, Viola. *Improvisation for the Theatre: A Handbook of Teaching and Directing Techniques*. Northwestern University Press, 1990.

Stauffer, Jill. *Ethical Loneliness: The Injustice of Not Being Heard*. Columbia University Press, 2015.

Still Lives. Devised by the ensemble. Directed by Tony McCaffrey. Different Light Theatre. Society for Disability Studies 24th Annual Conference, San José, California. 15–18 June, 2011. Ludus Festival, Leeds and PSi 18 Riley Smith Hall, University of Leeds. 28–30 July, 2012.

The Earthquake in Chile. Directed by Richard Gough and Peter Falkenberg. St Mary's Church, Addington, Christchurch NZ. Body Festival. 13–16 October, 2011.

The History of Different Light. Devised by Different Light Theatre. Directed by Tony McCaffrey, Christchurch Arts Festival, NASDA Theatre, Christchurch, 1–3 August, 2019.

The Lonely and The Lovely Parts One and Two. Devised by the ensemble. Directed by Tony McCaffrey. Different Light Theatre. Arts Access Excellence Concourse, Chatswood, Sydney, Australia. 30–31 October, 2012. Disability Studies in Education conference, Jack Mann Auditorium, University of Canterbury. 7–9 June, 2013.

The Peanut Butter Falcon. Directed by Tyler Nilson and Michael Schwartz. Armory Films, 2019.

The Poor Dears. Devised by the ensemble. Directed by Tony McCaffrey. Different Light Theatre. NASDA Theatre, CPIT. Body Festival 1–4 Oct 2009, University of Canterbury Platform Festival, 27–30 May, 2010.

The Shadow Whose Prey the Hunter Becomes. Devised by the ensemble. Directed by Bruce Gladwin. Back to Back Theatre. Carriageworks, Sydney, 28 September, 2019.

"The Winner" *The Fall Guy* Season 4, Episode 12. ABC, December 19, 1984.

The Wizard of Oz. Devised by the ensemble. Directed by Tony McCaffrey. Different Light Theatre. NASDA Theatre, CPIT. Ignition Creative Festival, 18–21 November, 2010.

Different Light Theatre. Guild Theatre, University of Melbourne. PSi 22 Conference 5–9 July, 2016.

Umathum, Sandra and Benjamin, Wihstutz, eds. *Disabled Theater*. Translated by Christopher Nöthlings. Diaphanes, 2015.

Voegelin, Salome. *The Political Possibility of Sound: Fragments of Listening*. Bloomsbury, 2018.

Whatley, Sarah, Waelde, Charlotte, Harmon, Shawn, Brown, Abbe and Wood Karen, and Blades Hetty, eds. *Dance, Disability and Law: InVisible Difference.* Intellect, 2018.
Williams, Moira. Access guide. Pre-conference presentation. Performance Philosophy Problems Conference, University of the Arts, Helsinki, June 2021.
Yergeau, Remi M. *Authoring Autism: On Rhetoric and Neurological Queerness.* Duke University Press, 2017.
Yo Tambien Directed by Antonio Naharo and Alvaro Pastor. Olive Films, 2009.

1 Setting the Scene

The Shadow Whose Prey the Hunter Becomes

Back to Back Theatre's *The Shadow Whose Prey the Hunter Becomes* (2019) could stand as a paradigm of the current state and potential future of learning disabled theatre. I offer an analysis of this performance at this point to provide clear, specific examples in the context of performance of the consideration of different meanings of voice in learning disabled theatre.

This was the last piece of live learning disabled theatre that I experienced before the period of the lockdowns and isolations of 2020 and 2021 due to the global pandemic. I attended the premiere season at the Carriageworks in Sydney at the end of September 2019. In May 2020, the Carriageworks was one of the first arts venues in Sydney to go into voluntary administration due to 'irreparable loss of income' because of the coronavirus pandemic (Bosely and Convery 2020) but subsequently reopened to the public in August 2020. This production is important and has acquired even more importance, I believe, due to its occurrence in the last days before the outbreak of the pandemic that also led to the cancelling of the company's international tour. The play, and its impact, remains, but that impact, for a period, seemed all the greater because of its suspension in time. The cessation of live performance in the human pause has now been largely superseded, but the implications of the pandemic for conventional practices of live performance are still being investigated.

It is a play that is crucially about voices and how they are given and taken away. The play emerged from the company's methodology of devising and development of working with the same small core of performers, offering them different challenges from one production to the next (Grehan and Eckersall 2013). This methodology testifies to Back to Back's commitment to taking time to listen the performers into speech and to provide supported opportunities for learning disabled artists in performance that are tempered with the rigour of continuing artistic self-criticism.

The play is set 'in a small community hall in Geelong, Australia' (Back to Back Theatre 2022) but what is not clear is the identity of the 'community' in this hall. Although community halls would normally be open to hire by any kind of group, perhaps the suggestion is that community is a placefiller term into which can be read any kind of social grouping, and that

DOI: 10.4324/9781003083658-2

community is, at heart, contingent, contextual, and ephemeral. It is not clear what the nature of the meeting is, what it is 'about', for what purpose, or for whom. This uncertainty is shared by early reviewers of the piece: 'The play centres around a group of activists who hold a public meeting' (Stone 2019). This description reveals the nice distinction between the play and its actors who perform represented actions, and the 'activists' who engage in supposedly actual or politically efficacious actions. Another review stated: 'Though it's presented as such, it's not your typical democratic forum' (Zhou 2019). This hints at a fundamental questioning that is implicit in *The Shadow Whose Prey the Hunter Becomes*. What might constitute a 'typical democratic forum' in a time when democratic processes and mechanisms of political representation are breaking down? Can we any longer rely on typical democracy? A third reviewer refers to a conceptual space and time 'when theatre disguises itself as civic action, or when civic action disguises itself as theatre' (Trezise 2019). This is, I will argue, a crucial confusion that the company wishes to exploit. One kind of public meeting is in effect staged within another, that other being the temporary community of performers and audience in theatrical performance. It is significant, however, that 'we' the audience are invited into this event and into this non-specific community hall meeting, with a mixture of both hospitality and hostility. This uncertainty and ambivalence characterizes the world of the play and its dramaturgical premise. An early section entitled 'Welcome to the meeting' complicates this act of hospitality with an acknowledgement of the historical hostility and violence enacted upon the indigenous people, original occupants of the land, in what has become known in Australian and other settler colonial contexts as a 'welcome to country'. There is, moreover, a lack of clarity as to who is the host, the chair, the person taking or in charge of the meeting. The allocation of the voice of authority is first proposed by Michael (Chan) to Sarah (Mainwaring): 'Over to Sarah who will start the meeting'. Sarah's response is characteristic of Saint Pierre's 'dysfluency' (2018): hesitations, pauses, followed by 'I can't remember what to say' and 'My mind's gone blank'. Another participant in the meeting, Scott, then consults a different voice, Siri, the voice of the online hive-mind – or of doxa? – to ask what to do 'when a disabled person panics'. Siri through an unspecified 'disability website' advises Scott to 'Keep the conversation concrete' hinting at the supposed inability of learning disabled people to engage in abstract thought and discourse. Scott contradicts this ableist assumption within a few lines when he says: 'Philosophically she should lead the group'. He goes on to give voice to a much more liberal doxa when he says: 'We should empower everyone to have a voice'. When the conversation turns to shifting the responsibility of running the meeting to Simon (Laherty) the following exchange occurs:

MICHAEL: I'm trying to understand the word 'empower'. I'm a bit lost.
SCOTT: It means, giving Simon a voice.

MICHAEL: Only if he's interested in it.
SARAH: Simon, do you want to be the one with the voice?
SIMON: Yes
SCOTT: Ok, there you go.
MICHAEL: Simon, do you know what you want to say to the public?
SIMON: No.
MICHAEL: I rest my case. (29)

Here, as is the case throughout the play, 'voice' as identity, as authority, or power is presented ironically. The assumption of authority is resisted by Laherty in terms reminiscent of Bartleby. He wants to claim the right to voice without necessarily knowing what to say, recalling Deleuze's telling observation that: '[w]e don't suffer these days from any lack of communication, but rather from all the forces making us say things when we've nothing much to say' (1990, 137).

The learning disabled artists who have 'historically been denied subjectivity' problematize identity and the 'production of subjectivity' (Manning 2020, 51). They do so by participating in a theatrical assemblage of the production of subjectivity, a polyvocal mix of voices in the head, politically correct voices, misapplied speech acts, and irony that requires careful listening into speech by an audience. With Back to Back, we the audience are invited to take what is said at more than its face value. This is not the hermeneutic identification of subtext, nor does it equate to dramatic irony, both of which presuppose a hierarchy of knowledge and a complicity that can connect the educated audience member with the inner workings of the character or the intended meaning of the playwright or play itself. Back to Back's invitation is rather to check our privilege, if we assume ourselves to be non-disabled, to listen to what happens to the speech acts that exemplify the 'saying what everyone thinks' or the clichés about disability and intellectual disability *when they are spoken by learning disabled actors*. This also includes the discourses of 'identity politics', in both an affirmative and an offence-taking sense. Disability and intellectual disability are likewise often referred to ironically, yet the play does present graphic examples of the very real implications and consequences of being diagnosed, labelled, and treated as intellectually disabled. Identification and disclosure of (intellectual) disability is likewise presented in all its nuance, encapsulated in Simon Laherty's splendidly aphoristic and dialectic statement: 'I'm okay with saying I have a disability as long as I don't have to talk about it'. The careful attention to the contextualization of utterances by the company, including the ambivalence that informs speech acts that are uttered in a theatrical space, affords the learning disabled artists the possibility of presenting characters, personae, and speech acts of dialectical complexity.

The production largely eschews the visual spectacle or epic layers of narrative that characterize the heightened theatricality of Back to Back's previous work to concentrate on the voices of the production in terms of not only what is said but how it is said and in what context. The theatrical palette is deliberately restrained: five actors, five plastic chairs, a trolley, a large piece of white polystyrene, a ladder, and some yellow masking tape. This strategy seems to suggest the urgency of the piece, an urge to get 'the message' across, paring back theatricalization to focus on 'what is said' the spoken or written text and the voices these contain. These include the Siri-type computerized voice, the expression of algorithms, the captions intended to clarify and amplify the non-normative voices of the learning disabled performers and the elaborate business of assigning the role of spokesperson or voice of authority.

Responding to this highly verbal piece requires the kind of listening that attends to both the saying and the said, a listening to what passes through, and around, and in between the words that are spoken by the actors and that are echoed – or at times travestied – by the captions that, projected from above and behind, accompany them and dominate them. It requires the kind of listening that pays careful attention to the speech acts of the actors, speech acts that are delivered, however, in a theatrical, and, therefore, subjunctive, and unreliable context.

At one point Scott Price refers to the captions scrolling behind and above the ensemble whenever they speak: 'You can tell we have disabilities as everything we say comes up on a screen' a triumph of tautologous logic and a tacit acknowledgement that what they say is almost immediately lost from them, captured by the captions which shadow what they say and translate, travesty, or traduce them to the audience. Throughout the performance, the captions appear to struggle to keep up with what the performers say. Sometimes they deliberately misunderstand and mis-translate. The captions are like the shadows whose prey we the audience become in the hunt for the meaning of what the performers say and who they are. As the captions are always a little late to capture what is said, do they seem to echo the struggle for utterance of the actor rememorating a script, or a person with intellectual disabilities overcoming difficulties with processing quotidian communication in what Yergeau has termed the 'violence of rhetoric's impatience' (65)? This delay in the capture and translation of 'what is said' renders Derridean différance in real (theatrical) time.

Sarah Mainwaring finds the captioning offensive and patronizing, shouting out: 'We don't speak a different language' which is then duly captioned on the screen behind her. She crowns her resistance to the captioning with: 'I don't want to be spat on and polished'. The phrase captures the stigmatization, 'spat on' and patronization 'polished' meted out to people with disabilities, often in a cognitively dissonant combination, or perhaps both attitudes are two sides of the same coin. The phrase also captures the 'spit and polish' of the unseen labour of this type of theatrical performance that takes the raw material of personal accounts of lived experience, group improvisation, and devising processes and polishes them up into performance texts that can be repeated and refreshed, whilst at the same time acknowledging that however real and extemporary the utterances may seem in the skilled hands of the performers, inevitably something is lost in the translation to dramaturgy. The phrase captures. It does precisely that, capturing in language, rhetorical language Sarah Mainwaring and her performance persona's ambivalent attitude to the meaning-making of theatrical performance. It does so momentarily in the transmission of affect of the performance event (which is also created by the power of resistance to being labelled and categorized embodied in the physical and vocal performance of Mainwaring's 'saying') leaving the complexities of the statement, the speech act, and the context to work themselves out subsequently in the spectator.

The title, *The Shadow Whose Prey the Hunter Becomes*, hints at the very process of how subject and object become confounded, and an exposing of the obsessive but ultimately futile desire to capture or 'get' meaning or identity. The provenance of the phrase as director Bruce Gladwin explains is generally French, connected to the colloquial phrase *lâcher la proie pour l'ombre* – to give up what one already has to go chasing shadows, and more specifically from Jacques Lacan. Gladwin refers to the borrowing of the phrase from Lacan in the following terms, as: 'the verbal mind-game where the identity of the protagonist and antagonist keeps moving around' (Mordue) and elsewhere: 'it was used initially to describe the ego and its elusiveness … it's not clear who the antagonist is in the scenario, like our own relationship with our own ego' (Stone). Hunting down the source of the phrase brings us to *The Triumph of Religion*:

> … psychoanalytic investigation of the ego allows us to identify it with the form of the goatskin bottle [outre], with the outrageousness of the shadow whose prey the hunter becomes, and with the emptiness [vanité] of the visual form. This is the ethical face of what I have articulated, in order to convey it, with the term 'mirror stage'. (34)

The title thus folds itself into the context of the production's own stated objective to search for and to transmit the subject, meaning, or message of a piece of theatre and the search for the 'identity' of the learning disabled performers. The Lacanian source suggests that this may be an identity that we who like to think of ourselves as not intellectually disabled may well be guilty of projecting onto people with intellectual disabilities, whilst all the while chasing the shadows or illusions of our own identity as sovereign subject. It may be that what we are supposed to 'get' from *The Shadow Whose Prey the Hunter Becomes* is our own implication in, and acknowledgement of, the processes whereby the subject is constructed and deconstructed. How do these concerns, and how does Gladwin's reading of an excerpt from Lacan, translate to, or relate to, the Back to Back actors in *The Shadow Whose Prey the Hunter Becomes*?

Setting the Scene   47

The answer is that the actors are cognizant of the processes of collaboration and devising theatre with Gladwin and others as this is something they have been doing over many years. They are equally cognizant of discourses that frame them, define them, and marginalize them as they are with strategies of resisting and attempting to free themselves from such discourses. They are seasoned and well-travelled performers, as acquainted with the rigours and pleasures of touring internationally as with the rigours and pleasures of being up there on stage, often, in the distinctive way of working of the company, in performance in which they are slipping in between character, persona, and some approximation of their own self, in a carefully rehearsed and finely timed giddy abandon. They are accustomed to the range and diversity of responses they receive in response to their performance in post-show discussions and casual conversations struck up in the theatre foyer.

This presence is not some guarantee of the authenticity of learning disabled identity but emerges from the rhetorical strategies of the actors themselves, slipping in and out of dominant discourses, slipping in and out of the theatrical frame, and slipping in and out of their own rhetorical devices: the kairos (Yergeau) of the well-timed, well-paced, well-intoned spoken line or action or reaction, the deliberately mis-timed, mis-pronounced, or misfiring utterance or gesture, and those emergent moments when performers and audience are caught up in really listening and attending to each other, and in which performer, audience, disabled, and nondisabled seem to slip the bonds of categorization.

The Shadow Whose Prey the Hunter Becomes is an exploration of theatre's capacity to investigate the self and knowledge and of course the promise of self-knowledge:

SARAH: What do you think about self-knowledge?
SIMON: I have very little knowledge on that.
SARAH: Have you ever pursued it?
SIMON: No, not at all.
SARAH: Self-discovery?
SIMON: No never.
SARAH: Any interest?
SIMON: None. (55)

and this exposes the 'self' of learning disabled theatre *qua* theatre in terms of ontology and epistemology. The ironic discussion of self-harks back to the first principles of Greek philosophy and theatre: the *gnothi seauton* of the oracle at Delphi and the tragic path to self-knowledge unravelled in Sophocles' *Oedipus the King*.

The origin story of *The Shadow Whose Prey the Hunter Becomes*, its stated point of origin is an account of slavery, of contemporary slavery in 'The Boys in the Bunkhouse', an article that appeared in the *New*

York Times Magazine (Barry 2014). Scott Price gives the following account:

> In the State of Iowa, in America, in 2013,
> 32 men with intellectual disabilities
> were found to be enslaved
> in a turkey processing plant
> For three decades .... (34)

The narrative intertwines the violence and exploitation committed against animals and learning disabled people in the service of an economy of consumption and the slavery that enables the narrative of *The Shadow Whose Prey the Hunter Becomes* with the kinds of slavery and exclusion that enabled Athenian theatre and democracy. Slavery is later referred to in a passage that manages to interweave compassion with acute social commentary and critique:

MICHAEL: Tell me this when Artificial Intelligence overtakes human intelligence how will people be treated?
SCOTT: I don't know, I haven't thought that far.
SIMON: Maybe slaves.
SCOTT: Like how we treat a chicken or a turkey?
MICHAEL: Yeah.
SCOTT: Or, a person with a disability. (45)

Back to Back offer throughout the play in their own oblique way an acknowledgement of what Moten and Harney in *All Incomplete* term 'the Socioecological Disaster' (45) and the histories that have brought us to it that include the creation of settler colonial states built on the exploitation of indigenous populations and on slave capital. To return to the welcome and hospitality at the beginning of the play:

MICHAEL: Welcome to the meeting. I'd like to acknowledge that we are standing on the land of the Wurundjeri people and we pay our respects to their elders – past, present, and future.
SCOTT: It's.
MICHAEL: Yep?
SCOTT: It's Wathaurong.
MICHAEL: Oh, Wathaurong. (mispronounces)
SCOTT: It's Wathaurong. (attempting to correct him)
MICHAEL: Whatever. (25)

This is learning disabled theatre as complex satire. The dialogue makes fun of how the performance of Land Acknowledgement can become routinized as merely a token gesture rather than indicate the depth of oppression and legacy of colonialism that it is meant to acknowledge, but perhaps never does so. With Back to Back, however it is also always already more complicated and intersectional. Michael Chan the actor who mispronounces the tribal name is Chinese-Australian who speaks English with an accent. Wathaurong is a transliteration of a foreign word an Aboriginal word gone into 'English'. What Scott or the audience deems acceptable pronunciation may be very different to how the Wathaurong pronounce their tribal identity that, like the Aboriginal people themselves, get left behind in the exchange.

The Shadow Whose Prey the Hunter Becomes is a play that is all about voices, the voices that have been stolen as much as the voices raised at a public meeting, the voice of being a spokesperson for learning disability – one of the actors, Scott Price, wears an 'Autism Pride' t-shirt, the ironic presentation of the voices in the head that 'correct' the voicing of certain opinions in the era of political correctness and identity politics, the oracle-like voice of Siri.

The Shadow Whose Prey the Hunter Becomes stages a non-specific 'public meeting' in the kind of bare, bureaucratic, and unlovely space in which such meetings conventionally take place: plastic chairs, microphones, and projected video. The audience does not know the location or purpose of this public meeting, but it is of course framed within another kind of public meeting that of a theatrical performance. The *theatron* or place of looking is presented as the *agora* or marketplace or public space, or the two are deliberately confused. It is a contemporary *agora* complete with heterogeneous, ill-fitting objects and décor, the awkward switching between live presence and the mediated, the oracular voice of Siri, and the chorus of social media. This learning-disabled theatre confounds the distinction between *demos* and *idiotai*. In Ancient Greece, the supposed site of origin of Western theatre and democracy, a culture based on slavery, *demos* meant the common people, the whole citizen whose voice and presence is the basis of democracy. *Idios, idiotai* meant variously the unskilled, the private person, the layman, the stay-at-home, those not engaged in public life, those who chose not to use their voice in the political process, those who, like Bartleby, would prefer not to. Many people caught a glimpse of what it is like to go from *demos* to *idiotai* in the lockdowns, bubbles, and isolations of the *pan demos* pandemic. Perhaps the real promise of the soothsaying of *The Shadow Whose Prey the Hunter Becomes* is the emergence of a voice located somewhere between *demos* and *idiotai*, a minor voice, aligning with Erin Manning's use of 'minor' (2016)

The minor presence of the learning disabled artists of Back to Back requires and repays careful attention. Their presence suggests and invites an undermining of the entitled self and different possibilities of mutual care and collaboration in both the *theatron* and the *agora*. *The Shadow Whose Prey the Hunter Becomes* (2019) stages the contemporary conflation of the *theatron* and the *agora* complete with the oracular voice of Siri and a chorus of social media. It is a play all about voices: voices signalling virtue, voices who cannot breathe, voices clamouring for rights, voices taking offence, and voices of entitlement that are in danger of drowning out the cries of the planet. There are also the quieter, less certain, less assured voices of the learning disabled artists. These are wryly humorous voices; they slip in and out of certainty, in and out of claiming the legal fiction of entitled selfhood, and alert us to the need for interdependence, collaboration, and conviviality.

References

Back to Back Theatre. *Back to Back Theatre Collection: The Shadow Whose Prey the Hunter Becomes, Lady Eats Apple, Super Discount.* Playlab Theatre Publication, 2022.

Barry, Dan. "The Boys in the Bunkhouse: Toil, abuse and endurance in the heartland." The New York Times Magazine. 9 March, 2014.

Bosely, Matilda and Stephanie Convery. "Carriageworks goes into voluntary administration citing 'irreparable loss of income' due to coronavirus." The Guardian. 5 May, 2020.

Deleuze, Gilles. *Negotiations. 1972–1990.* Translated by Martin Joughin. Columbia University Press, 1990.

Grehan, Helena and Peter Eckersall, eds. *'We're People Who Do Shows' Back to Back Theatre: Performance, Politics, Visibility.* Performance Research Books, 2013.

Lacan, Jacques. *The Triumph of Religion Preceded by Discourse to Catholics.* Translated by Bruce Fink. Polity Press, 2013.

Manning, Erin. *For a Pragmatics of the Useless.* Duke University Press, 2020.

———. *The Minor Gesture.* Duke University Press, 2016.

Moten, Fred and Stefano Harney. *All Incomplete.* Minor Compositions, 2020.

Saint Pierre, Joshua. "Fluency machines: Semiocapitalism, disability, and action." PhD thesis, University of Alberta, 2018.

Stone, Jacob. "Back to back returns with questions of (artificial) intelligence." Broadsheet. 26 August, 2019. http://www.broadsheet.com.au. Accessed 29 October, 2019.

The Shadow Whose Prey the Hunter Becomes. Devised by the ensemble. Directed by Bruce Gladwin.; Back to Back Theatre, Carriageworks, Sydney, 28 September, 2019.

Trezise, Bryoni. "*The Shadow Whose Prey the Hunter Becomes* review: Back to Back Theatre's exciting reframing of disability." In The Conversation, 30 September 2019.

Yergeau, M. Remi. *Authoring Autism: On Rhetoric and Neurological Queerness.* Duke University Press, 2017.

Zhou, Debbie. "*The Shadow Whose Prey the Hunter Becomes* review." Time Out, 5 October 2019.

2 Community Theatre and Myths of Community

Welcome to our world: hospitality, hostility, Different Light Theatre

If theatre in its relationship with audience, in its narrative forms and genres, and as a social and cultural practice, is a form of hospitality, then learning disabled artists are uneasy guests, uneasier hosts. One prevailing assumption in the development of learning disabled theatre is that 'theatre' is something that can be given to learning disabled people and that this gift will somehow enable them to give voice to their experience and to express themselves. We give voice to them. We give theatre to them. We allow them to find their own voice. Voice is given to the voiceless. We include them in our world. This book represents a critique of these assumptions. Any 'voice' of learning disabled experience expressed within spoken language will be caught up in the lexicon, grammar, and tropes of language within which dominant discourses prevail. In Hartman's words in *Scenes of Subjection* 'there is no access to the subaltern consciousness outside of dominant representations' (10). This occurs not only at the level of access to language – a stigmatized or disadvantaged access to language – but at the level of language itself, at the level of syntax: the relationship of subject and object, the relationship of subject to predicate in, for example, the learning disabled artists are present, and in the use of active and passive voices. The kinds of inter-relationships and interdependence that emerge in learning disabled theatre praxis are, therefore, hard to write about and talk about. They do not sit well in conventional grammatical and syntactic structures. It is important to analyze the agents or actants in the process of 'giving' itself. Who is doing the giving, what exactly is being given, what is involved or implied in this giving: what are the terms of this exchange?

This involves looking at the relationship between non-disabled and disabled people in a world constructed on ableism and a consideration of how deeply inflected with ableism are even good intentions to include, to empower, and to facilitate. What is taken, taken away, or taken back, in the process of the artists themselves giving voice? In Derrida's questioning,

DOI: 10.4324/9781003083658-3

Figure 2.1 John Lambie introduces Different Light Theatre. *The Wizard of Oz*, 2011. Image: Different Light Theatre, Stuart Lloyd-Harris.

'Who will decide whether this voice was lent, returned, or given? And to whom?' (1991, 7). What obligations are imposed upon learning disabled artists by being given the gifts of voice and theatre? One of these is the assumption that this will enable them to communicate the lived experience of learning disability, the authenticity or truth of this experience. Saint Pierre in 'Fluency Machines' offers a nuanced critique of this imperative imposed upon marginalized peoples both to tell the truth and achieve some therapeutic release as communication in the service of a market economy that forecloses any possibility of political resistance:

> Therapeutic truth-telling is an apolitical enunciation that indexes the model of authenticity. This mode of truth-telling is limited to speaking truth about oneself and here in a normalizing register. I argue that the insistence on an "authentic" voice generates an impoverished relation to oneself, to others, and the world; this practice of self-transformation will not help us escape "the veridictional cage of the market" (McFalls and Pandolfi 2014, 174) .... (28)

The giving of voice and theatre to learning disabled artists can be configured as being fundamentally and epistemologically caught up in Derrida's paradox of hospitality and hostility. In this, it is part of a much wider context of well-intentioned initiatives toward inclusion that ultimately reveal themselves to be inclusion on 'special' terms, or what might be described as the 'performance of inclusion', a performance that barely masks an underlying impulse to exclusion.

In 'Hostipitality' in *Acts of Religion*, Derrida details the smiling or joy of the host that should accompany the welcome or hospitality granted to the stranger entering the home but juxtaposes this with the weeping of women in the Tupinamba ceremonies of hospitality, 'their welcoming ritual associated with a cult of the dead, the stranger being hailed like a *revenant*' (359). This is the first figuration of the intertwining of hospitality and death in this seminar that Derrida tracks through to Old Testament sources in which unconditional hospitality taken to its limits would require the death and dismemberment of the host. These extremely high stakes of hospitality and the welcoming of the stranger then inform the emergence within hospitality of its contradiction and opposite, hostility:

> what belabors and concerns hospitality at its core [ce qui travaille l'hospitalité en son sein] what works it like a labor, like a pregnancy, like a promise as much as like a threat, what settles in it, within it, [en son dedans], like a Trojan horse, the enemy (*hostis*) as much as the *avenir*, intestine hostility, is indeed a contradictory conception, a thwarted [contrariée] conception, or a *contraception* of awaiting, a contradiction of welcoming itself. (365)

This and other writings by Derrida on hospitality have enjoyed a recent renaissance due to their relevance to the delineation of inclusion and exclusion in terms of economic immigration and the arrival of asylum seekers and refugees within Europe (Still 2010). I would argue that disabled people and in particular learning disabled people are likewise positioned as strangers or others that are always with us, but never part of us. They should, according to certain codes, be granted hospitality but this is always, to some extent, inflected with hostility. One reason inclusion and access may be so difficult to achieve is that the hospitality offered in inclusion contains within it, in the very visceral terms Derrida describes, a deep hostility. Disabled people, learning disabled people, and vulnerable aged people are particularly prone to being treated with a reception by the non-disabled that swings between the appearance of hospitality and an irrepressible hostility perhaps because such people represent the community of the normative the once and future revenants of an unsustainable normative wholeness.

Derrida reveals how the apparent 'selflessness' of acts of forgiving, giving, and hospitality is inherently self-contradictory:

> The other must not hear, [il ne faut pas que l'autre entende] one must not say that one forgives, not only in order not to recall the (double) fault but also not to recall or manifest that something was given (forgiven, given, given as forgiveness), something was given back again, that deserves some gratitude or risks obligating the one who is forgiven.

> At bottom, nothing is more vulgar and impolite, even wounding, than to obligate someone (by telling them 'I forgive you' which implies an 'I give you'). This opens a scene of acknowledgement (reconnaissance), a transaction of gratitude, a commerce of thinking that destroys the gift. Similarly, one must never say 'I grant you hospitality' or 'I invite you'. When one says 'I invite you' it means: I pay and we are inscribed in the circular commerce of the most inhospitable exchange possible, the least giving. (398)

The implications of the impossibility of unconditional forgiveness or unconditional hospitality can be found in an aporia underlying attempts to give access, to give voice. For non-disabled people to 'give' rights to disabled people is inherently a giving that is inequitable, that operates from the position of having the power to give. What Derrida's tortuous syntax describes is that the giver never really releases this power or relaxes this grip. In fact, the giver often tightens and twists their grip to compensate for the loss experienced, or the sense of obligation they feel is due to them, in their exercising magnanimity and generosity. The recipient can be burdened with the consequences of an almost irredeemable debt of gratitude and obligation. Derrida suggests that the gift that is given in forgiving, in giving, and in hospitality is often a Trojan horse.

Derrida reveals that these impossible tensions operate at a deep level within cultures and individuals. They play out in an extreme form in, for example, the treatment of the vulnerable in care in institutions. In fact, terms such as 'care' and 'home' that should denote comfort and solicitude, have at times become bywords for systemic negligence and violence. There seems to be a constant litany of revelations of how learning disabled people and vulnerable aged people have been subjected to abuse in the institutions within which they might expect care, shelter, and protection. Indeed, in the UK and other countries during the pandemic care homes were the locations where the full necropolitical force and hostility were released in terms of the provision of 'care for the vulnerable' without the slightest façade of hospitality.

Different Light Theatre: welcome to our world of theatre

I can trace how this aporia played out in my own earliest attempts to give the gift of theatre or to welcome learning disabled people into what I considered to be theatre. In 2004, I was invited to conduct ten weeks of theatre workshops with some 20 people at Hohepa Hall in Christchurch, within the Hohepa Community, a residential institution for the learning disabled people that had been in operation since 1965. These workshops led to the formation of Different Light Theatre. If I examine now with the benefit of hindsight what went on in these workshops, I am struck by the openness and enthusiasm of the participants subjected to the range of physical theatre exercises and improvisations in which I expected them to engage. I am also aware of the tensions that were already apparent in the establishment of a group or company ethos. The attempted establishment of a 'theatre company ethos' involved the performers' meeting expectations of physical commitment, ensemble work, and overcoming challenges and difficulties that I had brought to the workshops from my previous experience in making and teaching theatre. This followed a model of commitment, labour, and collaboration of a conventional Western drama school of the late 20th, early 21st century. This was not only a non-disabled model but an inherently ableist one, its assumptions being that working on one's physical, vocal, and mental 'blocks' would lead to virtuosity and a clarity of voice and body in performance. This represents a kind of theatre training model of what Puar in *The Right to Maim* terms 'neoliberalism's heightened demands for bodily capacity' (12). I applied this model to people who were either within a segregated institution or in a segregated section of the New Zealand secondary school system until they were in their 20s. They would have had very little experience of such demands. Whilst my ignorance of their capacities may have been at times felicitous as much as reckless, what efficacy this approach may have had was more by accident than design. On the other hand, running alongside the 'theatre company ethos' and to some extent in tension with it, there was a kind of 'male banter ethos'. The participants in the initial group were mostly male. A working relationship was developed in the down times from the work of theatre exploration and training that was based on a kind of gruff male-to-male benevolent antipathy or raillery that might now be described as 'banter', a term that has recently, and justly, fallen into deep disrepute. We were working out ways of being together as a group, finding out what we had in common as experience by engaging in the particularly New Zealand male phenomenon of 'rarking each other up': humorous teasing, well-intentioned chiding or chivvying, common amongst male sports teams or groups of manual workers. This was what emerged as our first attempts at an informal ethos. The first space of commonality that we went to was modelling a kind of New Zealand maleness. The irony of this situation was marked. Neither I nor the male learning disabled performers could in any sense be described as typical New Zealand males. It was as if we sought to redress the perceived uselessness and frivolity of improvisation and playing theatre games with a pretence of being blokeish workers. We thus combined a commitment to theatricality with a suspicious anti-theatricality, an uncertainty over the gendering of what we were doing masked by the adoption of the stereotypical male persona. Hospitality and hostility had already been internalized to allow the group to make theatre.

These personae and relationships later evolved and diversified over time, but it is perhaps symptomatic of the depth to which Derrida's aporia operates that this internalized tension emerged amongst ourselves even before the performers were to encounter how it would play out so much more vehemently in a myriad of situations as the company proceeded to perform publicly and to tour. The public sphere was where the group would encounter a range of variants of the uncomfortable braiding of hospitality and hostility: patronization, low expectations, infantilization, micro-aggressions, actual major aggressions, segregation, medicalization, pathologization, the denigration and diminution of the performers' capacity to act.

Constructing myths of community, finding ways of being together

The first three performances by Different Light Theatre, *A Different Light*, *The Birds*, and *Dante* were experiments in being together. They represented a seeking of community whilst attempting to deal with the singularities and diversities of the performers. These narratives were also inflected with various kinds of spirituality. This was in part a response to the strongly held faith of some of the performers. It was also a tactic towards building a group ethos of 'common good' as opposed to the post-therapeutic discourses of the relentless assertion, affirmation, and glorification of the individual self.

In 'Community Arts and Practices: Improvising Being-Together', Petra Kuppers has written of community performance, drawing on Jean Luc Nancy's *The Inoperative Community*:

> Storytelling and myth-making are important parts of Nancy's articulation of the inoperative community, a community that becomes inoperative at the same moment at which it offers relation. (102)

Nancy's community is established and dissipates in the sharing of the myth, the leaning into the circle. In his poignant articulation: 'Community is at least the clinamen of the '"individual"' (2004, 3) that leaning or tendency of the individual toward community. Lucretius' swerve of the atom that Nancy aligns with the tendency of the individual toward something that once achieved is exhausted until the next occasion of leaning and yearning.

The yearning for community that emerged in the first productions of Different Light Theatre was for a community different from that of the existing meanings of community around the performers. These were institutional communities: the Hohepa Residential Community part of a national network of institutions for the learning disabled run on the principles of Rudolf Steiner, the KiwiAble network of Christchurch City Council, the Southern Ballet Theatre the performance venue within the Arts Centre, the drama school at which I taught and some of whose students collaborated in the first three Different Light Theatre productions. The community of performers and audience that emerged in the early productions was a leaning toward ephemeral, improvisational, but somehow reiterative community, it was not an institution or solid state. To cite Kuppers again: 'no point of standstill, definition, or grounding of identity in ontology is possible in this conception of improvisational community' (102). There was an ebbing and flowing in the being together of the group and in those moments of emergent community within the circle of performers and audience. The kind of community theatre that constituted the early productions of Different Light was particularly suited to exploring this clinamen of the 'individual', both the individual performers whose life experience was subject to segregation and a limited network of relationships and those audience members not used to encountering people with learning disabilities in their everyday lives.

The local council had communicated to me that the funding for the initial workshops was in the interest of promoting 'positive images' of people with disabilities, but, rightly or wrongly, I felt that it was possible to promote all kinds of different images, to allow for contradiction in the images and representations of learning disabled people. Community performance often becomes an essay at performing community. Learning disabled theatre was for me an opportunity to experiment with performances of community and to expose the myths of community through the humour of the learning disabled performers and their capacity for contradiction and ambiguity.

Devising from myths and canonical texts

For the group's first public performance I chose a narrative framework very loosely based on Marlowe's *Dr Faustus*. This was in part the result of my misspent youth as a working-class student reading English at Cambridge. At the time my intentions were to allow the performers to present themselves as much as devils as angels, to allow for contradiction and ambiguity in their inhabiting of characters and presentation of themselves. It was also to allow them to encounter, in whatever form, a canonical text, the basic premise of which has been cited as one of the super-plots of Western myth and narrative. Looking back with the hindsight of 17 years, I can now see that the choice of the narrative was a particularly appropriate one. In terms of hospitality and hostility, Faust's pact with the devil Mephistophilis: 24 years of whatever Faust desires in exchange for the loss of his immortal soul, is perhaps the ultimate example of a gift with some serious strings attached. It would be a strain to suggest that the performers entered into a Faustian bargain of theatre and representation, however ambiguous the gift of theatre might be. Many of the performers were, however, familiar with the obligations of gifts with strings attached. Some of the members were residents of Hohepa, an institution that provided security, individualized care, and a range of occupational and artistic therapies, but at the price of segregation from the community and long-term separation from families of origin. In the case of one of the Different Light performers, John Lambie, who was in the role of John Faustus, he was one of the original intake of children to the institution who remained there for 50 years. Others were all too familiar with the ambiguous bonds of living within their family

58 *Community Theatre and Myths of Community*

Figure 2.2 Promotional flyer for *A Different Light,* the first performance by Different Light Theatre at Southern Ballet Theatre, Arts Centre, Christchurch, September, 2004. Different Light Theatre, Inez Grim. Features left to right Shawn O'Rourke, John Lambie, and Ben Morris.

homes or halfway houses and the tensions in the lives of people with learning disabilities between being given support and being able to assert some measure of independence. The experience of community for many of the performers was that of a relatively closed community provided by NGOs and post-charitable disability initiatives and enterprises.

A Different Light: first performance

In the first three performances, there was an emphasis placed on theatre as a collaborative and ensemble activity. I used exercises adapted from the work of Jacques Lecoq and Augusto Boal to help build and sustain a company ethos and collective solidarity. The physical theatre approaches to devising included exercises in the movement and properties of a physical theatre chorus as a kind of collective, organic character. The performers were taught that the physical theatre chorus moves on the breath as an organic being, and that it can operate using the commedia verbs of I see, I look, and I react. These verbs are marked by the breath and moved in the collective body, not in synchronization but organically, just as in the activity of a single body the arms move differently to the head, to the core, or to the feet. They were put through exercises on the four elements of fire, water, earth, and air, energies imaginatively and physically articulated passing through individual bodies and collective bodies, walking through various environments actual and imaginary and allowing that to affect their bodies, Lecoq's chorus of materials, observing and experiencing the movement properties of different materials such as paper, glass, wood, oil and finding their own version of these movement properties. They were introduced to physical theatre isolations utilizing various articulation points of the body and to Lecoq's Seven Levels of Tension. They were introduced to physical theatre archetypes, commedia-influenced physical and vocal characterizations, animal-human characterizations, and some elementary work creating machines, assemblages, and environments only using their bodies and the sounds they could make with their bodies. Much of the initial studio work was wordless. It was explained to the performers that the payoff for developing this physical theatre work was that they would be able to create whatever they wanted to onstage and would engage an audience through the movement of their bodies in space and time.

The performers approached this elementary form of training and inculcation of company ethos with great willingness, but according to their own lights. With hindsight, it is possible to see the ableist assumptions of this approach. The performers' bodies both individually and collectively were meant to achieve expressivity through a kind of *via negativa* or stripping away of learned physical behaviours. As Carrie Sandahl has pointed out in 'The Tyranny of the Neutral' much theatre training is inherently ableist in its pursuit of an eminently flexible body and voice to be used as a base for characterization.

One difficulty in pursuing this drama school model was the infrequency of training/devising workshops and rehearsal period: a mere three hours per week and then a 'production week' in the theatre. All needed to be negotiated around institutional/caregiver availability and transportation needs. The drama school model was also problematic as the performers in their daily lives were the subject of various operations and practices of care. These were, like medications, administered to them. A lot of time was spent on attempting to inculcate the drama school ethos of physical and vocal warmups, clearing an emotional, physical, and vocal path for bold offers and responses, and openness to the moment. This ethos was premised on the incapacity or disability of the student, who is supposed to achieve freedom from what is 'blocking' them emotionally and physically to become an ideal transparent instrument of communication, freeing their natural voice. This assumption of performer incapacity had to be revisited in the work with performers who had already been deeply incapacitated at an educational and social level. There was a strong ludic element to the exercises and we, meaning I, Kim TePairi Garrett, and a shifting roster of drama students from NASDA, attempted to provide an environment of care, support, and encouragement.

It became clear from the initial workshops at Hohepa Hall and the subsequent work on the first three productions that the performers' experience of 'theatre' was a kind of restricted version of what theatre was on offer in Christchurch in the first decade of the 21st century. The Court Theatre operated as a kind of repertory theatre producing seasons of re-presented theatrical and musical hits from relatively recent West End, Broadway, and occasionally Sydney productions with a sprinkling of new New Zealand work. There were large-scale pro-am musicals produced in large venues, occasional touring productions generally spectacular and on the circuits of the Australasian legs of tours. Secondary school theatre was very popular and well-resourced, although none of the Different Light performers who had attended these schools had been cast in any school production. There were touring companies of theatre in education that some of the performers had seen. Many of the performers had participated in or seen productions by Jolt Dance company. Hohepa Community provided eurythmy classes and from time to time invited local practitioners to involve the community in various types of performance. It also became clear in a variety of improvisation exercises that the imaginary of the performers was heavily influenced by daytime television, soap operas, Disney fare, and local television.

The performers' understanding of theatre was evident in the first three productions by Different Light. In *A Different Light* (2004), the first public performance that emerged out of the Hohepa workshops, the narrative was presented in part by a physical theatre chorus, dressed in stage blacks and bare-footed, along the lines of a drama school studio performance. The ensemble consisted of six male learning disabled performers and two female NASDA students. Amiria Grenell, a NASDA student and singer-songwriter, provided live musical accompaniment, and I provided a spoken narration.

On a bare stage in the black box space of the Southern Ballet Theatre the chorus represented different groups, crowds, and environments: an assemblage of devils or angels, or the desires, fears, and conflicts within Faustus. As a chorus, their function was also to connect directly with the audience. A chorus is a kind of community as a collective character. In working with the performers, we felt that this formation might offer the performers solidarity and support, bolstered by the onstage and backstage presence of the female drama students who also conducted group warm-ups and provided support and pastoral care during the process.

The group sequences were mostly non-verbal and accompanied by Grenell's gentle songs. They were intended to act as breathing spaces for performers and audience and to mark transitions in the episodic narrative. This episodic structure was in large part determined by the restricted devising and rehearsal schedule. In the devising process, the performers had been keen to incorporate material they had encountered on the internet. For some this was a source of contention with institutions and families who were concerned at the amount of time, the areas of interest, and the engagement in the murky seas of social media interaction that were taking place and that they felt needed to be policed. In *A Different Light*, this became Faustus's search for knowledge online, stopping off at various websites during which the stage became an elementary version of a computer screen.

Following the company ethos of collaboration, the chorus was a defining feature of the productions: the whole company was present onstage throughout. This meant that there were challenges to the performers' engagement when they were required to stay present but fade into the background in sequences that became more focused on protagonists. The chorus elements required time to stage, and the degree of 'ownership' of these sequences varied from performer to performer.

The individuals in the group were, however, in the process of developing, or having developed for them, their own performance personae, characters, and stock characters. This was an elementary form of typecasting that emerged from a combination of individual offers in the devising process, the perceptions of the characteristics of certain individuals within the group, and the requirement for inhabiting different characters in the naïve, pseudo-mythical theatrical narratives. Those of us who were non-disabled participants acting as directors and facilitators had a great deal of influence in how these performance personae emerged. Self-devising was a process of trying out possibilities of the self both for the group and the individuals. To illustrate this process, I will refer to specific performers. This is an account of 'first impressions' that is informed by my own position as director/deviser and at the time of writing further coloured by nostalgia and subjective and selective memory.

A note on introducing the 'voices' of the performers

In the following account I will introduce members of Different Light Theatre more or less in the chronological order in which they joined the company. This chronological order is not intended to suggest a narrative of progress and development but rather to give an indication of how the company changed and adapted to the inclusion of a succession of different members and how the negotiation of the terms of making theatre fluctuated and varied. Each introduction makes a distinction between the different voices of each performer. Voice is intended here not as a guarantee of 'character' or some immutable self of identity but rather the voice or voices of each performer that emerged in the process of making theatre. There is a danger in labelling the performers that such labels 'stick' and limit how each person is viewed. This is a particular danger for learning disabled artists who are constantly subjected to being labelled 'Down's Syndrome', 'autistic', or 'learning disabled' as if these terms gave some definitive account of who they are. The references to voices that follow are not to voices as in essential qualities of the person but to voices that emerged in the process of making theatre together. These voices were influenced, therefore, by the processes of theatre, theatricality, the creation of characters, and the promotional impetus involved in building and sustaining a theatre company producing public performance. Theatre does to some extent depend upon character and identity, but it is also a subjunctive space, an unreliable space, a space of imagination, a possibility that by its very nature does not guarantee veracity and authenticity. Character and identity are created, or rather their simulacra are. This can be an empowering and liberating experience for learning disabled performers as they can (temporarily) inhabit identities very different to those limited identities they are often assigned in a normative world. They can also experience a realization of the voices that speak through them. In the theatre, a script and a character is developed and learnt and becomes at once, to adapt Schechner's formulation, some arrangement of 'self, not-self and not not-self' (4). Voice as guarantee of self and identity is *in play* in theatre and thus self and identity can be undermined and reconfigured. Voice in its materiality, rhetoric, and theatricality is not the guarantee of self, of the entitled and immutable self upon which economies and institutions of power are predicated and which they in turn seek to determine. This *play* of voice in theatre has interesting implications for the perceptions of learning disabled performers and the possibilities open to them inside and outside the theatre.

The voice of the actor as person of *Mana*: John Lambie

To speak of the voice of Different Light founding member John Lambie illustrates some of the complexities of the notion of voice in this book. A performer with Down's Syndrome who joined the group when he was 45, Lambie's speaking voice was difficult for many to discern as he had a slight stammer and a distinctive slurring of his voice, due to partial deafness. This necessitated practice on the part of the listener to become acquainted with his distinctive articulation and pronunciation of words. Due to his skill in deploying a range of non-verbal tactics, however, the intention of his utterances was always clear. His was a voice and a presence to which transcription would not do justice. In a Metro News television report on the 2009 production *The Poor Dears* an interview took place with both him and me that ironically speaks of Lambie's agency in the creative process and desire for a wider agency in his life in which said agency is mediated through me:

TONY MCCAFFREY: Poor dear means somebody – Aww poor dear (extending the vowel sounds) (looking to Lambie).
JOHN LAMBIE: (picking up and imitating the intonation) Aww Poor Dear (he strokes an imaginary person in a potentially patronizing gesture, smiling.)
TONY MCCAFFREY: John doesn't like that do you?
JOHN LAMBIE: (firmly) NO!
TONY MCCAFFREY: Because he's *not* a poor dear (makes dismissive hand gesture)
JOHN LAMBIE: (imitating the intonation of the same sentence and the gesture) po po po NOT a Poor Dear
TONY MCCAFFREY: Not a poor dear
JOHN LAMBIE: No.
TONY MCCAFFREY: He's a man
JOHN LAMBIE: (imitating intonation): I'm a man
TONY MCCAFFREY: He has his own life
JOHN: Im Im Im I got my own life. (accompanied by emphatic gestures to underline his point)
TONY MCCAFFREY: He doesn't like to be pitied or-
JOHN LAMBIE: Yeah
TONY MCCAFFREY: He wants to do things for himself, don't you John
JOHN LAMBIE: YEAH bo (pointing to himself) myself
The article cuts him off in mid-flow to switch to images of another performer dancing with a cowboy hat (McCulloch 2009).

The irony of the interview illustrates some of the complexities of giving and taking voice in the learning disabled theatre of Different Light. The production was titled and developed around the idea of 'Poor Dears' which was a phrase taken from Lambie. The strange kind of 'facilitated communication' that occurred in the interview was my taking the lead in answering the TV journalist's question but responding by trying to honour what Lambie had communicated to me previously over the period of devising the performance. What emerged on screen, however, was Lambie appearing to imitate me as neither the interviewer nor I were prepared to make the temporal and ethical accommodation to allow Lambie the time to lead the answering of the questions.

The difficulties of archiving or transcribing Lambie's communications are also evident in an example from 20 March, 2011, that took place in the wake of the second more destructive and fatal Christchurch earthquake. Different Light Theatre were meeting in the International Buddhist Centre in the relatively undamaged west of the city and we were documenting on video the performers' responses to the disaster. This is part of a one-minute sequence filmed in the tea rooms in which Lambie stood up at the table and invited everybody in the group to his birthday party. Lambie's voice again presents problems for transcription due to his distinctive articulations and fulsome use of non-verbal cues:

JOHN LAMBIE: (in response to a general conversation about birthdays) Twenty fourth of March
(Chatter continues in the background.)
TONY MCCAFFREY: On Thursday?
JOHN LAMBIE says something that is difficult to decipher
TONY MCCAFFREY: (guessing) At Hohepa?
JOHN LAMBIE: (makes a gesture with his arms that suggests inclusion of the whole group present) All invite
TONY MCCAFFREY: Everyone's invited?
JOHN LAMBIE: All Light. Wa-wa-wa-wanna come.
TONY MCCAFFREY: All of Different Light that want to come?
JOHN LAMBIE: Yeah, bear. (A phrase Lambie used frequently to express emphatic agreement)
TONY MCCAFFREY: OK Where do we go, John? To Hohepa? To Rata or Koru or–?
JOHN LAMBIE: No (incomprehensible utterance) Here. (he gestures to indicate he means here)
TONY MCCAFFREY: He's inviting us here. (Buddhist Centre interviews 2011.)

As it transpired the choice of location was not entirely within John's remit. We attended the birthday celebrations organized by Hohepa Canterbury at the Lone Star restaurant in Riccarton, the same area of Christchurch as the Buddhist Centre. The attempt to record Lambie's communication indicates some of the limitations of the transcription of the spoken voice. The communication itself also illustrates how his emphatic attempts at autonomous decision-making were often overridden by the institution which had care of him.

Over the years I knew Lambie, two acts of communication stand out in the imperfect and highly subjective archive of my memory, and they were both acts of performance, expression, and communication that took place without spoken words. The first was in 2007 at a meeting with Arts Access Victoria when Different Light Theatre were performing on the tour of *Ship of Fools* to the Awakenings Festival in Horsham. I had been invited to give a presentation about the group's work and had requested that Lambie accompanied me.

As I proceeded to talk and show PowerPoint slides, Lambie spontaneously got up and started to perform his Ancient Mariner movement sequence from *Ship of Fools*. He did this precisely but without the usual spoken and musical accompaniment of the production. His precise, elegant, and deeply engaged movement, influenced perhaps by his years of eurythmy at Hohepa, provided a more eloquent, if non-verbal, expression of the work of the company. His performance was in apposition to my spoken presentation but was far ahead of my words in terms of affective power.

In 2010, while Different Light were touring a presentation/performance for Arts Access Australia, to the Powerhouse Museum, the group attended some workshops at the Carriageworks in Sydney. On arrival in the building, Lambie immediately responded to the physically and visually impressive interior with a movement sequence, his own ritual of inhabiting the space and welcoming it into his physical presence. The rest of the company and the staff of the venue respected this enough to remain silent and stationary throughout, until he had concluded, whereupon everyone in the atrium applauded.

Lambie brought to the group a range of performance skills: a finely attuned sense of inspiration of the breath, an ability to make eloquent physical offers, and articulacy in his movement. This was in part due to his many years of practice of eurythmy. From the earliest workshops we attempted, not always successfully, to work out ways of allowing him to speak and to take the time and make the effort to listen to him. Such was his presence, authority, or *mana* that it seemed appropriate to cast him in lead roles and to organize the performance around him. In *A Different Light*, he played the role of Dr John Faustus. He could suggest inner conflict through an acute awareness of the principle of movement that Lecoq has termed the 'push and pull dynamic': the moment of stillness that precedes the impulse to move, the sense of 'reculer pour mieux sauter' (to draw back in order to make a better jump). He had an ability to mark and maintain moments of stillness dynamically before finding the impulse to move that would then emerge as a lean, a walk, a change of direction, or the performance of a physical action toward or away from other bodies or objects on stage. He was particularly sensitive to moving in response to music, sound, and lighting effects. He was cast as Faustus because he had sufficient *mana* to present a character that devils and angels might fight over and about whom the audience would care. Mana in Te Reo Māori encompasses ideas of power, authority, ownership, status, influence, dignity, and respect derived from the god/atua. It is composed of mana tangata, derived from whakapapa or genealogy and mana huaanga, 'authority derived from having a wealth of resources to gift to others to bind them into reciprocal obligations' (Mutu 2011, 23). Lambie's mana was in evidence not only within a theatrical space. When he accompanied me and two other performers to a conference at Manukau Institute of Technology in Auckland, he was the only disabled member of the company that was invited to the kava-drinking ceremony that preceded the conference.

In the Marlowe text, Mephistophilis grants Faustus the opportunity to do whatever he desires for 24 years. In *A Different Light*, this included a ticker tape parade in a limousine, climbing the mountain of a human pyramid and planting a flag, an under-the-seas sequence, and a journey through planets and stars. Lambie through his considered physicality and use of the ambiguity of the push and pull dynamic managed not only to enjoy these moments of self-assertion but also to suggest the underlying hollowness of these achievements.

The group's second performance, *The Birds*, was a substantially truncated version of Carrière's and Brook's script of *The Conference of the Birds*. During the rehearsal process for this Lambie was ill, but this did not, however, prevent him from participating. Time was set aside for him to develop his own movement sequences that could be integrated into the material that had already been devised. He appeared as a bird of his own devising accompanied by a live flute improvisation. He emerged towards the end of the performance in a sequence in which the birds, realizing that their journey to find their King had revealed that the King had been within them all along, then lose themselves in the mirror of the King's Palace to be consumed in flames. This ending sequence suited Lambie. The movement was accompanied by Sufi music that steadily built momentum and tempo encouraging a kind of intensity of movement as a form of spirituality that was akin to the eurythmy with which he was familiar.

In the third of the company's productions, *Dante*, Lambie was again the central, eponymous character. This production involved a much larger ensemble and incorporated elements of music theatre and projected video. It again revolved around the dynamic and considered silences and stillnesses of Lambie's presence. It made use of his resemblance to images of the poet in paintings, and his friendship with Kim TePairi Garrett who acted as assistant director and as his Beatrice. It represented an opportunity for the learning disabled performers to devise material collectively and singularly from their experience using a framework of comics and other imaginings of hell, purgatory, and heaven. It was a way to facilitate at once both Lambie's desire to be the centre of attention and his generosity in the moment to other performers and the audience. The piece opened with a combined video and live sequence in which a recorded image of Lambie moved through a background of stars before he arrived on stage in front of this image suggesting that he had stepped out of the video. Lambie subsequently became a kind of a peripatetic focal point leading the audience into and through the different sections of the performance, very loose adaptations of the tiers of Dante's Inferno and Purgatorio until the production's concluding sequences which comprised videos of individual performers in their happy place or idea of heaven on earth. The final image of the production was a gathering of chorus members around Lambie with different kinds of practical lights, candles, and lighters preceding their merging into projected images of stars and planets.

The voice of the showman: Matthew Phelan

> PAMELA PHELAN: When he was eight he sat on the bed with me and said, 'Mum, I'm Down Syndrome, aren't I? I'm I'm different to other people.' And I said, 'Why why do you ask that, M.?' Because

in actual fact when they did the six year nets at Primary School they discovered he had a reading age of eight so he could actually read and spell better than most of the kids in his class. But he said, 'Oh just some things. I'm different. I can't skip and I can't stand on one leg and I can't ride a bike and people sometimes call me "Handicap".' And then I explained to him what Down Syndrome was and he had a bit of a cry and said, 'Is there a cure?' and I said 'No' and he had a cry and I had a cry.

MATTHEW PHELAN: I actually don't call it Down Syndrome, I actually call it Up Syndrome ... Why I love performing? Well, all my life and passion, my passion in life is performing. (Plains FM 2006)

As is indicated in this early encounter with local media, Matthew Phelan has a strong belief in performance and its importance in his life. He came to the group with a range of experience in acting and performance. He is very articulate, with remarkable powers of rememoration. His showman persona, ever on the edge of stepping over into showing off, is apparent in a news article on the 2006 production *Dante* by the local station, CTV:

Matthew Phelan: It is the best drama group I've ever been in and ahm ahm I just have a wonderful time (switches to a shot of Phelan moving out of a scene in rehearsal to stand directly in front of the camera lifting his eyebrows and looking and smiling into the camera). (McLean 2006)

In the archive of the 'video diary' footage taken backstage on the group's 2007 tour of *Ship of Fools* to the Awakenings Festival in Horsham, Australia, his contribution is ever alert to an imagined public:

Hi I'm Matthew Phelan, and I represent New Zealand as you can see and very soon we'll be performing on stage and hoping for the best as this is our last production we're doing and very soon we'll be leaving Australia and going back to New Zealand so thanks and ... keep up with us. (Awakenings interviews, 2007)

In fact, prior to departing for Australia, he had insisted on videoing a 15-minute film of his own introducing the Australian audience to the sights of Christchurch with a running commentary: the river Avon, the Botanic Gardens, the Arts Centre, his own flat, his computer, and his DVD collection. He also filmed footage as performers arrived for a rehearsal of *Ship of Fools* in the Arts Centre. He interviewed seven performers, non-disabled and disabled, in a persona, blending television presenter and stage performer. His conversations with performers Tola Newberry, a non-disabled Māori performer, and Ben Ellenbroek, a performer with Down's Syndrome, illustrate his technique:

MATTHEW PHELAN: Now this is one of my Different Light Theatre company friends. This is Tola. Kia ora (shakes hands)
TOLA NEWBERRY: Kia ora.
MATTHEW PHELAN: OK and this is Tola who's part of our Ship of Fools production and he has been working with us very hard and ehm and he's ehm yeah he's very into character and we really enjoy his hard work. (Turning to him and gesturing to the camera) Would you ehm like to say anything?
TOLA NEWBERRY: Ehm. Well I've enjoyed it.
MATTHEW PHELAN: Yeah?
TOLA NEWBERRY: It's been fantastic, yeah.
MATTHEW PHELAN: Yeah?
TOLA NEWBERRY: Fooling around with these guys on the Ship of Fools
MATTHEW PHELAN: Well that's great and thank you for your time, Tola (shakes hands again.)
TOLA NEWBERRY: Thank you, buddy.
MATTHEW PHELAN: (to camera) Cut.
...
MATTHEW PHELAN: (puts his arm around Ellenbroek, who reciprocates, and looks into the camera) OK. And this is one of my other Different Light friends. This is Ben Ellenbroek and he's been working very hard with us on this brand new production we're doing, the Ship of Fools. (looking to Ellenbroek) Would you like to say something about what we're doing? (He shakes his head 'No') about this production?
BEN ELLENBROEK: (shuts his eyes, thinking) We're performing on behalf of Matthew's show. 'Here's the captain's Sunday lunch'. That's my line.
MATTHEW PHELAN: Yep. That's his favourite phrase and ehm and thanks for your time, Ben and we hope we all have a great time working hard and we're going to really enjoy this next time and it's great having you on board, Ben. (In an effusive gesture he offers his hand to shake, shakes hands warmly and immediately does a throat-slitting gesture and mouths 'Cut!') (Phelan interviews, 2007)

As a showman, one of his favourite experiences in the early productions was the curtain call. At times he seemed quite content for this not only to revolve around him but even to be for him exclusively. He would include in his curtain calls impromptu speeches testifying to his belief in the company, intertwined with his own Baptist evangelical spiritual beliefs.

Immediately after the short season of *A Different Light* we held an after-party that included a mock awards ceremony complete with certificates and speeches spoken into a microphone. This ceremony lasted at least twice the length of the 40-minute performance. This was for many of the performers the first access to the appurtenances and paraphernalia of public performance and conventional theatre: dressing rooms with lights on the mirrors, technical rehearsals, dress rehearsals, half-hour calls. This was an introduction to the distinctive spaces and times of theatre as well as the pressures and challenges. We as non-disabled facilitators emphasized that this was an opportunity to show what the performers could do and not what they could not. We were at that time promoting a narrative of overcoming adversity in the very act of making theatre.

Phelan's showmanship was very useful in the early performances of Different Light as he easily established a direct relationship with audience, and he was capable of learning and 'owning' spoken text: difficult text, copious amounts of text, to facilitate the progression of conventional theatrical narrative. He took such pleasure in his technical abilities that even when he appeared to overstep the mark in terms of the contract of the demands of attention between performer and audience, he was always capable of redeeming this. He was capable of combining a shrug in acknowledgement of his hogging the limelight with an inclusion of the audience into his own elated sense of being in performance. It was always interesting to observe the skill with which he could manipulate an audience, even when he had overstepped the mark of demanding attention. This might consist of a few too many knowing looks or impromptu spoken asides or in a curtain call speech that seemed to be outstaying their welcome. What was more interesting was to observe the places he went to physically and emotionally when he too became aware that he had strained the audience's hospitality in accepting his extended imprecations and extemporizations. This was in effect to see the actor working the crowd beyond the point that it wished to be worked. His showman's demeanour and elated physicality worked overtime in the knowledge that he could only prevail upon the audience for a few moments more before he would have to make his reluctant final bow and leave the stage.

In devising and improvisation, he presents a complex character who on the surface exalts in the light: lightness of touch of narrative, character, and verbal humour, but who is in turn fascinated by the dark: fear, loss, and the more negative aspects of human existence. His redeeming features as a performer are, precisely, his sense of *redemption*. He pushes the audience's credence and tolerance to the point of breaking until he always, winningly, redeems the contract that had seemed in danger of being broken.

In *The Birds* he was in tune with the spiritual metaphor of the piece and acted as narrator. In *Dante* he met the challenge of learning and delivering the opening lines of the Divina Commedia in the original Tuscan Italian. He did so line by line, each of the lines then being presented in English and Te Reo Māori, accompanied by bongo drums beating out a rhythm increasing in intensity and tempo. This represented a kind of presence as affirmation. Phelan's own ethos and practice of performance informed the dramaturgy of the group at that time: Here is something difficult, something virtuosic. There. I can do that. We can do that. Now you know you can pay attention to us and what we do next. At the end of the piece, there was a section in which various performers were presented on video talking about their ideas of heaven. Phelan's contribution was the first in this sequence, but it was not presented on video. With a voiceover describing heaven as a land of grace – or Graceland – Phelan arrived onstage in a sequined jumpsuit, wig, and sunglasses in the first of his appearances with the group as Elvis Presley. To the strains of 'A Little Less Conversation', Phelan occupied centre stage, lipsynching, adopting the hieroglyphic poses and hipshaking of Elvisness, in front of a chorus of seven drama students. The background dancers came forward and lifted him off the ground in a pose where he could extend the cape of his jumpsuit as wings, inhabit an elated body, and soar above the chorus. This sequence never seemed quite enough for Phelan, particularly when it came time to the dismount. In the acknowledgement of each performer's idea of heaven of the closing sequence, Phelan added his own words:

> My idea of heaven is seeing people walking around with new spirits in grace, wonder, and love.

The showmanship of Phelan/Elvis was a consistent self-affirmation and promotion, but his faith always held open the possibility that this self could be a channel for something else, that the performance of self might prove to be speaking in tongues.

The voice of the actor as self-protagonist and antagonist: Ben Morris

For Ben Morris the tongues that emerged in the self-performances of the early Different Light productions would have been the tongues of flames. Morris' self-presentation aligned with his oft-repeated self-description as 'Hot-fire Ben', accompanied by a steaming hot finger gesture, and the bright flame colours he favoured wearing on stage. His contributions to the group's early media interviews were characterized by a similar dynamism and energy:

> BEN MORRIS: I think it's really exciting on the first and the last nights because you're really *geared* and *amped* you know and it's really full on .... We just got rave reviews in the eh press and media ehm which is – which is fantastic. Next year we're ehm hoping to raise money ehm to go to Washington DC ehm yeah so that will be a great opportunity. (McCulloch, 2009)

An extract from the tongue-in-cheek 'video diary' of the Awakening Festival tour shows that this energy was often channeled into wordplay, the verbal spritz of the group's in-jokes, and his view of himself as a brightly coloured presence in the world:

TONY MCCAFFREY: Shawn and Ben do you want to talk to the video diary?
SHAWN O'ROURKE: (smiling broadly) Nah.
TONY MCCAFFREY: What complaints have you got?
SHAWN O'ROURKE: Ehm
BEN MORRIS: Yeah. Ehm We've got ehm. On tonight's menu we've got the Circe's saucy special on tonight that includes savs, hot chilli sauce ehm lots lots of pepper ehm
TONY MCCAFFREY: How about the flies, have they gone away?
BEN MORRIS: Nah. (Adopting a broad Aussie accent) those damn flies haven't gone away. Ehm we're actually expecting some wild dingoes and like Kenny the Kangaroo. He's gonna fight the Kiwi Shawn.
SHAWN O'ROURKE: Five rounds
BEN MORRIS: I'd say it'd be a major battle tonight.
...
TONY MCCAFFREY: Got anything to say Shawn?
SHAWN O'ROURKE: Nah. (He smiles broadly.)
TONY MCCAFFREY: Any complaints? Any message for New Zealand?
SHAWN O'ROURKE: Nah
TONY MCCAFFREY: Ben, any complaints?
BEN MORRIS: Yeah. (Showing a plastic milkshake cup): This orange is so bright that I have to wear Ray Bans. And today (showing two buns and biscuits). I'm feeding Benjamin and Nathaniel. (Referring to his first and middle names) (Awakenings interviews, 2007)

In videos uploaded to YouTube by a small group of performers in 2009, Morris took the lead in a kind of humorous promotion of the group:

Four actors look into camera, BEN MORRIS, JOHN LAMBIE, MATTHEW PHELAN, SHAWN O'ROURKE
BEN MORRIS: Hi, we're cast and crew from A Different Light, Ohio, Orlando, America. We-we have done such performances as *A Different Light, The Birds, Dante,* and *Ship of Fools* and just recently we have done *Frankenstein's Children.* Also this year we're doing *The Poor Dears.* (JOHN LAMBIE starts to make bunny ears behind SHAWN O'ROURKE'S HEAD.) Look out for ... for me (laughs)
SHAWN O'ROURKE: Or me cos I'm the handsomest guy here you know.
MATTHEW PHELAN: And I'm also what you call the King of Rock'n'Roll, baby.
JOHN LAMBIE joins in still wiggling his bunny ear fingers and smiling but his spoken contribution is not decipherable. (The actors of chch, YouTube 2009)

In another attempt at the YouTube self-promotion message Morris varied his self-introduction in the following way:

> BEN MORRIS: Hi I'm Sir Royal Class Morris and I've been in this company (the others start mock booing him, he laughs and continues) for … for decades and it's just really really fun (he laughs.) (diffltnz, YouTube 2009)

He was constantly reinventing himself and presenting a different persona. In an interview conducted within days of the second fatal earthquake he makes characteristically oblique reference to character and persona and interweaving his own experience in making theatre:

> BEN MORRIS: One of the scenes that I draw back from either *Birds* or *Dante*. You know how I'm not sure we had Catriona and Ben Ellenbroek and we kinda like all and I was kinda like in the centre and ehm and it's sort of like two girls came up … came up to me and then we kind of like had a curtain and stuff and we pretended that we were throwing underwear and socks and stuff like that. That's the kind of thing that I was drawing on sort of before but sort of relating to but sort of sort of go further just sort of draw on that concept but go … go further …. When I said to you about people's real emotions you know like I say like if you see in a movie or say like in a sitcom a situation could be say like a married couple you know something could go wrong like a woman finds another guy and they might do something and it kind of like builds and they sort of … sort of get angry ehm is the fact that I sort of think that maybe this this earthquake would have rattled a lot of people's nerves … I sort of think that I think also I think a lot of people's sort of real ehm real emotions sort of flare up you know its they sort of get angry because ehm because of the quake. That has – it's not just coming from me. (Buddhist Centre interviews, 2011)

During this interview Morris did not take the path of speaking directly about his personal experiences of the earthquake as others in the group did. The transcription above contains the kinds of periphrasis and tangents we had all become accustomed to with Morris and his explorations of what he found 'real' in performance or how was looking to go further in creating 'reality' on stage. In his subsequent years with Different Light, Morris explored the same highly voluble, though often circuitous, voice in pursuit of what he felt was 'real' and 'deep and meaningful' (his terms) that was often in tension with processes of characterization that involved the adoption of theatrical or cinematic or televisual personae. Time and again he made interesting offers whilst at the same time keenly editing, and frequently censoring, himself. Morris did have some experience of attending Jolt Dance and had a distinctive and fearless style of highly energetic dance and movement improvisation. His verbal improvisations were characterized by his desire to present the complete variegated contexts of any narrative or anecdote. This desire often prevented the arrival of said narrative at anything approaching a destination that would be satisfying to the neurotypical sensibility. His extreme willingness to be helpful in all kinds of different ways and his desire to make multiple offers often obstructed his ability either to help or make offers.

In *A Different Light* we cast him as Mephistophilis, Marlowe's conflicted devil. One major feature of Morris' participation in the early productions was his anxiety at learning spoken and movement text and the timing or 'cueing' process on which even naïve conventional theatre depends. This tension led to his anxiety over 'getting things wrong'. He would spend so much energy in his anxiety at regurgitating lines and movements that when speech and movement did emerge they did so in ways that seemed alienated. No one was harder on Morris' perceived deficiencies than he himself. As we continued to work with Morris, to offer him greater opportunities and challenges, we attempted to devise strategies for rehearsal and performance that might ease the burden of his own expectations of himself. In *A Different Light*, he began to find ways of turning the at times punitive energies he was directing against himself into the service of creating the performance persona of Mephistophilis, a troubled devil caught between impulses to act and self-repression.

In *The Birds*, he channeled his energies into the hither-and-thithering raven, sent out of Noah's ark to wander back and forth fretfully. In *Dante*, he benefitted from working with a number of drama students in the ensemble in the more music-theatre/dance based sequences and felt confident enough to take on more spoken text and dialogue. When offered the opportunity to be filmed to present his idea of heaven he chose to be filmed dancing in a brightly coloured shirt in a room on his own. He accompanied this film extract with onstage lines delivered directly to the audience: 'My idea of heaven is style, movement, dancing, and hot chicks. Speaking of hot, I'm supalicious hot'. He then delivered his characteristic gesture of licking his index finger and making a hissing sound. Morris' subsequent development with the company was particularly interesting, in many ways remarkable, but remained fraught with anxiety.

The voice of the actor as 'beformer': desiring and resisting performance: Ben Ellenbroek

In the archive of the early performances of Different Light Ben Ellenbroek presents an interesting contradiction: a performer both engaging in and resisting performance. This is apparent in the earliest filmed improvisations in 2007 in one of which he chose a persona as a member of a gang, the Hornby Helldogs:

> BEN ELLENBROEK: (wearing a crash helmet and motorcycle gloves in front of a wall covered in graffiti) This is Diesel. (The others in the group chant his name) Yeah. We are Different Light from the characters we met from Tony, he's a cool dude but there is a favourite actor and that's me. (Hornby Helldog interviews, 2007)

In this brief improvisation he indicated that he both wanted to be a character other than himself and to signal that he was only playing a character.

He made a brief contribution to the backstage video diary of the group that I took at the Awakenings Festival in 2007:

> BEN ELLENBROEK: (Gesturing for me to come to him but then waving away the camera when I reached him):
> Put that away will you? ... Hello my name's Ben from Different Light. This is the world actress out here called Tony. We are here. There is a very strong smell in this place. It's Shawn O'Rourke. (Awakenings interviews, 2007)

These brief contributions indicate his divided attitude to performance and his desire to seek commonality through the in-jokes and blokeish banter of the group.

Another aspect of his presence and participation was shown in the rehearsal video which played silently in the foyer of the theatre before *Dante* the group's 2006 production. This managed to capture Ellenbroek engaging in his own kind of personal performance during the downtime of rehearsals. Ellenbroek came to the group with his own particular take on performing. He seemed to be most expressive in performance when he was not required to present it in front of an audience. When he felt that he was unobserved it became fascinating to watch him improvise movements, spoken text, and extra-daily high-pitched and sing-song voices. During the downtimes of the devising and rehearsal process, Ellenbroek would launch into intense improvisations. These consisted of quite lengthy verbal, quasi-musical, extemporizations, accompanied by highly stylized movements that fascinated those of us who viewed them, but that never seemed to be reproducible on stage. To be more precise, the kind of theatrical performance the group was being directed towards by myself and other non-disabled facilitators at that time could not accommodate his contribution. In fact, he often struggled to make the stage. Immediately before each public performance he would habitually disappear, often winding himself up in the black stage curtains and not emerging, even in the face of copious amounts of cajoling, imprecation, and pleading, until he was ready. He and I could improvise situational and nonsensical dialogue together for extended periods, but these likewise did not reach the stage. He professed a great love and desire for performance, or, in a distinctive neologism that he coined, 'beformance'. This was a *conscious* neologism. He knew and used the word performance in other contexts, but for him 'beformance' covered a range of activity that included his impromptu improvisation. It included his extremely unusual vocal choices and pitching that were guaranteed to derail conventional mimetic characterization and character interaction, but that in effect took his performance to a completely different place. Over the years of knowing him, I had a feeling that part of him felt that theatre was neither a very male nor a very adult activity but something toward which, in principle, he was attracted.

In *A Different Light*, his vocal contributions were characterized by so much energy and attack in the onset of the voice that there was little breath left for the rest of the sentence. In any group vocal work his voice was pitched very high and stood out from the others. It was as if he was creating his own convention of vocal performance. His physical contributions to the performance, however, were generally characterized by sensitivity, lightness of touch, and delicacy.

In *The Birds*, he portrayed the Nightingale who refuses to go on the journey to find the King because they are so in love with the Rose and all they want to do is to sing songs of love to the Rose. This characterization allowed Ellenbroek to focus his attentions on another person, one of the female drama students, and for once allowed him to use onstage his distinctive vocal/musical and movement improvisations. In *Dante*, he was afforded an opportunity to develop both his penchant for stylized, almost baroque movement and his positioning himself as an elegant version of a commedia lover. He appeared in a slapstick version of the story of Paolo and Francesca with Catriona Toop, the drama school student who had played the Rose to his Nightingale in *The Birds*. His choice for the heaven/happy place sequence was a film of him in 18th-century costume and wig with a playscript and skull in hand. He then came out in the same jacket and wig to announce: 'My idea of heaven is ACTING!' with an inordinate emphasis on the last word. Ellenbroek later left the company, amicably. It would have been interesting to have afforded him more opportunity to explore what he understood by acting, performance, or 'beformance'. Ellenbroek's participation whilst he was with the company remains for me a memory of a contribution never fully realized in public performance. This aligns with my experience of failure in learning disabled theatre. Time taken does not always equal success or achievement, the process does not always recuperate what is lost but merely indicates what might have been.

The voice of the actor as worker and stage technician: Shawn O'Rourke

Shawn O' Rourke was another performer who was usually a man of few words in the various video interviews of the company. Matthew Phelan's interview with him for *Ship of Fools* is indicative of his blokeish standing within the group:

MATTHEW PHELAN: (approaching O' Rourke and putting his hand on his shoulder, O'Rourke continues to smile throughout the following)
And this here, this is Mr Shawn O'Rourke and we all call him the bloody Australian big man and he loves his (O'Rourke elbows Phelan in the ribs playfully, Phelan laughs) big bacon burgers and I guess his favourite scene would be 'Sir Shawn' So Sir Shawn tell me what you're doing on your ship.
SHAWN O'ROURKE: (in character as Sir Shawn) Ramming people that won't get out of my (he mouths the f-word) bloody way!
MATTHEW PHELAN: Yeah that's great. And we all enjoy the show. And this one (indicating O'Rourke) well he's just as happy as a pig and easy and really enjoying himself and really enjoying this production. Thanks for your time Shawn O' Rourke. (Phelan interviews, 2007)

One exception to his laconic contributions was in the interviews that took place in the immediate aftermath of the 2011 quake:

SHAWN O'ROURKE: Ehm. On the day of the earthquake I was in at Alpha (a day-facility for about one hundred people with intellectual disabilities in central Christchurch.) Ehm. Thought it was going to be just an-another small aftershock but turned out not to be. So I hid under a table and then Kate and all them came down check on us guys ehm then we decided to evacuate everyone from the building. And then send everyone home. So. Yeah. That's about it.
TONY MCCAFFREY: How did you get home?
SHAWN O'ROURKE: Old boy dropped me off home.
TONY MCCAFFREY: So were there people at Alpha quite upset?
SHAWN O'ROURKE: Yeah there was quite a few people ehm upset and scared.
TONY MCCAFFREY: And did you have to look after them a bit.
SHAWN O'ROURKE: Ehm Yeah. I think we all. Yeah we looked after each other. (During this last sentence he is on the verge of crying).
TONY MCCAFFREY: You've done well. You've been really strong.
LOUISE PAYNE goes to hug O'Rourke who is now crying.
TONY MCCAFFREY: (to the group) Shawn looks after a lot of people at Alpha
BEN MORRIS, THERESA KING and others go to hug him as he cries and then recovers himself. (Buddhist Centre interviews, 2011)

O' Rourke brought to the group a genuine sense of humour, good comic timing, and soon developed an admiration for, and obsession with, the role, or the stereotype, of a theatre technician. The stereotype of a theatre technician in the context of community theatre is somebody who facilitates the whole process and techne of the art form but who retains a stubborn anti-theatricality, who is particularly suspicious of the capricious, egotistical demands of actors. This is a figure that also seems to hold a fascination for Back to Back Theatre in their presenting of this hidden labour onstage by actors-as-technicians in a number of productions and in the dramaturgy of the first section of *Lady Eats Apple* (2016) which presents technician-like figures at the start of the performance who later emerge as Gods in a distinctive version of the creation myth. O'Rourke instantly became fascinated by these quiet, efficient people in black who exercised power, literally, who had technical expertise, a gunslingers belt with a range of tools and equipment, and rolls of magic gaffer tape, who coiled cables like lassoes and ventured up ladders with little regard for their own safety. They were the stagehands who were hands-on with all the magic-making effects of theatre: they made theatre work. When we later travelled to the Awakenings Festival in Horsham, Australia, we managed to obtain special permission for O'Rourke to spend some time sitting up in the lighting box with a group of technicians as they called the show and operated all lighting, sound, and special effects for two days of performances. This exalted position high up above the performance and the auditorium, this control centre, was in effect O'Rourke's idea of heaven. In *The Wizard of Oz* (2010), we managed to incorporate O'Rourke into the narrative as an impossibly over-equipped onstage super-technician whose job it was to attach and operate the laser lights that came out of the Wizard's (Glen Burrows') wheelchair whilst the other actors danced around them, not so much to conceal this normally hidden labour of theatre, but to celebrate it.

    In *A Different Light*, O'Rourke was cast as the Good Angel a smiling, remarkably gentle presence who tried to dissuade Faustus from signing the bargain with Mephistophilis. His good humoured and caring persona was also an asset as he took charge of the set of props for the production and could inculcate discipline in this area without being punitive. In *The Birds*, he devised a character of a smoking, drinking, partying bird that wore sunglasses and wanted to sample the high life and get high. He also played the Chamberlain of the King who twice refused the group of birds entrance to the King's Palace in rough, down to earth, archetypal Kiwi terms: 'Bugger off!' but who when the birds are wandering off, seemingly unsuccessful in their quest, relents. O'Rourke's self-devised line 'OK then I'll let yous in' consistently prompted laughter at his vernacular phrasing and accent. O'Rourke played the Chamberlain as a stereotypical Kiwi worker who has a job to do but who was basically a decent sort who can be persuaded to bend the rules and use their discretion. In *Dante* he brought a similarly well-observed sensibility to bear in the creation of Chef Pepe in one of the sequences in Hell in which various members of the ensemble went into Hell's Kitchen only to be cooked as their favourite food. In response to the question 'What's on the menu tonight, Chef Pepe?' O'Rourke devised what was almost an advertising slogan manner of delivery as he smiled and said 'Something HOT and SPICY!' with a glint in his eye and his voice as he used a giant inflatable fork to stir the chorus round as ingredients in a giant frying pan. The video sequence he chose to have filmed was of him working at Riding for the Disabled brushing a horse, wheeling and dumping a wheelbarrow full of horse manure and holding the bridle of a horse that then seemed to kiss him. His onstage narration to accompany this sequence was: 'My idea of heaven is horse riding, beer, and food. With the horses I love I muck out and groom'.

The voice of the actor as ethical citizen: Stuart Craig

> STUART CRAIG: I just love actually working with the people and meeting different people. (McCulloch, 2009)

Stuart Craig brought to the group a tremendous sense of responsibility and his own brand of authority that consisted in supporting and encouraging others in the building and sustaining of the group ethos to the point that it almost seemed a civic duty and that earned him the soubriquet of the Mayor of Christchurch. On the opening night of the first production, we were able to obtain for him a card addressing him as such and wishing him and the others well from the then Mayor of Christchurch, Gary Moore. He also brought a voice that was clear but delivered at a great volume; his lines appeared to be delivered *AS IF HIS LIFE DEPENDED ON THEM*. This seemed to represent his way of offering maximum support to the others in the group and to the project. In devising and rehearsal the most common phrase heard from him was 'You people are AWESOME!' and if there were any issues or struggles his was always a rallying cry of support. In the 'heaven' sequence in *Dante* he chose to be videoed in white hat and apron working in the bakery where he had a part-time job, accompanied by the words: 'My idea of heaven is I work in a bakery and I bake cherry pies and I make cakes and I work in the garden'.

The voice of the actor as person of faith: Michael Stanley

> MATTHEW PHELAN: And here I am again and this is another one of my Different Light Theatre friends. I'd like to introduce Mr Michael Stanley. (He shakes hands with him. Stanley shakes with one hand and gives a thumbs-up gesture toward Phelan with the other.)
> MICHAEL STANLEY: Hello. How are you?
> MATTHEW PHELAN: Are you enjoying this production we are doing right now at Southern Ballet?

Community Theatre and Myths of Community 79

MICHAEL STANLEY: Yes.
MATTHEW PHELAN: Could you say your ehm lines from the ... the fisher ... ehm
MICHAEL STANLEY: Fisherman. Yes. And Jesus said unto them, 'Come ye after me and I will make you to become fishers of men'. (He speaks enunciating the words very clearly and supporting them with gestures.)
MATTHEW PHELAN: That's great.
MICHAEL STANLEY: YEAH!
MATTHEW PHELAN: Thank you for your time on the video camera and I'd like to introduce some more of my friends from Different Light so thanks Mr Stanley and enjoy yourself. (Phelan interviews, 2007)

In the interview on the last night of *The Wizard of Oz* (2010), he again focuses on his lines from the show:

TONY MCCAFFREY: Some video for the making of DVD.
MICHAEL STANLEY: Yes
TONY MCCAFFREY: Do you want to say hello
MICHAEL STANLEY: Hello
TONY MCCAFFREY: And who you play....
MICHAEL STANLEY: I play the trolley 'Would you like fries with that?'
TONY MCCAFFREY: What other lines do you have?
MICHAEL STANLEY: He won't hurt anybody anyway. (He accompanies this by moving his head exaggeratedly from side to side to look at those around him as he did in the performance.)
TONY MCCAFFREY: And what else?
MICHAEL STANLEY: Is it a problem of processing? (Complete with the habitual gestures he used in performance). (Wizard of Oz interviews, 2010)
In the 2011 interviews, after the earthquake, he spoke about events as reported in the media, and more reluctantly and obliquely about his own experiences:
MICHAEL STANLEY: I know about the CTV building that was destroyed too. And also the Christchurch Cathedral and the Christchurch Catholic Cathedral.
TONY MCCAFFREY: So what happened to you on that day? Were you at Hohepa?
MICHAEL STANLEY: Ahh yes. When there was ehm a s-a water of sand there (a reference to liquefaction) and also ehm there was a aftershock. Yeah.
TONY MCCAFFREY: What were you doing?
MICHAEL STANLEY: We were sitting down in-in outside and also going sitting down in the ... Hall. Yep.
TONY MCCAFFREY: Can you remember what you were doing when the shake happened?

MICHAEL STANLEY: It was rock It was rocking when I screamed help. And also ehm ehm ehm ehm there was ehm ehm emergency that happened Someone from ehm the daybase. Yes.
TONY MCCAFFREY: So were you in a class? Were you doing anything?
MICHAEL STANLEY: We're just-we're in cafeteria at lunchtime. (Buddhist Centre interviews, 2011)

In 2012, he was interviewed with his then-girlfriend Natalie Walton about *The Lonely and The Lovely* the Different Light soap opera project in which the lines between characters and actors were often quite blurred:

TONY MCCAFFREY: Who is your character?
MICHAEL STANLEY: Ehm. My character is ... What is it? Ehhh ... Marty!
TONY MCCAFFREY: And what does he do?
MICHAEL STANLEY: He's doing the ehm bar manager.
TONY MCCAFFREY: Cool
MICHAEL STANLEY: Yes
TONY MCCAFFREY: Marty's bar.
MICHAEL STANLEY: Marty's bar.
TONY MCCAFFREY: And does he have a partner?
MICHAEL STANLEY: (turning to Natalie Walton) Yes Ehhm Roxie.
NATALIE WALTON: Yes.
TONY MCCAFFREY: Cool. And does she-what does she do?
MICHAEL STANLEY: She is doing the .... What is it? The-the bar.
TONY MCCAFFREY: With you?
MICHAEL STANLEY: Yes.
TONY MCCAFFREY: How long have you known each other?
MICHAEL STANLEY: Ehhhm. Two thousand and eight.
TONY MCCAFFREY: So ... four years?
MICHAEL STANLEY: Four years. Yes.
TONY MCCAFFREY: How did you meet?
MICHAEL STANLEY: Going to Able Tours.
NATALIE WALTON: Able Tours
TONY MCCAFFREY laughs
MICHAEL STANLEY: (smiles) Yess. Great.
TONY MCCAFFREY: That's how Michael and Natalie met. Through Able Tours. So what I'm saying is that Marty and Roxie is maybe different than Michael and Natalie.
NATALIE WALTON: OK
MICHAEL STANLEY: Yes. (*The Lonely and the Lovely* interviews 2012)

Stanley came to the group with a very quiet and gentle energy. He had a firm sense of his Catholic faith and of his close family who had migrated to Aotearoa/New Zealand from the Philippines. He was consequently familiar with the angels and devils of Faustus in *A Different Light*. Grounded in the experience of elementary contact improvisation with Jolt Dance he made interesting physical offers, his movements emerging more from his core than merely from the arms and the upper body. In the Seven Deadly Sins sequence, he presented Sloth rolling his head as he spoke lethargically and seemingly constantly in danger of falling asleep, propped up the physical theatre chorus. In *The Birds*, he presented a highly effective version of the Parrot who has become so used to their cage, their swing, their little bath, and bell that they are unwilling to join the other birds on their journey. In response to the other birds' requests for him to join them, he responded with: 'I'm comfortable in my cage. I can't come. I'm comfortable on my swing' in a cage of bamboo sticks and swinging on a bamboo stick all provided by the physical theatre chorus, who then left him alone on stage holding onto two bamboo sticks held vertically in front of him and still swinging and repeating 'I'm comfortable in my cage'. Stanley's sincerity allowed the audience to laugh along with his characterization, which naively hinted at the infantilization and internalized institutionalization of learning disabled people. In *Dante*, he chose to be filmed shooting hoops in the grounds of the Hohepa community, unerringly finding the basket each time. He chose to speak the lines: 'My heaven is basketball, dribbling and bowling and ... and ... my ... and the heaven is God'. His hesitation over what he had intended to say redeemed by the certainty of his faith.

I have offered these specific examples as an account of first impressions. The early work of the group consisted of the development of a repertory company constructed in response to the individual talents, predilections, and concerns of the company members. The devising workshops, rehearsals, and performances were an attempt by us, the non-disabled facilitators of the group, to inculcate a community ethos. The next chapter looks at the group's turn to dramatic theatre. The intention of this shift was to allow the learning disabled performers to find the joy of exploring and inhabiting characters that were to some degree other than themselves, of collectively telling stories with the twists, turns, and revelations of dramatic theatre, and the particular engagement with audience such theatre engenders. Pursuing conventional dramatic theatre, however, meant the company engaged with the temporality of developing process into the product, a temporality of efficacy, rush, and momentum that came into conflict in interesting ways with the temporality of care and support required to involve the learning disabled artists.

References

A Different Light. Devised by the ensemble. Directed by Tony McCaffrey. Southern Ballet Theatre, Arts Centre, Christchurch. 15–17 September, 2004.

Boal, Augusto. *Games for Actors and Non-actors*. Translated by Adrian Jackson. Routledge, 1992.

Carrière, Jean, Claude and Brook, Peter. *The Conference of the Birds*. The Dramatic Publishing Company, 1971.

Dante. Devised by the ensemble. Directed by Tony McCaffrey. Different Light Theatre. Southern Ballet Theatre, Arts Centre, Christchurch. 16–19 September, 2016.

Dante Alighieri. *The Divine Comedy*. Translated by John Ciardi. New American Library, 2003.

Derrida, Jacques. *Cinders*. Translated by Ned Lukacher. University of Nebraska Press, 1991.

———. "Hostipitality." *Acts of Religion*. Edited by Gil Anidjar. Routledge, 2002, pp. 356–421.

Different Light Theatre. Hornby Helldogs interviews, CPIT, 9 June, 2007. Different Light video archive.

———. Video interviews by Matthew Phelan, Ship of Fools rehearsals, Arts Centre, Christchurch, 25 September, 2007. Different Light video archive.

———. Video interviews at Awakenings Festival, Horsham, Victoria, Australia. 12–15 October, 2007. Different Light video archive. https://www.youtube.com/watch?v=5BYkacTLX6U&t=394s

———. "The actors of chch' and 'diffltnz," YouTube videos, 7 June, 2009. https://www.youtube.com/watch?v=bq3BrO-f3Xg https://www.youtube.com/watch?v=I3odS89Xc04

———. Wizard of Oz backstage interviews, NASDA theatre, 21 November, 2010, Different Light video archive.

———. Video interviews at the International Buddhist Centre, Christchurch, 20 March, 2011. Different Light video archive.

———. The Lonely and the Lovely interviews, 16 September, 2012. Different Light video archive.

Hartman, Saidiya V. *Scenes of Subjection: Terror, Slavery and Self-Making in Nineteenth Century America*. New York: Oxford University Press, 1997.

Jolt Dance. https://joltdance.co.nz Accessed 11 October, 2021.

Kuppers, Petra. "Community arts and practices: improvising being-together." In *The Improvisation Studies Reader: Spontaneous Acts*. Edited by Ajay Hebble and Rebecca Caines. Routledge, 2015.

Lady Eats Apple. Directed by Bruce Gladwin, Back to Back Theatre. Hamer Hall, Melbourne, 9 October, 2016.

Lecoq, Jacques. *The Moving Body: Teaching Creative Theatre*. Translated by David Bradby. Methuen, 2000.

Marlowe, Christopher. *Dr Faustus*. Edited by Roma Gill. Methuen, 2008.

McCulloch, Craig. Metro News, CTV news article, 4 October, 2009. https://www.youtube.com/watch?v=OLVT1cQwX40&t=34s

McFalls, Laurence and Mariella Pandolfi. "Parrhesia and Therapeusis: Foucault on and in the World of Contemporary Neoliberalism." In *Foucault Now: Current Perspective in Foucault Studies*. Edited by James D. Faubion, 168–187. Polity, 2014.

McLean, Matthew. Metro News, CTV news article, 3 October, 2006. https://www.youtube.com/watch?v=K3M2qb4Z08c

Mutu, Margaret. *The State of Māori Rights*. Huia, 2011.

Nancy, Jean Luc. *The Inoperative Community*. Trans. Peter Connor, Lisa Garbus, Michael Holland and Simona Sawhney. University of Minnesota Press, 2004.

Plains FM half hour radio feature on A Different Light Theatre, 13 August 2006.
Puar, Jasbir K. *The Right to Maim: Debility, Capacity, Disability*. Duke University Press, 2017.
Saint Pierre, Joshua. "Fluency Machines: Semiocapitalism, Disability and Action." PhD thesis, University of Alberta, 2018.
———. *Cheap Talk: Disability and the Politics of Communication*. University of Michigan Press, 2022.
Sandahl, Carrie. "The tyranny of the neutral." In *Bodies in Commotion: Disability and Performance*. Edited by Philip Auslander. University of Michigan Press, 2005.
Schechner, Richard. *Between Theater and Anthropology*. University of Pennsylvania Press, 1981.
Still, Judith. *Derrida and Hospitality: Theory and Practice*. Cambridge University Press, 2010.
Super Discount. Devised by the Ensemble, Directed by Bruce Gladwin. Back to Back Theatre, Wharf Theatre, Sydney. 20 September–19 October, 2013.
The Birds. Devised by the ensemble. Directed by Tony McCaffrey. Different Light Theatre. Southern Ballet Theatre, Arts Centre, Christchurch. 9–11 February, 2006.
The Wizard of Oz. Devised by the ensemble. Directed by Tony McCaffrey. Different Light Theatre. NASDA Theatre, CPIT. Ignition Creative Festival, 18–21 November, 2010.

3 Dramatic Theatre and the Temporality of Learning Disabled Theatre

From community theatre to dramatic theatre

The previous chapter gives an account of Different Light's early attempts at the community theatre, a model that valued participation over the artistic or aesthetic aspects of performance and that sought to find community both within the group and between the performers and the audience. The group's next three productions and related activities sought to emphasize the theatricality of the group's work through a framework of conventional dramatic theatre, Aristotelian theatre that prioritizes plot or linear narrative arc (mythos), and individual character arc (ethos). For many learning disabled theatre companies this is a recognized path of progression, a turn from post-therapeutic performance to dramatic theatre and the aspiration to professional performance and remuneration of the learning disabled performers. For Different Light, the rush involved in this turn to dramatic theatre revealed ethical and political limitations. Increasingly, the attempt to create dramatic theatre was confronted with the need for a different temporality of process and performance that aligned more with notions of 'crip time'. These tensions led to a reconfiguration of the hierarchies of creation to take account of listening others to speech. It led to exploring methodologies of theatre-making and performance more attuned to the access needs of the performers and that sought a redefinition of conventional theatrical and semantic kairos more aligned with Lipari's formulation of 'kairos as akroasis'.

> ... *kairos* is an ethical virtue inextricable from *akroasis*, it is an attunement to others and the dance of circumstance. It is not timely in the mechanical sense of efficiency or serendipity, or as a well-timed shot into the goal, or timely as an intervention in the future "just in time." Instead, *kairos* is the tangle of braided nonlinear moment choosing us—speakers and listeners—as we move rhythmically together in harmonically attuned, responsive movement. (213–4)

During this period straining and striving for conventional theatrical kairos was reconfigured in terms of more contemplative, considered, and caring possibilities for the relationship between performer and audience. This process questioned what constituted good or 'professional' acting: the resonant and on the breath placement of the voice, clear changes in tempo, pitch, and other vocal and physical qualities to signal new thought by new breath, that are so often used as instruments to 'mesmerize' or subordinate the senses of the audience to the will of the conventionally virtuosic actor. My experience is that learning disabled actors are quite capable of inhabiting the charism and aura of such performance on their own terms, but they also open up other more interesting possibilities of actor–audience engagement.

This shift in methodologies and intentions by Different Light was not part of a linear or teleological process toward more enlightened, equitable, and just practices of learning disabled theatre. It was rather two steps forward, one step back approach, or at times more like two steps forward, three steps backward, and two steps to the side approach. As time went by and we all spent more time with each other we attempted to 'develop' as people and as theatre-makers. The non-disabled facilitators attempted to engage the learning disabled performers more meaningfully in theatrical performance. In retrospect this urge to 'development' revealed an imbalance in power relations, which meant each initiative of improvement promoted by the non-disabled facilitators came up against further reiterations of the epistemic injustice to which learning disabled people are subjected.

Ship of Fools, Frankenstein's Children, The Poor Dears

The next two productions *Ship of Fools* and *Frankenstein's Children* resembled conventional dramatic theatre. I pursued this strategy with the intention of giving the performers the opportunity to create and inhabit characters other than themselves. *Ship of Fools* was also an attempt to hold together an ensemble of both learning disabled and non-disabled performers through a tour to the Awakenings Festival in Australia. Participation at that Festival, however, revealed some of the contradictions and limitations of a non-disabled-led model of learning disabled theatre. *Frankenstein's Children* was the first performance in which only learning-disabled performers were on stage. The latter's use of various kinds of stage technology, however, were attempts at supporting and guiding the performers onstage, particularly with regard to the temporality of theatre: cueing, turn-taking, and narrative structure, that ended up controlling the contributions of the performers. Both of these experiments revealed that a top-down imposition of theatrical structure and discipline only allowed the performers limited possibilities to invest and participate meaningfully in the production. This realization led to the adoption of more free-form and performer-led strategies of creating and performing narrative and characterization in *The Poor Dears*. In addition, the inclusion of the very different voices of performers such as Glen Burrows, Isaac Tait, and Louise Payne helped to encourage and provoke new ways of working and being together.

Ship of Fools: inclusion as a journey

Ship of Fools (2007) was the last 'mixed ability' production including onstage the seven learning disabled performers of the first three productions with five drama students and me. It was first performed at the Southern Ballet Theatre in the Body Festival in Christchurch to a local audience that had been slowly growing over the three years of the group's existence. It subsequently toured to the Awakenings Festival of All Abilities in Australia. The Awakenings Festival had been in operation since 1996, its main patron is the pianist David Helfgot, and it took place in Horsham, a small city in Victoria with a population of some 16,500 people. For the three days of the Festival the streets of Horsham were filled with disabled people, dancing to the outdoor music performances and moving between venues that offered theatre, dance, and movement. Different Light performers were interviewed by Anthony Bartl, a quadriplegic journalist, who wrote a review of *Ship of Fools* in *The Big Issue* Melbourne. We held a workshop for groups of disabled people from different parts of Australia which was facilitated by both non-disabled and disabled members of Different Light in which we shared some of the games, exercises, and strategies of physical, verbal, and narrative improvisation that we had developed over three years. We also collaboratively presented the brief history of the group to date and two of the performers, Matthew Phelan and Ben Morris, were interviewed by a local radio station. The performers also attended a range of workshops during the Festival, on-stage make-up and clowning. It was an introduction for the performers to the disabled arts community in Australia.

On advice from the City Council's KiwiAble network we operated a 'buddy' system of one non-disabled person supporting each learning disabled performer for the duration of the Festival, including sharing accommodation. Along the way, we shared experiences that became part of the group's collective memory: filling in departure cards at Christchurch airport entailed an acknowledgement that the reason for travel was to perform at an overseas festival and that people could put their occupation as 'actor'. This led to some dialogue with border officials in both New Zealand and Australia that formed the basis for later scenes in *The Poor Dears*. Border officials post-9/11 treated everybody with suspicion. The questioning of the Different Light performers as to the purpose of travel was informed by this, but also served with a side of ableism and patronization. This included the reference to the group of 20-something adults as 'children' or 'kids', the directing of questions' over the heads of the learning disabled performers to those of us in the group who were non-disabled, and the expression of amazement mixed with a suspicion that they were going overseas to 'perform'. The environment of Horsham for the three days of the Awakenings Festival was, by contrast, more inclusive and accepting.

The narrative and dramaturgy of *Ship of Fools*

Ship of Fools was designed as a production for touring and the narrative framework of the piece was an odyssey through the history of the treatment of 'the different'. The title of the piece was taken from Foucault's *Madness and Civilization*. The narrative of the production encompassed metaphors and tropes associated with various ships containing various fools.

A recurring pattern for the structure of the group's performances had now been established. This involved ensemble sequences out of which emerged individual actors presenting fantasy sequences connected with the broad themes of the narrative. Ben Morris as a kind of Ulysses took a shower in which various Sirens appeared and in which he gently teased the audience that he was disrobing. Matthew Phelan played Captain Cook 'discovering' New Zealand. John Lambie was the Ancient Mariner from Coleridge's poem, carrying the albatross around his neck. Ben Ellenbroek developed his courteous 'lover' persona in a kind of pas de deux with Julia Guthrey and a piece of flowing red silk. Shawn O'Rourke portrayed a brash New Zealand Pork Baron in his luxury yacht seeking to ram a vessel of asylum seekers rather than give way. Michael Stanley presented a sequence based on *Matthew* 4: 18–20 in which Christ calls out to the brothers Simon and Peter to cast aside their nets and follow Him. Stuart Craig was given the spotlight in a sequence as the Mayor of Christchurch, the Odyssey's Cyclops as one-eyed Cantabrian, delivering a rousing stump speech in Craig's high intensity, high volume style. Once each of these individual sequences had been presented, the piece reverted to an ensemble format led by two doctors in white coats, played by Matthew Phelan and me, inducting the ensemble as patients into SeaView Mental Hospital. These two characters brusquely dispensed treatments from the 19th century – chloral hydrate – the 1950s – diagnosis through the Diagnostic and Statistical Manual of Mental Disorders (DSM) and electro-convulsive therapy – and 2007 when the patients, now referred to as clients, were liberated from the institution but only with liberal depot doses of antidepressants and mood stabilizers and released into 'the care of the community'. As the lights faded at the end, the ensemble reached out to the audience, asking: 'What community? What community? What community?'

Being called out

Looking back on *Ship of Fools* two incidents stand out as significant in the subsequent development of the devising and performance methodologies of the group. The first occurred backstage at the Festival, during the warm-up. Ben Ellenbroek as was his custom was making an impromptu speech calling on the group to do their best and represent New Zealand. During this speech, he turned the attention to me as 'the world actress here called Tony'. Leaving the interesting confusion of gender aside, he called me out. He 'called me out' in the North American sense of the phrase: to expose or identify (a person) as acting in a dishonest or otherwise unacceptable manner; to challenge or confront (Oxford English Dictionary [OED]). He drew attention to my behaviour, my presence as a non-disabled person at a disability arts festival in a 'mixed-ability' ensemble. He had some justification in calling me out. My positionality within the company at that time could best be described as ubiquitous. In this production, I not only took on the roles of actor, director, and co-devisor, but also that of nascent researcher. The second occurred after the performance. Towards the end of the piece the two white-coated doctors ran through the ensemble and the audience sprinkling glitter and chanting the names of medications like magic spells:

> Fluoxetine Paroxetine Escitalopram Citalopram Sertraline Venlafaxine Duloxetine Bupropion Mirtazapine Reboxetine Quetiapine Risperidone Olanzapine Clonazepam Carbamazepine.

I had googled Prozac derivatives and found the list of polysyllabic names that sounded to me like incantations. The function of the chanted list at the end of the play was to represent the (neo)liberal use of depot medications in support of the current strategy of de-institutionalization. After the noisy and very appreciative reception of the piece by an audience composed mainly of disabled people, an audience member came up to me afterwards and informed me that they were currently taking some of those same anti-depressants the names of which we had sprayed out around the auditorium. What for me represented somewhat superficially undertaken research for a performance represented for them lived experience: prescribed, circumscribed, painful, and painfully painless experience. They likewise called me out.

Ship of Fools was the last Different Light performance in which I or any other non-disabled performers appeared as onstage support for the learning disabled performers. In every subsequent performance only learning disabled performers were present. This was influenced by attending some of the community learning disabled theatre at the Festival in which a director would appear at the front of the stage, like a conductor, to cue in learning disabled actors' lines or movements, joining in with the spoken or sung text. During one of these performances, John Lambie got out of his seat and stood in front of the audience, behind the director faithfully imitating their every move and direction to the cast. Lambie's intervention called out the charity or non-disabled saviour model of learning disabled theatre and made me look to my own practice.

One year after the *Ship of Fools* performance, Louise Payne joined the company on *The Sunnyside Project* a two-year performance research project on Christchurch's Sunnyside Asylum. She had been a patient in the institution and was part of a class action taken against the New Zealand government for abuse within the psychiatric system. In *The Sunnyside Project*, she devised a sequence giving an account of the contents of the bright yellow lunchbox of empty medication packaging that she carried around with her as a testament to the drugs she had been administered in Sunnyside. On her release, she discovered these were now being prescribed to the general population, including children. The following text is a transcription of her improvisation:

> The first one on the market was Prozac manufactured into 20 capsules 1940s sort of green tapering down into a beautiful cream colour. Made the cover of Time magazine because it was so beautiful. With this starter booklet which accompanies it where you have black and white trees but after a few weeks on this you can walk into the colour with the daffodils apparently. And even the checklists for your so-called depression anxiety are in the shape of Prozac pills. You can get Prozac beanies, Prozac lamps, you can get junkets to Bali, or you can't your doctor can, the stationery I save it, the tee shirts. The next SSRI – Venafaxine – originally brought out as 75 mg per capsule – so fast, so heavy they reduced it to 37.5 mg. Venafaxine – it'll take you there. But will it get you back? And I really do mean that. It's a kick arse drug. Olanzapine. Anti-psychotic. If you're taking this (Venafaxine) you might need this to bring you back. White wafer like communion. Gone before you know it. No non-compliance, you can't spit it. Truly make you feel like Muppets. Will knock you out 8-12 hours. And here we have the anti-psychotic when you're not really having an anti-psychotic – the Clayton's effect – Quetiapine: innocuous tiny tiny orange, put you on your butt maybe 3 or 4 hours but they like to tell you that that will dampen down your anxieties. It's more like hammering them. Me I prefer your good old fashioned 5mg YELLOW VALIUM.

I cite this in full as Louise Payne's distinctive voice, with its mixture of humour and pain called out my superficial methodology of a few minutes' Google search.

At this early stage of the group's development the negotiation of the specific voices, personae, and performance identities of the learning disabled artists was still very much on my terms as director. I constructed a narrative and thematic framework within which the artists were afforded or allowed contributions. I had still to learn to listen to the learning disabled artists. Learning to attune to their contributions involved uncovering the inequities in my successive attempts to empower, to liberate, and to create collaboratively. Learning to listen entailed a continuing discovery of the reiterative ways in which normative, neurotypical forms of power reasserted themselves in the work, despite, or more accurately because of, my intentions to empower the learning disabled artists.

Frankenstein's Children: only the learning disabled actors are present on stage

In light of the experiences of *Ship of Fools*, *Frankenstein's Children* (2008) was the first Different Light production in which only learning disabled actors were present on stage. It was presented in the Body Festival in the NASDA theatre, a 90-seat black box studio space located in the drama school in which I teach. This afforded the Different Light actors greater access to a theatre space for devising and rehearsal. The piece had a cast of nine performers, the seven from the previous productions, with the addition of Verity Carter, a female performer with Down's Syndrome, and Glen Burrows, a performer with cerebral palsy and motorized wheelchair user. The production was the first to incorporate a set, designed by Christchurch artist Chris Reddington and a more substantial and integrated use of video projection designed by Stuart Lloyd-Harris. It was subsequently presented at the Christchurch Town Hall opening the National Residential Intellectual Disability Provider Group (NRID) Conference on 8th July, 2009.

The production persisted with the established format of ensemble sequences out of which more individualized sections emerged. The intention was to develop less of a skit-based format in favour of a more coherent narrative arc. The ensemble consisted of a group of white-coated scientists who, having mapped the human genome, were now intent on creating genetically modified human beings with no more disorders, dysfunctionality, or disability. Matthew Phelan was cast as Professor Frankenstein, the leading scientist, a lonely person seeking in 'Project Eugene' to create a perfect being in his own image.

The opening sequence, titled 'Mapping the Human Genome' was a combination of ensemble movement and video projection. Matthew Phelan sat upstage centre with his back to the audience in front of the video screen. To the left and right framing of the stage were tables covered in white cloths, which were lit with LED lights of changeable colours. At the upstage end of each platform of tables were cartoonish, two-dimensional representations of complex laboratory equipment. As Phelan sat there, the projected video showed a montage of X-ray images of human anatomy and MRI brain scans. The voices of the performers could be heard speaking about their ideas of the perfect human being. These were recordings taken directly from the group's improvisations in the devising process. As this continued, the chorus of scientists, including Burrows in his motorized wheelchair, moved around the laboratory space as Phelan very slowly turned around to look at them and face the audience.

The projected video showed various stages in the process of mapping the genome that increased in tempo and intensity in time with the accompanying music as the performers jumped around in a choreographic representation of scientific research. The video behind them reached breakneck speed and then became calmer as Frankenstein announced that they had now mapped the human genome. Frankenstein stated that they could now create a perfect human being, but to do so they must experiment on themselves, and called for volunteers. At first, nobody volunteered. Somebody suggested Professor Burrows. The group gathered round to watch Glen Burrows type out his reply which they repeated letter by letter as it spelled out F U C K O F F. Professor Stuart Craig suggested that there was something wrong with Professor Burrows' keyboard.

Figure 3.1 Glen Burrows in rehearsal. Image: Paul McCaffrey for Different Light Theatre.

The voice of the actor through assistive devices: Glen Burrows

Glen Burrows' arrival at Different Light Theatre was a transformational experience in that it changed how the company created performance, sought to provide care and support, and tried to work out different ways of being together. Burrows is not learning disabled in terms of diagnosis but experiences similar disablement in trying to travel to and attend rehearsals, in contributing his voice to the processes of devising and performing, and in moving through an ableist world. His commitment over 14 years to working with the company, performing, and touring is remarkable. The adjustments needed to accommodate Burrows' participation are many but the joy he experiences and shares with the company, his *mana*, has compelled us to re-examine what we mean by support, care, access, and inclusion.

When the group was invited to present *Frankenstein's Children* in the Christchurch Town Hall, a long ramp had to be built for him to access the stage. After he joined the group, we became accustomed, when travelling, to sending scouts on ahead to check for wheelchair-accessible routes and to waiting for wheelchair taxis that failed to arrive. In *Frankenstein's Children* Burrows participated with full commitment to every devising and rehearsal session and to every vocal and physical warm-up, even if he had to extemporize how to do so. At that stage, Burrows had a limited range of options for 'voice'. Firstly, his own speaking voice with which he struggled to articulate. We were keen to hear this voice as he was extremely expressive in his use of pitch and tone and, between us, we found ways of sharing a certain amount of vocal but non-verbal communication. He also had a laminated book of common phrases, letters of the alphabet, and, at his request, a list of obscenities. At this period, he used a Dynavox speech synthesis device but that entailed quite a lot of delay whilst he inputted text. It was also prone to freezing, when it would need to be sent to Sydney for repair. He later acquired an iPad which suited him a lot better in terms of being able to play music and write text in his own time but his impaired motor control, even in his good hand, made it difficult for him to benefit from text-to-speech applications. It was also difficult for him to 'speak' using these applications and move at the same time as he needed his hand to operate the joystick of his wheelchair. In terms of proxemics on stage and moving through the space, we tried to inculcate a practice of letting Burrows go where he needed first and then adapt the movements and positioning of others to him, but sometimes amidst the pressures and anxieties of performance some actors forgot this practice and Burrows was required to execute extraordinary many-point turns in his wheelchair or suddenly to improvise a path to avoid collision. The more we subsequently learned about what was necessary for Burrows to be part of the theatre company and to engage in activities that the rest of us took for granted, the more we tried to find ways to facilitate his meaningful and engaged participation in all aspects of performance and in friendship with other performers. This involved, however, such a fundamental challenge to all aspects of making theatre that often we did not achieve anything approaching our intentions or Burrows' desires.

Given his own time, however, he was able to produce writing and quite comprehensive rehearsal and production notes. The following is an example of his notes from the 2016 production *The Three Ecologies of Different Light*:

> What the fuck are they doing they will thinking and end we dont tell them till later on
> We all are in our dressing room waiting and getting ready to we start the show
> Josey does some moves and sings Come on and do the blue beat woooh – ohh
> A chicky chick a chicky chicky chang chang
> Peter says my baby dose the blue beat I luyn it to
> Matthew dose the king, a chicky chick a chicky chicky Chang Chang
> Andrew does his crying bit
> Ben dose funny voice like a witch It gets in2 your blood Qi and keept on your toals and makes you really swing
> Iasick and I say yeah baby do the blue beat in hut hop kind of way
> This is all about John and his Parss home
> We all count to 50 and move and put own arm up à do look up in a pods And llayarond with own velceits getting lound dr sofer
> I got some work but sold come I am busey for the show al of it for obey for July used like some songs 2 songs Frigie and Slash sweet child of mine and Shania twain something songs to get them ready to go Tony is writing our pages up for our show in July John Had been there for 50 years were in 19 65 whne he were 7 years old
> (Burrows' writings, Different Light archive)

Through the vagaries of the connection with the keyboard of Burrows' motor control of his good hand, these notes are a clear and accurate record of the rehearsal process of the opening sequence of *The Three Ecologies of Different Light*. I remember telling the performers that the opening was a kind of WTF?! sequence for the audience which would become clearer later, and which was all about our honouring the 50 years that John Lambie had spent within the Hohepa Canterbury institution since his arrival in the initial intake of children in 1965. The notes clearly indicate Burrows' ability to contribute and participate if given sufficient time, a time not generally afforded him in group rehearsals.

The pursuit of Burrows' voice(s) was and is a constant in the life of the company. The video archive of Different Light after the earthquake in 2011 contains footage of the group trying to give Burrows time to speak using the methods available to him at that time. This was on a day when his Dynavox was frozen, so he used a set of laminated cards on which were written the letters of the alphabet, times, places, objects, common phrases, and, at his insistence, swear words. He was questioned about the day of the quake:

TONY MCCAFFREY: Were you at Berrywood? (the name of the home for young people with physical disabilities in which Burrows was a resident)
GLEN BURROWS: (speaking) Yeah (whilst searching through the laminated files)
TONY MCCAFFREY: When it happened?
GLEN BURROWS: (speaking) Yeah.
TONY MCCAFFREY: So, what happened?
He uses the letters of the alphabet to spell out words. Louise Payne, Ben Morris and Isaac Tait attempt to read/anticipate his words.
LOUISE PAYNE: We – were – out – side – had –
(He searches through the laminated cards and chooses 'staff')
LOUISE PAYNE: With staff?
GLEN BURROWS: (speaking) Yeah
TONY MCCAFFREY: Did you feel the shake, Glen?
GLEN BURROWS: (speaking) Yeah
TONY MCCAFFREY: Were you scared?
GLEN BURROWS: (speaking) Yeah
LOUISE PAYNE: Did you stay in your chair?
GLEN BURROWS: (laughing and speaking) Yeah.
(The other performers find his laminated cards containing swear words and the discussion dissolves into laughter over these (Buddhist Centre Interviews, 2011)

This sequence of the group's attempts to listen to Burrows lasted seven minutes.

In 2013, preparing the *Canterbury Tales* project, each performer picked out prompt questions from a bag that they would ask members of the public in the interviews for the site-specific performance. The questions included some about experiences of the quakes, of disability, and some other random prompts to storytelling. In the video, archive of this process Glen Burrows participated with the help of Isaac Tait:

Burrows pulls out a question.
ISAAC TAIT: A story that starts, 'My first love …'
TONY MCCAFFREY: And Glen says?
Burrows types on his iPad.
ISAAC TAIT: (repeating the computerized voice of the iPad's text-to-speech software) Kirsten and I were drinking. Jack Daniels. We were drunk. (Canterbury Tales interviews, 2013)

Due to my perception of time constraints and inadequately considered methodology many of our processes afforded Burrows the merest sliver of opportunity to contribute. We attempted to supplement these by separate visits to Burrows at his home and encouragement of his making written contributions in his own time. In the group's later performances *Three Ecologies of Different Light*, we attempted to acknowledge the particular performance ecology that would be needed to include Glen Burrows.

Female voices in Different Light Theatre: Verity Carter, Natalie Walton, Theresa King, Rebecca Flint, and Caroline Quick

The inclusion of Verity Carter in Frankenstein's Children was an early attempt to disrupt the all-male environment of the company. Carter was treated by the others with respect throughout, but her participation was constrained by her being in a boyfriend-girlfriend relationship with Ben Morris at the time. She was the first female learning disabled member of the company to appear onstage in a public performance. There were female actors who participated in the Mixed Ability performance classes that were now running on Saturdays, but she was the first to be able to make the commitment to the extra time and work needed for performance, and to express enough confidence to brave the male-heavy environment of the company at that time.

In the first few years, access to the company for female actors was often determined by their place in heteronormative relationships with male members of the company. Verity Carter joined the group in the period of her relationship/friendship with Ben Morris, as subsequently did Rebecca Flint. Caroline Quick joined the group when she was engaged to group member Andrew Dever, Natalie Walton with Michael Stanley. Theresa King joined the group as she could share transport to and from Hohepa Canterbury with John Lambie. Louise Payne was a notable exception to this pattern as she arrived and negotiated her participation very much on her own terms, as much later did influential female company members Josie Noble, Biddy Steffens, and Angie Douglas.

The male-heavy humour and banter of the early stages of the group's development, combined with the familial and institutional perceptions of young learning-disabled women as more vulnerable rendered the inclusion of female actors more problematic.

In the video archive of the 2007 'Hornby Helldogs' improvisations in which the participants were encouraged to develop streetwise gang characters Verity Carter made the following contribution to the mockumentary video format:

VERITY CARTER: Hi I'm Lucy and I joined the Hornby Helldogs in – twenty years ago and I really kinda like it here and – Yeah. (Hornby Helldogs, 2007)

The brevity and politeness of this contribution was in marked contrast to the much more voluble contributions of the male performers. Occasionally in the early years, improvisation and devising exercises would reveal other aspects of the female actors. In an exercise in which the performers were invited to design and describe their idea of a room in an imaginary Different Light House, Natalie Walton's contribution was as follows:

NATALIE WALTON: Small family. Lot of people died. Sad girl. Bedroom. Britney Spears. To live with Michael (Stanley, her boyfriend) and do a flat. Dance in my room. Try to be happy but really … sad … miss my mum and parents. (Different Light archive)

In the post-earthquake interviews in 2011, Theresa King, a Hohepa resident gave her account of the day of the quakes:

THERESA KING: (smiling throughout) We had earthqu- pantry mess in the pantry. Things smashed. Annnd I helped- I helped John. He had a bad fall. From the shakes. Annnd stay safe and safe in the house. And I nearly got a bit scared and I got into the bed and had a torch. Then I was a bit scary. And then I didn't want earthquake to come back no more. (Smiling and shaking her head in an affirmative gesture) We wanted to get back to normal. (She continues to shake her head affirmatively) That's the end. (Buddhist Centre interviews, 2011)

In the video interviews about the soap opera characters each performer had chosen in preparation for *The Lonely and the Lovely* Rebecca Flint spoke of the character she chose, Lisa Goodchild:

REBECCA FLINT: She's a reception de- receptionist. Sh-she is looking for relationship, but she doesn't know who. But she doesn't know who. She's a little bit (six second pause) nervous. She's a little bit nervous about the ins and outs of how – how it will work out …. She is looking for love, but she finds it hard.

In contrast to these more reticent participants, Caroline Quick in the same video interviews was in complete control of her character's back story, her motivations, and the soap-style on-again off-again relationship with her character's husband, Danny Sebastian, played by her then-fiancé, Andrew Dever.

CAROLINE QUICK: I'm Bernadette who goes to Auckland because of my job … a modelling agent and I told Danny about it, and he wasn't happy about it and so me and him have a fight about it and so I said to Danny 'Stuff you' I'm going to Auckland because I had a promotion.

TONY MCCAFFREY: Why didn't he want to go to Auckland as well.
CAROLINE QUICK: Because he said to me that he didn't love me .... The marriage was in tatters, and I found out something from Osgood because Osgood's been texting me and keeping me updated with what's been happening and Osgood was telling me ehm that Danny ehm just became a waiter at Marty's bar and he also told me that he had an affair with someone. I was really upset and that's when I decided to end my marriage by getting the divorce papers and sent them off. I came back to Christchurch because my job got transferred to Christchurch again and I wanted to sort things out with Danny. I found him putting his arm around two gorgeous ladies. So, I yelled at him and walked off. (The Lonely and the Lovely interviews, 2012)

In all honesty, the group was ill-prepared to include the young women who attempted to join Different Light in this period. As with the participation of Glen Burrows, their voices, for the most part, required greater sensitivity to be listened to speech. The *Frankenstein's Children* narrative confirmed the group's gender stereotyping as it presented a world of men within which the sole female struggled to be heard. This neglected aspect of the company's development was not really addressed until the later arrival of Louise Payne and others.

Frankenstein's Children: the production and the characters

Frankenstein's Children was an opportunity for Matthew Phelan to claim the centre stage as the showman. He was the focal character around whom the narrative revolved. He was the leader of the group of scientists driving them on in the quest to create the perfect human being in the Project Eugene experiments, each of which resulted in failure. The first involved Ben Morris being hoisted high above the stage on a counterweight harness and 'genetically modified'. This turned Morris' character into an automaton that could speak only in scientific jargon and gobbledygook. The second involved trying to genetically modify Shawn O'Rourke's character, but a particularly virulent and resistant 'Irish gene' destroyed this attempt. In the last experiment, Frankenstein created a metallic robot. This was an attempt to replicate his twin brother who had been disabled, but perfect in Frankenstein's eyes, and who had died young. In frustration at only creating a clunky metallic version of his twin, his last act was to instruct the robot to destroy him, its creator, so that he might finally be reunited with his twin in death.

The Frankenstein character was an attempt not only to play to Phelan's strengths but also to encourage him to explore a more conflicted character. At the end of the performance in the Christchurch Town Hall, however, Phelan returned to his element when he spontaneously made a speech to the assembled audience of the National Residential Intellectual Disability

Provider Group conference, the then Mayor of Christchurch, Bob Parker, and other local dignitaries:

> Ladies and gentlemen, I hope you enjoyed our show. I hope we did a really good show and thanks so much for the round of applause and support. On behalf of all of us, I'm Matthew Phelan and on behalf of us, of A Different Light, thank you very much for watching our show. It's our pleasure. Thank you very much, good night, thank you, God bless you.

John Lambie played the older scientist who did not agree with the objectives and methods of the brash and domineering upstart Frankenstein. He also played John Haydon Langdon Down the founder of Earlswood Asylum for Idiots who gave his name to Down's Syndrome. In this sequence, Lambie, dressed in bowtie and frock coat, was accompanied by projected images of Earlswood Asylum, its residents, and specially constructed theatre. He arrived into a kind of schoolroom setup in which the scientists put their white coats on backwards and sat in rows to present the 'idiots' of the asylum's historical name whilst Phelan remained as Dr Frankenstein in their midst. Whilst Lambie walked around writing in a journal, Phelan's voice-over cited extracts from Down's 'Observations on an Ethnic Classification of Idiots' (1866). At certain points in this recitation, the chorus reacted. When the voice stated: 'They require highly azotised (salted) food with a considerable amount of oleaeginous (oil content)' the chorus members took out bags of salted snacks, solemnly held up one to the audience and then ate it. When the voice stated: 'The face is flat and broad, the cheeks are roundish and extended laterally .... The eyes are obliquely placed' (260). The chorus exaggeratedly mocked these 'observations' by squashing up their faces with their hands, blowing out their cheeks and blowing raspberries, squinting up their eyes and wrinkling their foreheads. A performer with Down's Syndrome portrayed Dr Down interacting with another performer with Down's Syndrome who gave voice to his observations. Meanwhile, a chorus of learning disabled actors mocked his observations of idiots whilst the voice-over intoned: 'They have considerable power of imitation, even bordering on being mimics. They are humorous and a lively sense of the ridiculous often colours their mimicry' (260). It was a theatrically naive attempt to speak back to the earliest document on Down's Syndrome. In the devising process, I had presented extracts from the document to the ensemble, and it was their responses that were presented in the scene.

In a subsequent sequence Lambie, as the older scientist, and Verity Carter as his assistant brought Morris's Eugene One to a woodland safe zone complete with animated landscape and birdsong. Lambie and Carter gave Eugene One the chance to speak in this more peaceful environment, but he still could only come up with jerky spasmodic movements of the head and body and confusion of jargon/gibberish. This was an opportunity for Lambie, not one of the most vocally fluent speakers in the group, to slow everything down and teach Morris how to say simple words like 'Hello' and 'Good' and 'Help' It was again a flipping of the script of social interactions that valorize speed of communication over connection and taking the time and trouble to speak and listen, lessons that we had all been experiencing in our interactions with Glen Burrows.

Ben Morris' role was that of a shy, younger scientist not able to object vociferously enough to avoid being experimented upon who then became the failed experiment, Eugene One.

Shawn O'Rourke was put in charge of various technical elements within a production that relied quite heavily on theatre technology. He supervised the harness and hoist sequence, the use of the smoke machine, and the onstage costume change into the metallic robot. Stuart Craig and Michael Stanley played the roles of scientists and participated in all of the ensemble sequences, including inhabitants of the Earlswood Asylum. Ben Ellenbroek played Frankenstein's dead twin and his robot killer.

Whilst only learning disabled performers were present on stage in *Frankenstein's Children*, the production used a range of technological devices, strategies, and prostheses intended to support their presence but which rather determined and controlled their participation. The intention was to showcase the abilities of the learning disabled performers on stage. In the pursuit of this intention, however, we threw all manner of theatre technology at the performers and the production: video projection, animation, voice-overs, captions, sound effects, smoke machine, counterweight flying, more elaborate scenography and costuming, and in a 30-minute performance, many hundreds of lighting and sound cues that required intense co-ordination by two operators. This elaborate framing of theatre technology did not so much support the learning disabled actors but rather the expected *kairos* or good timing of conventional theatre, the tight cueing, and new scene/new energy demands of conventional dramatic narrative.

In one scene in the production however, a different approach emerged. This was the forest scene with John Lambie, Ben Morris, and Verity Carter. This was presented as an 'environment' within which the learning disabled artists were more left to their own devices. to discover and negotiate their own sense of kairos, to take their own good time to inhabit performance that allowed for variation of actions and responses and that did not straitjacket them into hitting certain spatial and temporal marks.

The production also raised questions in terms of what might constitute the aesthetics and politics of the group. It was becoming clearer that the political *content* of the performance, such as the existential threat of eugenic agendas in a number of countries in the first decades of the 21st century, was in danger of being imposed upon the learning disabled artists by those of us who were non-disabled. These 'political' subjects may well have been developed in discussions in the devising process, but it was still far too easy for me and for other non-disabled facilitators to control the themes, subjects, or material for devising that were brought to the table in the process of theatre-making. The next production, *The Poor Dears*, attempted to address the politics and aesthetics of the selection of the company's material and dramaturgy but it also revealed deeper epistemic injustices underlying our methodologies of making theatre.

The Poor Dears

The title of the next production came from John Lambie. He had a particular antipathy towards the phrase being applied to him, particularly in the pitying, patronizing expression 'Ah, poor dear!' He asserted that he was not 'a poor dear' nor did he wish to be treated like one. *The Poor Dears* was an attempt to expand the reach of the Different Light project, the original group of seven performers was joined by five new performers who had come from associated projects and initiatives to develop and promote Mixed Ability theatre in Christchurch. These included the extra classes that we were running on Saturdays at Christchurch Polytechnic Institute of Technology which comprised a group of about 20 learning disabled students. It also included some overlap with two years of development of *The Sunnyside Project* investigating the memories and legacy of Sunnyside Hospital, formerly Sunnyside Asylum. I had also obtained funding from Adult and Community Education to run a ten-week professional development project in mixed ability theatre at CPIT to encourage drama teachers, theatre practitioners, and people working in the field of learning disabled care to learn more about the possibilities of learning disabled theatre. This project ran alongside the devising process and rehearsals for *The Poor Dears* and was documented in a 40-minute video by Paul McCaffrey. This video was later used in presentations about the work of the company at the Society for Disability Studies conference at Temple University, Philadelphia in June 2010 and, with the performers present to answer questions, as part of a Keynote presentation at the Arts Access Australia conference at the Powerhouse Museum in Sydney in 2010. These related activities constituted an attempt to prolong the lifespan and extend the outreach of the company beyond the annual theatrical production and public performance. New members of the group and new creative facilitators: artist, musician, and video and sound designer Stuart Lloyd-Harris, and of musician and artist Demarnia Lloyd, and the developing skills of Assistant Director Kim TePairi Garrett and of the group members themselves all contributed to a reconfiguration of the group's practice.

The Poor Dears was the least conventional theatrical narrative in the group's development to date. The premise of the narrative was the efforts by a learning disabled theatre ensemble to get past Border Control into the 'US', meaning both the United States and the 'us' of inclusion. Border Patrol consisted of various computerized, algorithmic tests, none of which seemed to make allowance for difference and diversity. At a certain point in this process individual members of the group made their case for inclusion through diverse modes of performance and self-presentation, none of which ultimately matched the criteria for inclusion.

The voice of the psychiatric survivor and activist: Louise Payne

Louise Payne joined the group through a call Different Light Theatre put out in the local newspaper, *The Press*, for former patients, staff, and others with experience of Sunnyside Hospital to participate in *The Sunnyside Project*. Sunnyside Asylum was founded in 1863 and, as Sunnyside Hospital, was closed in 1999. The historic buildings were knocked down and the land was blessed and cleansed by the Ngai Tahu iwi, the original inhabitants, who had associated the area as a place of healing. Linden Grove, a housing estate, was built in its place, the promotional material for which advertised the estate as occupying a 'historical location' without in any way referring to the specifics of that history.

Payne had been a patient at various times in her life. She had suffered various kinds of abuse at the hands and the electrodes of the institution and was part of a class action taken against the New Zealand Government for abuse within the psychiatric system. This action was ultimately successful but for Payne, the success consisted merely of the Government's acknowledgement. Financial compensation arrived shortly before she died suddenly in 2015 of late-stage lung cancer. She had a history of contracting pneumonia, of heavy smoking, and of self-harming. Payne was an activist, wordsmith, and artist who worked with the materials of her own often painful experience. As well as substantial involvement in *The Sunnyside Project* she started attending the Saturday mixed ability theatre classes and acted as an adviser on a NASDA final year production of Anthony Neilson's *The Wonderful World of Dissocia*. She joined Different Light Theatre on *The Poor Dears*. She encouraged Isaac Tait, Matthew Phelan, and Ben Morris to participate in open microphone performance poetry and improvisation nights at various venues in Christchurch and to participate in demonstrations and workshops promoting the Green politics that she advocated. She also brought to the group an engaged feminist perspective as well as developing and sustaining genuine friendships with the mostly male members of the group. She took considerable trouble to visit Glen Burrows in Berrywood, the home he inhabited for young people with cerebral palsy. She and her friends also navigated the exigencies of the city's wheelchair taxi network, and, in summer, adapted utility vehicles to transport Burrows around town. These efforts greatly augmented his ability to participate in social activities. She greatly influenced the subsequent development of the group. The following is a transcription of an interview with her in the immediate aftermath of the 2011 earthquake:

LOUISE PAYNE: I was downstairs at Alan-at Alan's and I had to go upstairs to get something and I was going under my bed when it hit and my arm got really smashed because I have a 1930s metal bed. Every time I tried to get up I kept getting smashed down ehm everything was smashed. Everything I own was smashed. The first earthquake I could help people, the second earthquake I slid into a corner outside and just started sobbing and rocking and tapping and screaming. Ehm. And. (she rocks backwards and forwards in her seat, an eight second pause during which she starts to shed tears)

TONY MCCAFFREY: How was Alan?

LOUISE PAYNE: Alan was in town and I got really worried about Alan because Alan was right in the middle of town. And. It was just chaos where I lived the ehm somebody helped and I got myself together a bit. When I couldn't stop tapping in public and things. Ehm went and helped out at the Rest Home ehm and they brought all the injured in from the other Rest Homes because one of them had partially collapsed at Beckenham so they were ferrying the injured. So I helped look after the elderly people for a couple of hours. Was really really worried about Alan. Alan came home probably about three and a half hours later and that was a big sigh of relief. My home's really special to me like everybody's home is special to them. Ehm. And to see my things all smashed and all of it in disarray cos it's normally (high-pitched, pinched sound) Perfect! OCD perfect. Ehm everywhere smashed TV PC laptop smashed shakes (her head) and the weirdest thing is that I have 'Jovial Dummy' from 1940s mannequin – she didn't fall down. But what did fall down was all these stars that I'd had all over the place and they all fell down so there was like multi-coloured stars all over my floor so that made me smile. (Buddhist Centre interviews, 2011)

The voice of the Gonzo poet: Isaac Tait

Isaac Tait joined Different Light working backstage on *Frankenstein's Children*. Tait is a talented visual artist who attended Christchurch Rudolf Steiner School, whose stated emphasis is on educating the whole person, 'Head, Heart, and Hands' (Rudolf Steiner School website), and on the value of the creative arts and spiritual development. Tait brought to the group a quiet voice often at odds with the more presentational aspects of theatrical performance and a different set of cultural reference points from his fascination with various forms of the historical avant-garde. His distinctive and quieter presence further reconfigured the dynamics of the group. From the outset, he and Glen Burrows struck up an affinity, and he was, and remains, extremely attentive to aiding Burrows' participation in the group. Tait is a keen observer of the social, cultural, and political sphere in Aotearoa New Zealand and continues to explore various personae and performances and practices of the self: gonzo beat poet, Buddhist, and artist. At the Australasian Association for Theatre, Drama and Performance Studies (ADSA) conference at Auckland University of Technology in 2017 as well as performing with Different Light he presented solo standup poetry and comedy in the breakout sessions of the conference. His contribution from the floor, quoting *Hamlet*, concluded the final plenary of the conference. Tait's contributions proved at times difficult to accommodate when the group was more committed to dramatic theatre, but the current, post-pandemic, turn to more online, filmed, and research-minded activity suits his contributions much more. In the post-earthquake interviews Tait contributed the following, a much more emotional account than we had become accustomed to from him in his contribution to the group's devising and rehearsal processes:

ISAAC TAIT: (after several false starts and pauses, in a quiet voice)
Ehm … ehm … ehm. I was on the bus going to work. And I was on the number I think I was on the number 10 bus going eh down Victoria Street and when it started ehm you could see all these – it felt like a ca-car crash like all the roads were like (he waves his arms up and down) bumpy and that and ehm you could see all the people just coming out of their buildings and being scared and people being terrified and that and when when I got to got to my work wasn't open (he is starting to cry) and I couldn't go to work so I didn't know what to do Ehm then I then I helped my grandma up cos she had fallen and a guy came over next door and helped me help my grandma and just stayed there for a while and so I call my mum and we went went to my brother's house and he was all right cos he was working and stuff cos he feeds the people from Orion and my work gave me a care package cos I work for McDonalds and they gave me food and stuff. (Buddhist Centre interviews, 2011)

When interviewed about the creation of characters in the devising process for the soap opera *The Lonely and the Lovely* Tait was reluctant to make the kinds of moral judgments on the characters that the soap opera format prompts in the viewer:

TONY MCCAFFREY: I wanted to ask you about the relationship between Osgood, played by Andrew Oswin and Danny played by Andrew Dever and they have this car crash, what do you make of it?
ISAAC TAIT: It's a great scene.
TONY MCCAFFREY: Can you tell me some more about what happens in it?
ISAAC TAIT: It's kind of dramatic. They start off being best friends learning how to drive and then they're driving somewhere. They build up

suspense and have a fight and stuff .... Danny is cheating and lying to his wife and she doesn't know but Osgood knows.
TONY MCCAFFREY: Are you on the side of Osgood or Danny?
ISAAC TAIT: I'm on-neutral .... They were arguing-miscommunicating with each other. The crash was no-one's fault. (The Lonely and the Lovely interviews, 2012)

In the preparation process for *Canterbury Tales* when performers were responding to the random questions that they would ask the public to answer his response was:

ISAAC TAIT: (pulling a piece of paper out of a bag, he reads) 'If I could change anything about myself it would be ....' I would like to listen more and talk less. Listen to what people have to say and ehm maybe trust people more. (pulling out another piece of paper) 'A story that you don't understand' (he re-reads and repeats the prompt) A story that you don't understand. Ehm. Pretty much anything I don't understand. I don't understand some people and how they treat some people with disabilities like that like the way that they do when you when they apply for jobs and they don't get them. (Canterbury Tales interviews, 2013).

The voice of the timekeeper: Damian Bumman

Damian Bumman joined Different Light backstage on the first performance of *Frankenstein's Children*. Due to the unavailability of a performer, he subsequently took a major onstage role in the version of that play that was performed in Christchurch Town Hall. He has a particular fascination with time zones and time differences, something that emerged when he travelled to Sydney with the group, and a superb memory for time-related information: dates, ages, and durations. In improvisations and rehearsals, he displayed a skill in learning lines of spoken text and an attraction to slightly grotesque characters. This suited the kind of narratives and characterization the company was pursuing at that time, in *Frankenstein's Children*, *The Poor Dears*, and *The Wizard of Oz*. After a period of absence, concentrating on his work at a bakery and other activities, he has recently rejoined the company in its post-pandemic form.

In the interviews that were part of the preparation process for *The Lonely and the Lovely*, he spoke of his opinions of other characters and about a character in the soap that he had chosen and developed:

DAMIAN BUMMAN: I like the characters like Bernadette and all that kind of stuff. She's about to get married to Danny Sebastian but they get divorced. Danny cheats on her with Roxie. I think it's ridiculous for him having sex with Roxie and all this confusion. If he keeps cheating on her I don't think they have a relationship.

Dave Knobbs is a dangerous guy. Firstly, he asks for $700, and he gets fired from his job and he goes around asking women for some money. Well, I think he's a bit of a dodgy fellow

TONY MCCAFFREY: Now you have been in the story as the Mayor of Christchurch.

DAMIAN BUMMAN: Yeah. Bob Drake. That character Bob Drake that I play was actually based on Bob Parker, but his name is Bob Drake, but he goes around assisting all the earthquakes and make sure there's money there for the rebuild of the new city. He's trying to rebuild the city, make it into a better place.

TONY MCCAFFREY: Is he married?

DAMIAN BUMMAN: Yeah. He's married.

TONY MCCAFFREY: So, what does his wife do?

DAMIAN BUMMAN: His wife does ehm history.

TONY MCCAFFREY: History? She teaches it?

DAMIAN BUMMAN: Yeah. In high school.

TONY MCCAFFREY: Who are the characters that you like in *The Lonely and the Lovely*

DAMIAN BUMANN: I like Bernadette. Because she's nice lady and she puts up with Danny. Dr Kate, well she's lovely. She works really closely with Glen's character

TONY MCCAFFREY: Jason Hart

DAMIAN BUMMAN: Jason Hart. And she helps people who've been sick.

TONY MCCAFFREY: Is everybody nice?

DAMIAN BUMANN: Everybody's nice ... except for Dave Knobbs. (The Lonely and the Lovely interviews, 2012)

The voice of the high achiever: Andrew Oswin

Andrew Oswin, a performer with Down's Syndrome made a brief but intense contribution to the devising processes and performances of the company. He appeared in *The Poor Dears*, *The Wizard of Oz*, and *Still Lives Christchurch* and participated in the development process of *The Lonely and the Lovely*. A strong, imaginative, and opinionated person who was heavily involved in sports in addition to his part-time job, his contributions to devising and theatre-making processes often took distinctive turns to black humour. This is evident in a rehearsal and ideas workshop for the soap opera that was recorded on 20 May 2012, and uploaded to the Different Light website. This was a discussion of what to do with the character of Danny Sebastian who had been left in a coma after a car accident that occurred when he was driving with Oswin's character, Osgood Anderson, and something had happened that distracted his attention and caused the crash. The discussion then turned to what Osgood would do when he visited his best friend Danny in a coma in the hospital.

ANDREW OSWIN: (smiling) I could always pull the plug.
TONY MCCAFFREY: But then we lose a character. Two characters. Because you would be sent to prison. For life
ANDREW OSWIN: Oh yeah.
LOUISE PAYNE: It would be nice to see you shine and not you kill someone. What if Dr Kate said Osgood, we need to talk about this (why Danny is in a coma)
ANDREW OSWIN: I don't want to.
BEN MORRIS: Maybe it could be a dramatic ending without being a cliffhanger.

Oswin made unpredictable offers in the improvisation process, often 'blocking' or shutting down improvisational offers, but was also quite capable of thinking through the narrative possibilities of given situations. This was the case in a car scene in which Osgood was supervising learner driver Danny Sebastian. Danny had confided his infidelities to his best friend Osgood, who upbraided him, which then distracted Danny and caused a crash. In a solo interview about the car crash scene, Oswin explained:

ANDREW OSWIN: In the car I turn quite angry to Danny because of how he has been treating Bernadette, binge drinking of disorderly alcohol. My character would say that I thought Bernadette was a fine, beautiful woman. I thought she was better to you, but she is to me. The accident happened slightly out of range. I told him to focus on the road. But he didn't because he only wanted to look at me all the time. Because he just wants to spill everything out at me about what's been happening. He knew that I was raising my temper about how he had treated Bernadette and he was completely gobsmacked and shocked. (The Lonely and the Lovely interviews, 2012)

This accounted for his character's desire to pull the plug on Danny in a coma. The adoption of the soap character and the processes of improvising performance allowed him to explore other possibilities and other identities, but ultimately it was not something he chose to pursue. While working with the group he later became prone to fainting during the pressures of the production week for the performance of *The Poor Dears* and scenes from *The Wizard of Oz* presented at the University of Canterbury Arts Festival and withdrew from the company.

The Poor Dears: the production

The Poor Dears had a more abstract narrative framework that was intended to encourage greater input and ownership by the actors. At one point in the production, the performers held up t-shirts printed with legends such as: 'I'm not ignoring you, I'm just autistic', 'It's called Down Syndrome you fucking retard!' 'Keep staring … I might do a trick' and 'I'm with stupid —}' a mixture of slogans taken from the discourse of disability activism and ableist slights and slurs normalized as humorous banter. These were part of a first attempt to produce a kind of anti-marketing for the company that incorporated the poster for *The Poor Dears* which was deliberately anti-spectacular: a light blue square surrounded by dotted lines on a white background and written on the square: 'Insert image here'.

The narrative framework of the piece put the performers through a Border Patrol surveillance process. Automated voices ordered the performers into a particular formation in the space to conduct a US Border Patrol ID test, US standing for both United States and 'us' and ID standing for both identity and intellectual disability. The first question asked by Border Patrol was 'What is your name?' to which various members of the group responded 'We Are Not The Poor Dears', the name of the (fictional) learning disabled theatre company. The Border Patrol algorithm proved incapable of processing this name, despite the protestations of the group, each time condensing it to 'The Poor Dears'. Eventually, in order to have any chance of proceeding with being processed they had to agree to this name and the complete negation of their self-identity. The automated voice algorithm questioning their nationality conflated New Zealand with Australia, forced them to choose a (US) State in the manner of online application forms, and processed their occupation – 'theatre company' as 'unemployed'. When asked if they had any history of mental illness, Isaac Tait produced a copy of *History of Madness* by Michel Foucault. This temporarily threw a spanner into the works of the processing machine.

The performers then 'controlled' the stage. They presented sequences that had emerged in the devising process. These included a short play written by Isaac Tait entitled *Is it Normal? Any different?* This was the first complete text by a member of the company that was presented in a public performance. Tait's play was an assemblage of voices from snatches of conversation in cafes, bars, and on the streets of Christchurch and his everyday dealings with his support worker: 'Into the world the greatest person in the world: the community worker'. The support worker was played by Louise Payne, herself no stranger to community care, who asked the Isaac Tait characters or surrogates that proliferated on stage the usual how are you questions intercut with a recurrent phrase, part accusation, part mantra, part existential cri de coeur: 'Is it normal? Any different?' The montage included reference to drugs, being adopted, blame and recrimination, crime and punishment, and the vague possibilities of love, until the arrival onstage of a mannequin named Peaches. Tait lay down on the ground and caressed Peaches. This intimacy was then rudely interrupted by a Christchurch crowd who levelled confusing accusations at Tait to which he responded: 'THIS IS NOT A MUSICAL' and the piece ended.

The devising methodologies for Tait's scene that were controlled by Tait himself contrasted starkly with those for the scene that followed it,

Matthew Phelan's Elvis poem. Phelan's piece was a solo that was developed in an extemporized form of 'facilitated communication' that was devised between him and me over a period of weeks. The poem addressed his long-standing relationship with, and desire to imitate, Elvis Presley. We traced points of similarity between Phelan and Presley that included a strong Christian faith, a powerful love for the mother, a dead twin that connected with Phelan's character in *Frankenstein's Children*, the experience of being bullied at school for stuttering, a sense of feeling different, Presley being part-Cherokee Phelan being called 'handicap' at school, a sense of uniqueness in not sounding like anybody else, the desire to perform, and the loneliness of doing so. Phelan's poem was spoken into a large onstage microphone on a stand as he was backlit, dressed in a version of the black leather jumpsuit of Elvis of the 1968 Comeback Special that had been custom-made to his specifications. It was underscored by the live accompaniment of a simple, slow tempo looping, rolling riff on electric guitar, bass, and drums, an extended vamp that never broke out into a recognizable tune or resolved itself. It was a virtuoso performance that always drew applause from an audience. In response to this Phelan repeated 'Thank you very much' whilst adopting the hieroglyphic poses of Elvis.

At the end of the poem there was a section referring to Presley's mother's funeral that included lyrics from 'Will the circle be unbroken?' This was a prefiguration of John Lambie's scene. During the rehearsal period, Lambie's mother died. I recall being told by a support worker that as Lambie was categorized as intellectually disabled, he did not 'qualify' for grief counselling. I subsequently spoke to Lambie about his mother's death and elements of this conversation emerged in the performance. Lambie, of Scottish Presbyterian stock, had no time for the sentimental pitying of 'poor dears'. Equally, Lambie as a man with Down's Syndrome, institutionalized for most of his life, was not granted any meaningful time or support to grieve.

Previous elements of the abstract narrative: the tolling of a bell in the opening sequence, the abstract scene of an old woman on her own unsure of what she is seeing, and the funeral of a mother, the main subject matter of the song 'Will the Circle be Unbroken?' all served as prefigurations of Lambie's scene. This was sparse and consisted of Lambie walking in slow motion downstage and then upstage in a corridor of light, backlit and frontlit. At the same time, in the persona of a health professional, Louise Payne read 'notes' from his case. These consisted of abstract linguistic examples 'John is eager to please' and 'John is easy to please' interwoven with citations from the Book of John 19: 26–27: 'Woman behold thy son ... son, behold thy mother'. The sequence ended with a movement sequence performed by Lambie as two other performers repeated the words: 'I remember the day you told me. I wasn't very happy about that. I remember the day you told me. I'm not very happy about that'. These were the words Lambie had said when I asked him how he had heard of his mother's death.

In the scene that immediately followed, Michael Stanley tried to make his way diagonally from upstage left to downstage right as other members of the company literally held on to his coattails of a long ecclesiastical-looking coat and as he carried a crucifix in front of him representing the large crucifixes he often wore around his neck. In the Lecoq-type push-pull dynamic of this scene, Stanley would push to make progress and be pulled back by the accompanying chorus. A Gospel song accompanied his progress, a cacophony of voices his being dragged back. He eventually arrived centre stage, stood his ground, and delivered the prayer 'Hail Holy Queen, Mother of Mercy' the *Salve Regina* of Roman Catholicism that he knew by heart, even when being distracted by an antagonistic chorus. The next scene opened with Theresa King again sitting in a rocking chair, looking at a pair of cowboy boots and a black Stetson on the ground Country music played in the background as she got up and dusted the hat and placed it on a table, and then dusted the cowboy boots and placed them upstage. She then took the hat off the table, held it to her heart, and gently swayed, dancing with it to the music. While she did this Ben Ellenbroek arrived wearing a white Stetson. He stepped into the boots and approached King. As the music swelled they danced with each other, expanding their movements into the space, a swaying, circling partner dancing that they both enjoyed. At a certain point, however, he leaves the stage. She was left still dancing and holding the black hat to her heart. When she noticed that he had gone, she slowly put the hat on the table again and sat back in the rocking chair, bowing her head as the music and the lights slowly faded.

These three scenes that used very few words or the words of a well-known prayer or a song were early experiments in creating environments within which individual members of the group could improvise and extemporize. The toolbox that they had been given was, however, still 'given' to them – with all the problems of inequity that relationship implies. In addition, the emotional tone of the onstage supports they were given steered them towards engagement in certain emotional – and sentimental – narratives and theatrical semiotics. At this point, it is interesting to note how the negotiation of theatre-making and narrative content of these scenes consisted of variations of a push-pull dynamic: a giving in to flights of fantasy or memory that was then taken away by some form of reality principle at the end of each scene. Lambie is 'forced' to give voice to his feelings despite the patent inadequacy or absurdity of language to deal with deep feeling, Stanley's doubts or struggles resolved in the borrowed words of a prayer, King's fantasy/memory returning to the 'reality' of the aloneness of the rocking chair. The chair moves but in a movement that is yet static, on the spot, like life within an institution. These scenes that derived from the percepts of the performers were processed into theatrical concepts and metaphors still negotiated by a non-disabled facilitator with particular assumptions of the kind of narrative and dramaturgy that might engage an audience.

The next three scenes that foregrounded individual performers were attempts to include positive energies to redress the apparent emphasis on the lack and loss of the previous three. In 'Shawn Lights the Scene', Shawn O'Rourke was given the opportunity to bring his fascination with being a stage technician onstage. He was required to manually operate three lights on a mobile lighting tree to illuminate a scene in which John Lambie danced onstage with a large lump of dough that he threw on a table and, after rolling up his sleeves, and proceeded to knead vigorously and joyously. This was a sequence based on a happy memory of his mother making bread. He then danced off again, accompanied all the while by cumbia music, with which he was familiar from eurythmy exercises focusing on swaying of the hips and torso. O'Rourke's job was to react in the moment or anticipate how and where Lambie would move and to light the space for Lambie to inhabit and through which to move with joy.

The next scene was a relatively simple one involving Drew McLean. McLean was a young Māori performer who briefly joined Different Light from the Saturday group. He made distinctive and interesting contributions to *The Poor Dears* and *The Wizard of Oz* and then he and his family moved on after the earthquakes. McLean spoke directly to the audience about his experience of different schools in Christchurch, and where he had his heart broken and had developed his love of motorcycles and guitar music. This provided a deliberately clumsy segue into Glen Burrows arriving onstage in his motorized wheelchair zipping around and cornering at speed doing circuits of the space, whilst carrying Ben Morris on the back. When he eventually stopped, Shawn O'Rourke ran on as a roadie with Burrows' electric guitar and amplifier setting up Burrows to play chords to a live backing of drums and bass and the ensemble arrived onstage to dance around Burrows. Burrows had had an electric guitar for some time, but it had never been tuned. This was the first time he had played in public with a tuned guitar.

At the end of this sequence, the ensemble left the stage and Ben Morris remained on the stage centre in a spotlight in front of a microphone. He proceeded to take his top and trousers off and, standing in his boxers, started to rub baby oil on his body, the microphone picking up the squelching sound. The ensemble returned and approached the audience miming rubbing themselves and the audience with oil and exclaiming 'Oh, baby, baby!' as they did so. These cries were intended to suggest both the (usually) hidden desires of learning disabled people and the infantilization to which they are subjected.

Just before they reached the audience the Border Patrol alarms sounded again and they were instructed to go back to their earlier formations. They were subjected to further surveillance and security measures including the removal of their shoes and of Burrows from his wheelchair and repeatedly browbeaten by automatic voices asking 'What is your name?' until they acquiesced and as a group identified themselves with the phrase 'WE ARE

THE POOR DEARS' When they did so the soundscape from the beginning of the performance sounded and they exited the stage in the same formation they arrived, to the accompaniment of a tolling bell, exiting through the haze into the sidelight offstage.

The documentary

The 40-minute documentary that was made by Paul McCaffrey during the rehearsal and production process of *The Poor Dears* is a kind of alternative archive: largely visual and non-verbal. The video includes carefully observed footage of the performers in the pre-time and the down-time of rehearsals: showing the nervous tics and habitual gestures of the actors about to enter the stage or sitting watching the technology of the production being assembled or watching other actors in the spotlight. It includes the actors' reactions to my giving them direction or correcting them.

The dramaturgical strategies of *The Poor Dears* dramaturgy represented a paradigm of the processes of giving and taking voice in performance, sometimes intentionally, often unintentionally. In the narrative world, the group was given a chance to perform as a learning disabled theatre company but not really listened to. Individual performers were given the opportunity to present solo sequences from their own contributions to the devising process but the dramaturgical framing of these pieces was taken out of their hands. For many of the performers, it was a performance that in the colloquial expression 'took it out of them': they committed to devising material that was personal to them in a manner that physically or emotionally challenged them. The processes of negotiating the material and the aesthetics of presenting this material was still heavily reliant on non-disabled creatives and facilitators, musicians and technicians, and on me as director. Questions remained as to what was gained and what was lost by the performers and by the audience in putting out fairly personal material for performance. Methodological doubts remained as to how to facilitate different levels of creative autonomy. Firstly there was the approach that we took with Isaac Tait of leaving him to create his own text. The difficulty with this approach is that all material for devising is inevitably influenced by the given starting points or stimuli and the context in which material is devised: the often unspoken ethos and expectations of the wider group. Secondly, there was the approach that was taken with Matthew Phelan, a kind of facilitated communication of stylized or 'poetic' text negotiated over a long period of time to seek to match the material to his experience and to find a mode of performance that seemed best to suit his persona. The difficulty with this approach was that of ventriloquizing the performer's 'voice' and typecasting Phelan into what were perceived to be his strengths in performance. Thirdly the approach taken with John Lambie was suspiciously reliant on intuition and potentially exploitative of his experience, sentimentalizing his grief on his behalf, and, ironically, rendering him a 'poor dear'. Perhaps this was not ironic, given the ways in which theatre, once created, speaks back to the creators.

The three performances presented by Different Light at this stage of the group's development inevitably spoke back to the group and the inequities and imbalances in power in the process of making theatre. With hindsight, it is possible to find parallels between Captain Cook in *Ship of Fools* and we the non-disabled facilitators who were claiming to have discovered the artists in people who were already artists. We were planting our colonialist flags imposing the language of dominant discourses and the disciplinary formations of conventional theatrical narrative and dramaturgy in the far-flung lands of the learning disabled. Like Professor Frankenstein in *Frankenstein's Children* the stage was becoming cluttered with failed attempts to create perfect actors in our own image. In trying to present 'NOT the poor dears' how much had we helped to create narratives of lack, grief, and loss that rendered the learning disabled artists *The Poor Dears*? Theatrical performance has a way of speaking back at yourself, taking the characters you create, and what they have said and throwing them back at you. Making theatre is a reflexive process: you make theatre, and it also makes theatre out of you. At this stage in its evolution Different Light Theatre was performing itself into some kind of emergent being: a ship of fools, Frankenstein's children, (not) poor dears.

References

Bartl, Anthony. "Festival of life." The Big Issue Melbourne No. 292, 20 November–3 December, 2007.

Coleridge, Samuel Taylor. *The Rime of the Ancient Mariner*. Caxton Press, 1968.

Different Light Theatre. Hornby Helldogs interviews, CPIT, 9 June, 2007. Different Light video archive.

———. Video interviews at the International Buddhist Centre, Christchurch, 20 March, 2011. Different Light video archive.

———. The Lonely and the Lovely interviews, 16 September, 2012. Different Light video archive.

———. Canterbury Tales interviews, Ara Institute, 10 November, 2013. Different Light video archive.

Down, John Langdon Haydon. "Observations on an ethnic classification of idiots." *London Hospital Reports*, vol. 3, 1866, pp. 259–262.

Foucault, Michel. *Madness and Civilization. A History of Insanity in the Age of Reason*. Translated by Richard Howard. Routledge Classics, 2005.

Frankenstein's Children. Devised by the ensemble, directed by Tony McCaffrey. Different Light Theatre. NASDA Theatre Body Festival 9–12 October 2008 NRID Conference, Christchurch Town Hall. 8–10 July, 2009.

Lecoq, Jacques. *The Moving Body: Teaching Creative Theatre*. Translated by David Bradby. Methuen, 2000.

McCaffrey, Tony. *Incapacity and Theatricality: Politics and Aesthetics in Theatre Involving Actors with Intellectual Disabilities*. Routledge, 2019.

McCaffrey, Tony, McCaffrey, Paul, Parker, George and Garrett, Kim TePairi. *The Sunnyside Project*. Devised performance funded by Creative New Zealand. Developed 2007–2010 for Christchurch Arts Festival 2010, cancelled due to earthquakes, 2010–2011.

Neilson, Anthony. *The Wonderful World of Dissocia and Realism*. Methuen, 2007.

"Our Time." Society for Disability Studies Conference, San Jose, California, 17–20 June, 2009.

Rudolf Steiner School, Christchurch website. https://www.ch.steiner.school.nz/about-our-school/. Accessed 8 October, 2021.

Ship of Fools. Devised by the ensemble. Directed by Tony McCaffrey. Different Light Theatre. Awakenings Festival, Horsham, Victoria, Australia, 13–15 October, 2007.

The Poor Dears. Devised by the ensemble. Directed by Tony McCaffrey. Different Light Theatre. NASDA Theatre, CPIT. Body Festival 1–4 October 2009, University of Canterbury Platform Festival, 27–30 May, 2010.

The Wizard of Oz. Devised by the ensemble. Directed by Tony McCaffrey. Different Light Theatre. NASDA Theatre, CPIT. Ignition Creative Festival, 18–21 November, 2010.

4 Intertextuality and Intermediality

Performing Responses to the Disabling of the City

The Wizard of Oz, Still Lives, The Lonely and the Lovely

The company's next three productions were all heavily affected by, and informed by, the Christchurch earthquakes of 2010 and 2011. *The Wizard of Oz* was the last attempt to create a theatrical narrative that could accommodate a large ensemble of performers. It involved the same ensemble that had appeared in *The Poor Dears*. The narrative was chosen democratically. I had asked the performers to choose the story that would be the basis for the next performance that we were due to present in the Body Festival in Christchurch at the NASDA Theatre at the end of September 2010.

In March 2010, a group of nine of us: seven performers, one care-person for Glen Burrows, and I, travelled to Sydney to give a presentation at the Arts Activated Conference: Arts, Access, Excellence at the Powerhouse Museum. We presented a 40-minute documentary video: *Is It Normal? Any Different?* The title taken from Isaac Tait's play that included footage from rehearsals and the performance of *The Poor Dears* intercut with workshop sessions of the Saturday Mixed Ability class at Christchurch Polytechnic Institute of Technology (CPIT, Ara) and of the nine-week Professional Development initiative on Mixed Ability Theatre. The performers then answered questions from the floor. At the conference, the performers attended a Keynote by Jenny Sealey of the UK's Graeae Theatre, one of the longest established disability arts groups in the UK, who was there to share the experience with disabled artists and organizations who had participated in the Opening Ceremony of the 2000 Sydney Olympics, as she was planning the Unlimited Festival at the 2012 London Olympics. The performers also attended workshops and presentations and met up again with Australian disability arts performers, artists, and organizers they had first met at the Awakenings Festival in 2007.

As was becoming customary when we travelled together, we were caught up in unforeseen situations and difficulties, particularly concerning transport and access for motorized wheelchair user, Glen Burrows. Some of these mishaps were the result of my own lack of preparation and failure

Figure 4.1 Different Light Theatre in performance: *The Wizard of Oz*, 2011. John Lambie and the company. Image: Stuart Lloyd Harris for Different Light Theatre.

to provide enough support for the whole group. I had been advised to take more care and support personnel for the eight learning disabled performers but had been unable to do so in the rush to secure funding and arrange travel and accommodation. In the downtime from the conference, we took the bus out to Bondi Beach, but the driver was not familiar with the use of a ramp, obliging us to lift the wheelchair onto the bus. When we arrived at Bondi, we lifted Burrows onto some blankets on the sand near the carpark where we parked his wheelchair. This was an uncomfortable arrangement for him, but we were able to contact Bondi Surf Rescue a group of whom came running over with a Sandcruiser, a specially designed wheelchair with large, inflated wheels that allowed us to take Burrows onto the beach and into the sea.

Later that evening as we were returning to our accommodation, we came across a group of dancers from the Sydney Ballet Company rehearsing on some grass near the Harbour Bridge and some of the performers joined in with their warmups and as we left them, we turned to see a fireworks display illuminating the Sydney Opera House in the distance. On another occasion, as we were walking up the steep gradients of the Rocks in Sydney, John Lambie fell over onto his face. I took him to a nearby emergency doctor who because of Lambie's 50 years, an age the doctor considered advanced for a person with Down's Syndrome, called an ambulance to Sydney Hospital to have tests and scans, which, thankfully, revealed no cause for concern. Some of these incidents later found their way into *The Wizard of Oz* performance: Oz became Australia.

On our return, whilst we were in the later stages of rehearsal for *The Wizard of Oz*, Christchurch was hit by a 7.1 earthquake at 4.35 am on 4th September. There was no loss of life, but substantial damage to many buildings and the city experienced wave upon wave of aftershocks. In the immediate aftermath of this quake, the Body Festival was cancelled. When *The Wizard of Oz* was later presented in the Ignition Festival at the NASDA theatre on 18–21 November, it was informed by the performers' experiences of, and reactions to, the earthquake.

The Wizard of Oz and the archive

The keeping of an archive of devising and performance processes became more important at the time of *The Wizard of Oz*, in part due to the heightened awareness of having escaped disaster. The quakes exposed issues relevant to the members of the company: the precarious place of disabled people within both the disaster and the disaster capitalism of the recovery, and the trauma and the post-trauma that people experienced – and that many argue still affects inhabitants of Christchurch. The quakes also occurred at a stage in the development of Different Light in which there was an urge to move beyond the learning disabled performers' acting as a display of 'talent': look what I can do! I'm just like you – almost. There was a desire likewise to move beyond the tropes associated with learning disabled people as, variously, slow, confused, emotionally open, hugging, touched by the divine, of simple faith, cute, infantilized beings in whom the prospect of sexuality and desire was foreclosed, quaint imitators or mockers of the normal, who were yet excluded from the normal.

This increase in documentation included interviews with the performers in the immediate aftermath of the second deadly quake in 2011, video recording of rehearsal processes, footage of the performers backstage, and of improvisation and devising workshops. Video also became an important tool for the company's self-examination. It introduced to the performers other ways of working and performing allowing multiple takes and retakes that might be more congenial to their engagement with performance and afford the accommodation of 'crip time'.

The following is a transcript of backstage video taken in the NASDA theatre on 22nd November, 2010, the last night of the season, only 11 weeks after the first 7.1 earthquake. The performer contributions were upbeat, particularly upbeat as they were a preface both to the last night and to the after party:

BEN MORRIS: I'd just like to wish everyone a really fantastic time and ehm all the all the make-up artists. Especially these.

...

THERESA KING: I'm Dorothy.
...
ANDREW OSWIN: In this show I am a doctor and also a monkey. Ooh ooh aah aah (makes monkey gestures) policeman.
...
MATTHEW PHELAN: Well of course I am scarecrow, Dorothy, Toto, and Tin Man. And some lines with the little light (he uplights his face with a small torch as he does in the opening sequence) I'm a little bit scared of dying.
TONY MCCAFFREY: Which you wrote.
MATTHEW PHELAN: When my grandfather died in Tauranga, he saw a light and just before he died, he had a face bright as a child. (*Wizard of Oz* interviews, 2010)

In mid-March, a few weeks after the second quake, video interviews took place at the Buddhist Centre that were an attempt to allow the performers to speak to each other of their experiences and to keep the group together at a time when most theatres and rehearsal spaces were inaccessible. It was also a chance to include in the group performers who had joined from the Saturday morning classes, Josie Noble, Andrew Dever, and Peter Rees, who would go on to become an important part of the group's next phase of development:

JOSIE NOBLE: Yeah I was in – right in the Central Business District (CBD) area when it happened. I just finished my first day of work experience at WorkBridge. Ehm and I was just about to get lunch in the café next door ehm and then and then the earthquake happened ehm I was confused and scared ehm and I was holding onto the – the bench thing in the café. And then the ladies they got me out-s-side and they looked after me and I got my lunch. Ehm the plan was that I would get a taxi home but it didn't happen. Ehm so ehm ehm and my mum ehm just finished her orientation meeting in the hospital and she was at the Moorhouse lights and she thought someone was pushing against the car but it was the earthquake. So then she wanted to get home and see how I was. Ehm yeah so it was all scary and I saw a ewhm dust coming up from the ehm from the next – down the road when ehm it all smashed. Ehm. And. That's about it.
ANDREW DEVER: Well I was at SkillWise (in the CBD) when the earthquake happened. All I remember is it was 12.51. It was straight after lunch. We went back to our groups. The teacher went down to the second floor just to drop something off. And then-and then all of a sudden (he sways from side to side) start – everything started to move and started to shake madly things fell over smashed and we-we couldn't-we couldn't get we-we Ahh. Sorry. We-Sorry. And then we-we left the room where we was and there was no staff. We tried to walk up to the staff room

but we couldn't see anyone and then we walked towards our bags and we just sat down on the ground. We waited-we waited till the shaking stopped then we walked downstairs in pure darkness. We had torches and then we walked downstairs in the dark and then we went out onto Gloucester Street. Everything around us was-was smashed. So what we did was we tried to walk down Chancery Lane but the church there that got smashed up so we got cut off. So we had to walk up Gloucester into Colombo Street and we stayed in Victoria Park.

PETER REES: On the day of the earthquake, I was in the central city in SkillWise. I was sad, scared. My father was at work his work was badly damaged. The walls caved in. The computers and the desks fell and smashed so they can't get in and ehm and ehm we had no power no power no lights for half of the night and ehm and I went with my mum to see how my grandma was and ehm we took a thermos, and we shared some stories. A friend of mine from my dad's work died in the earthquake and we went to the funeral on Thursday morning. The end. (Buddhist Centre interviews, 2011)

The Wizard of Oz

The devising process for the performance was not an attempt at a mimetic version of the 1939 film but rather an exploration of how individual performers and the ensemble connected with the characters and world of the film. The first scene drew on improvisation in which performers had talked about their fears. This took on greater resonance in the adrenalin-charged environment of the aftershocks. Matthew Phelan had talked about his fear of death, and the light that his grandfather said that he saw before he died, and the child-like brightness of his face that Phelan observed the last time when he saw him. He then expressed how this informed his fear of death. Phelan feared that when he died, he would not be able to find that light and, therefore not know where to go and to find the body he was supposed to be in at the Second Coming. This fear was so powerful that he did not want to talk about it onstage and we re-allocated the lines that Phelan had devised to Isaac Tait who added his own matter-of-fact coda: 'The Wizard of Oz is a very old film. And all the people in it are dead now'.

In the next scene Phelan delivered a recital of a substantial section of text from the film that he knew by heart, playing both The Scarecrow and Dorothy. The corresponding scene from the film was projected silently in the background. These were the only moments of direct imitation of the film in the production and they were intended to show Phelan's particular skill in learning dialogue, but also to problematize fidelity to *mimesis* in performance. Phelan was capable of reciting much more dialogue, possibly the whole film, as he had watched the DVD of the film repeatedly, some 40 times, and knew it by heart. As his virtuosic one-man dialogue continued downstage right, the other members of the company arrived in the shadows upstage left, and slowly waved to him, actions which he was far too busy caught up in his recitation to perceive. The stage was thus balanced by Phelan on one side and the ensemble on the other. The audience were invited to hold in balance both Phelan's virtuosity and the distance from engagement with others this created.

Theatrical techniques of collage, intertextuality, intermediality, and ambivalent citation were applied to interweave the world of the 1939 film with the performance personae of the learning disabled artists of Different Light Theatre. The main narrative premise of the film is, of course, connected with self-perceptions of (dis)ability: lack of heart, brain, courage, and home. Each of the Different Light performers was associated with a particular character from the film but the connections were ambiguously presented. Matthew Phelan was the Tin Man, his favourite character, but the character's lack of heart and rigid movements also spoke to Phelan's intractable desire for imitation of the original film. Glen Burrows was the Wizard, a reference to his reliance on technology, viz his motorized wheelchair. The production exaggerated this reliance: laser lights were attached to his chair, computerized voices stood in for his own, and projected video amplified his presence. He was not the charlatan revealed in the film, but the production drew attention to the mediatization involved in representing his 'presence' on stage questioning what might constitute that presence. Isaac Tait was the Scarecrow whose clothes were stuffed not with straw but with scraps of paper containing fragments of Tait's poems. Ben Morris was Toto the dog with highly stylized make-up and an Elizabethan ruff collar. He suggested a conflicted, divided self, caught between aspirations as an actor and the animality of the character. John Lambie, and Ben Ellenbroek when Lambie was unwell, played an 18th-century composer, a black and white character in a technicolor world, a person out of time with the rest of the narrative. They inhabited a world of a slower tempo, accompanied by classical music. Theresa King presented a version of Dorothy in the Western-style shirt and jeans she used for her hobby, country dancing. The red slippers were trainers decorated with red sequins. Michael Stanley presented a muted version of the Cowardly Lion, Shawn O'Rourke was busy onstage throughout as an over-equipped super-technician, Drew McLean presented a sinister male version of the Wicked Witch of the West. Louise Payne was the leader of the Police/Flying Monkeys and presented a Yellow Brick Road sequence of anti-depressant medications. Damian Bumman and Andrew Oswin were Police/Flying Monkeys. Bumman also presented the two Songs of the Munchkin. The text of Song One was abstracted from his experience of bullying and being accused of harassment. It was punctuated by his exhortations to himself not to cry, despite the voices around him levelling non-specific accusations at him, until finally he discovered he was crying. Song of the Munchkin Two gave expression to Bumman's keen interest in different time zones that became evident when he travelled with the group to Sydney. He gave the audience the actual time at that moment in Christchurch, Sydney, Melbourne, Brisbane, and Adelaide and then proceeded to give updates by the minute in real time until he stopped, questioning these precise times given the possibility that his watch might be wrong.

It was becoming clear that the more the group pursued improvising and devising from personal experience the more this called into question the assumptions of practices of improvisation outlined in texts such as Keith Johnstone's *Impro: Improvisation and the Theatre*. His foundational concepts of Status, Spontaneity, Narrative Skills, Mask, and Trance depend upon an assumption of normativity and ability even though he prefaces the whole book with an account of a two-minute film he made about 'Cripples' and his encounter with a 'Psychotic Girl' (15). Throughout the book, he refers to giving permission to the 'psychotic thought' and 'madness' that will somehow liberate spontaneity and imagination. After the improviser has been through the initial comic phase of wanting to make people laugh at their improvisations, and then the 'obscene' sexual and scatological phase they will proceed to the improvisatory 'gold' of inherent creativity, somehow clearing a path to depths somehow drawn out of the unconscious. In exploring such improvisation practice with the learning disabled performers it became clear that some account needed to be made for the social, familial, and institutional constraints and policing that many of the performers experienced with regard to the expression of illogicality, absurdity, or connection with sexuality and bodily functions, aspects of experience that provide such core material for 'normative' theatrical improvisation.

The Wizard of Oz provided a theatrical framework within which to explore the feelings of the characters/personae of the learning disabled actors based on a book and film intended for children that is at times frightening, sentimental, melodramatic, and grotesque. In addition, the tornado that is the catalyst for Dorothy's journey had an obvious counterpart in the earthquakes that interrupted the production. The sense of anxiety couched within the children's narrative of the story of Oz was apparent in the first Toto the dog sequence. This was introduced by a looped recording from the soundtrack of the film, Auntie Em saying: 'Now you just help us out today and find yourself a place where you won't get into any trouble'. This phrase itself was then echoed by Dorothy: 'Some place where there isn't any trouble .... Do you suppose there is such a place, Toto?' The question resonated in the production, questioning the imperative to present 'positive images' of learning disabled people, whilst at the same time acknowledging the difficulties of exploring 'negative' thoughts and behaviour in performance. The subject matter of Different Light Theatre up to that point involved issues – of love and death, of frustration and exclusion – discussion of which were discouraged in the networks of institutional or familial care around the performers.

Intertextuality and Intermediality 121

The interweaving of 'personal' material, character, and theatrical narrative

In the production, Ben Morris presented the character of Toto the dog. This character spoke in the manner of a highly intelligent and sensitive person who was treated as a naughty, cute dog and made to perform tricks by Dorothy and the rest of the cast. The dog sequence was based on experiences Ben Morris had introduced in improvisation and devising workshops. Morris enjoyed inhabiting the character of Toto, having his face made up exaggeratedly, in a style reminiscent of Heath Ledger's Joker and sporting an Elizabethan ruff but his sense of anxiety at the vulnerability he was exposing in devising performance text from his own experience still troubled him, however much theatricality cloaked this experience.

The negotiation of character, persona, and person was also in question in a sequence in which Glen Burrows 'spoke' using a computerized voice coming through the theatre's speakers. He attempted to convince the audience that it was 'really him' and to prove it he would 'spin around onstage', which he proceeded to do. He then told the audience about the experiences that he and Tait had in Oz in Sydney, as video was projected of the firework display in front of the Sydney Opera House and of Burrows being taken into the sea in the Sandcruiser wheelchair at Bondi Beach. The scene questioned what constituted Burrows' presence, highlighting the split between his live and mediatized appearance and the ambiguity of the computerized voice saying that it was 'really him'.

Isaac Tait read scraps of paper that he found about his person as the Poet/Scarecrow. These included reference to a disagreement in the rehearsal process between him and me and which he had turned into a fragmentary poem that dealt with the tension between his writing and my direction that he needed to find a way to deliver his own text more clearly and effectively. This text concluded with the lines 'I wrote this. Tony, let me say it. Tony pesters Isaac till he cries. Isaac does the poems. This is not theatre. This is not performance. This is not Isaac'. These lines referred to differences and disagreements in the devising and rehearsal process and exposed the tension between my support of the learning disabled performers and my intended push toward the 'rigour' of theatrical performance. This ambiguous presence that theatrical performance based on self-devised work affords was further apparent through a lens of intermediality and intertextuality in a scene entitled 'John conducts Judy'.

Intermediality and intertextuality: Judy Garland and Different Light

In this scene the ensemble lay upstage on their stomachs facing away from the audience looking up at the cyclorama/projection screen on which an extract from the 1963 black-and-white film *A Child is Waiting* was projected, whilst downstage left Lambie/Ellenbroek in 18th-century costume conducted the scene facing the audience. This scene had been informed by Lambie's intervention in the Awakenings Festival referred to in Chapter 3. The film scene was one in which Judy Garland, in her penultimate film, as the music teacher at the Crawthorne State Training School for the Mentally Retarded tries to teach the pupils to sing a song for their end-of-year performance. She sits at the piano surrounded by a group of pupils as she bashes out each note on the piano, clearly enunciating and singing each syllable of the song. She then instructs the group to copy what she sings line by line. They attempt to do so but the result is a cacophony of incorrect pitching and tempo. She persists, her eyes forming tears, but she commends the group with an exaggeratedly approving 'Very good, very good!' At this point, one of the pupils vents the frustration of all present by banging hard and discordantly on the piano keyboard. At this point, the Different Light ensemble also banged and drummed on the floor of the stage in sympathy with this frustration. The projected scene continued as an ever more tearful Judy Garland attempts to teach the same lines of the song in the same way but achieves no noticeable improvement in the performance of the pupils. The screen then froze on Garland's tearful face as an excerpt from the soundtrack of the *Wizard of Oz* film was played in which the Wicked Witch speaks of concocting something with 'poison' in it, a poison that is attractive to the eye. Louise Payne then stood up in front of the projected image of Judy Garland and with the help of two assistants, Damian Bumman and Andrew Oswin, opened up her yellow plastic smiley face lunch box of medication. She guided the audience through her Yellow Brick Road of Selective Serotonin Re-uptake Inhibitors (SSRIs), anti-psychotic medication, narcotics, and mood stabilizers first used within psychiatric institutions but now available as a pathway out of anxiety for the general population.

At the end of this sequence the Yellow Brick Road song from the film played and Matthew Phelan took over the stage and the audience's attention. He delivered a speech of his own devising about Judy Garland which combined some basic biographical information about the actress: her issues with addiction, and her death from an overdose, with Phelan's own feelings for her as his favourite actress and his desire to meet her in heaven and the Yellow Brick Road dedicated to her memory. The screen then switched from the black-and-white image of Garland in *A Child is Waiting* to the technicolour image of her as Dorothy in *The Wizard of Oz* in the company of the Scarecrow and the Tin Man singing 'If I Only Had a Heart'. Phelan, now dressed in a silver jacket and with a silver funnel on his head then sang along with the Tin Man as the ensemble reprised their slow wave to him to get his attention. This was interrupted by the arrival of Drew McLean as the Wicked Witch. The Witch wrapped Phelan and the rest of the ensemble in an industrial-sized roll of clear plastic. As he did so the projected video in the background switched from the technicolor *Wizard of Oz* back to the black and white of *A Child is Waiting* and a scene in which the director of the Crawthorne State School, played by Burt Lancaster, takes Judy Garland into the locked ward of an institution for 'retarded' adults to show her the future of their pupils if they do not make some kind of effort to teach them. Institutionalized adult males scream, shout, and laugh uncontrollably as one patient tries to eat a rubber ball, and another stumbles across the room in a mocking kind of dance as Judy Garland looks on in incomprehension and pity. Whilst this video was projected, the performers reprised and repeated fragments of spoken text of previous scenes in the piece until, as more and more joined in, their different voices created a cacophony. This gradually stopped as they heard the sound over the speakers of Sarah H. singing. Sarah was a participant in the Saturday Mixed Ability Theatre class who was not comfortable with, nor accustomed to, verbal communication, but who loved to sing. Her voice was instantly recognizable to the group and she had agreed to let us use a recording of her voice singing 'Somewhere over the Rainbow' to end the performance. Sarah's singing was in tune, pleasant to listen to, and, at the same time, on her own terms with regard to phrasing and lyrics. It was not the voice of a trained singer, but that of a person to whom the song obviously meant a great deal.

The Wizard of Oz was an attempt to shift the terms of negotiation between non-disabled facilitators and learning disabled artists in making theatre. It exposed tensions in the process of devising and the assumptions of an early 21st-century drama school model of improvisation. These assumptions of the function and efficacy of improvisation are that the (trainee) performer needs to be challenged to explore greater psychological depth and spontaneity in devising material and creating character or persona, narrative, and affective moments of performance. These assumptions are themselves interestingly challenged in learning disabled theatre. *The Wizard of Oz* intended to offer the learning disabled artists a narrative text of their choosing. There was, however, a telling joke within the company, made by Ben Morris, that I had allowed the performers to choose the text but had then twisted it to become a much darker narrative than the performers had been expecting. Whilst it could reasonably be argued that the darkness was already there within the *Oz* narrative, this joke does reveal a significant tension in the evolution of the company's methodologies and aesthetic. My concern had been to allow exploration of more contradictory and nuanced representations than 'positive images of disabled people'. It was becoming clear, however, that as Different Light Theatre productions evolved that there was a danger that I and other non-disabled facilitators were imposing aesthetic frameworks in which disability was viewed as either inspiration or as loss, grief, and tragedy. Listening and paying attention to the learning disabled artists needed to be more responsible and responsive to allow the politics and aesthetics of the group to emerge rather than to be imposed top down from non-disabled participants. Ethical questions arose concerning the emotional and psychological content of improvisation and material devised for public performance. These were exemplified in Matthew Phelan's refusal to speak the lines he had devised communicating his fears of death and resurrection at the start of *The Wizard of Oz*, Isaac Tait's doubts over the efficacy of performance, using words that he had devised, and was then 'required' by me to perform, and the tensions apparent in Ben Morris' presentation of character/persona/self. There was also a range of complex ethical, practical, and political issues raised by Glen Burrows' access to voice and participation in the company. These questions emerged as the city experienced the second 6.3 earthquake of 22 February 2011, which resulted in the deaths of 185 people, and which caused far greater damage to the buildings and infrastructure of the city. *Still Lives*, the next performance project, was developed to address the impact of this disaster and the ethical, aesthetic, and political issues emerging within the company.

Still Lives, *The Earthquake in Chile*, the earthquakes in Christchurch

Still Lives was an attempt to focus on these issues by creating a performance involving only three performers: Glen Burrows, Ben Morris, and Isaac Tait. In the meantime, regular workshops continued with the rest of the company whilst attempting to cope with the exigencies of the immediate aftermath of the quakes, the lack of rehearsal and performance spaces in the city, the difficulties in transportation, and the disruption to established routines and peoples' fears of being in buildings together in a city that was still experiencing substantial aftershocks. Different Light Theatre resumed workshops and rehearsals within weeks, on 13 March in the Fo Guang Shan Buddhist Centre in the less damaged western side of the city. The effects on some of the performers, on their living conditions, and on their habitual round of employment and broadly therapeutic activities were much longer lasting. *Still Lives* was intended as a 20-minute performance at the Society for Disability Studies (SDS) conference 15–18 June in San Jose, California but was reconfigured in two further iterations, one involving the whole Different Light company in Christchurch in November 2011, and the second a more developed 40-minute version that was presented as part of the Ludus Festival of Performance that was held concurrent with the Performance Studies international conference, PSi #18, in July 2012 at the University of Leeds.

Still Lives San Jose: voice and access

The title *Still Lives* accrued different meanings as the project developed over two years. It was initially intended to suggest still life painting as the depiction of that which is overlooked and apparently without narrative (Bryson). The stillness was in part derived from the new-found appreciation of stillness amidst the rumblings and shakings of aftershocks. Christchurch became a 'disabled' city in which people experienced the same kinds of restrictions on movement and access to which disabled people had long been accustomed. In fact, the city became increasingly inaccessible to disabled people as streets were buckled or covered in silt and familiar landmarks disappeared. In the immediate aftermath of the quake early grassroots initiatives at sociality and conviviality emerged. These included the sharing of access to water and the outdoor cooking of food. The subsequent progress of the official central government recovery were, however, characterized by inequity and inaccessibility: disabled people were still overlooked. The earthquake was inclusive of all, the recovery, it turned out, was not.

The stillness of *Still Lives* also referred to the stillness of the lives of the disabled young men who were the performers, in terms of the limited possibilities for movement available to each of them. Dave Calvert has written perceptively about the particular dialectic of stasis and dynamism in the consideration of learning disabled performance (2017). The stillness of the title was also an invitation for the audience to consider their engagement as spectators as acts of contemplation rather than expecting the dynamics of conventional dramatic theatre. The still of *Still Lives* also came to encompass a temporal dimension. The people of the city were still waiting for access to spatially and emotionally central areas of the city many years after the quakes. The three young men were likewise slowly aging as they waited for meaningful employment, access, and inclusion to social lives.

The piece was intended for an initial performance at the Society for Disability Studies (SDS) conference in San Jose, California and we knew, therefore, that it would need to include different modes of access for an audience composed of scholars, artists, and activists many of whom were either physically disabled or d/Deaf or blind/visually impaired. The production aimed to integrate questions of access into the post-dramatic performance mix, drawing on the experience of companies such as Graeae and Back to Back. This approach to questioning the access of theatrical performance aligned with the communication difficulties and access needs of each of the three performers, Burrows, Morris, and Tait, which had emerged in the company's exploration of performance over the past seven years.

The opening of *Still Lives* attempted to present the similarities and differences of the three performers and to question what the stage showed, and what the audience might be 'seeing'. Morris and Tait sat strapped to chairs as Burrows sat in his wheelchair and a computerized voice (male, United States accent) gave three descriptions of what the stage showed. The three descriptions of Morris and Tait were of their hair colour, their eye colour, and their height, whereas all three descriptions of Burrows were the same: 'Glen is in a wheelchair. He has cerebral palsy'. The implication was that many people would only see this aspect of Burrows' appearance.

The computerized voices used in the production included two male and two female voices, with US and UK accents. These were used in a variety of ways to present a mockery of voices of authority, or as voices presenting relentlessly positive narratives of disabled experience that the live voices of the performers undermined. For example, there was a section that introduced Burrows' options for movement. This was based on some improvisation trust exercises we had conducted at Burrows' home, in which two participants gave movement instructions to a third who was blindfolded. In the performance, the US female voice spoke of Burrows' magic powers and his ability to move UP and DOWN and LEFT and RIGHT and IN and OUT. Whilst Burrows performed these manoeuvres with his motorized chair the other two struggled to make their chairs do the same. The IN OUT sequence increased in tempo and volume and became a crude physical innuendo for sexual activity but also introduced the theme of IN and OUT, inclusion and exclusion, in the disabled city and in social life, that would be developed throughout the piece. The final section of Burrows' introduction concerned his home: 'a palace' according to the US female voice, 'a care home for young people with physical disabilities' according to Ben Morris' live voice on stage; where he had 'servants who looked after his every need' (US female voice), 'where every intimate act required the help of others' (Ben Morris) 'Not quite every intimate act eh, Glen?' (Isaac Tait). The US female voice went on to say that he had everything he could possibly want, a statement that was challenged by the voices of all three performers saying 'EXCEPT ...' and when counter challenged by all four computerized voices in succession with the question 'Except what?' Tait replied that he was waiting for a princess to come along and kiss him, and Morris expanded this thought: 'And turn him from a handsome prince into somebody with a chance to be a sexy beast'. The piece was an attempt to interweave the discourses of childish fantasy with the desires of each young man.

Ben Morris' self-introduction was accompanied by a recording of his own voice alternately attempting to relax and soothe himself and to work up his anxiety and frustration. He spoke in his own live voice to introduce himself using the same formula as Burrows had: handsome prince, lovely laugh, and sexy speaking voice. Whereas Burrows' special powers had been his magic chair, Morris defined his as the ability of his attention to go in and out at speed. The 'palace' he referred to was Christ's College, the private school he had attended for a period until the bullying to which he was subjected became too much and he had wanted to respond by making his fists go IN and OUT as he punched those who had bullied him. He too had everything he could want – except he was still waiting for the princess and at the end of his introduction, as at the end of Burrows,' all three performers joined in the refrain 'Still waiting. Still waiting. Still waiting ...'.

Tait's introduction was his attempt to present moments of quietness and stillness and what might emerge from them in the newly empty quake-damaged parts of Christchurch and from his memories of being bullied. His ironic 'palace' was the golden-arched McDonalds where he worked part time and to which he went 'IN and OUT' in the repetitive rhythm of alienated labour, made worse by the bullying to which he was subjected by other staff and customers, and which also kept him 'still waiting': still waiting at tables, still waiting to be recognized as an artist, still waiting....

These three individual introductions were then followed by a sequence in which all three performers sat at a table and attempted to communicate with each other using phones and tablets. The apps they used came up with standardized expressions of greeting, questions, and answers that offered a simulacrum of social interaction. Due to his impaired motor control in his one 'good' hand, Burrows increasingly struggled to keep up with the speed of the interaction and in frustration then used his own speaking voice which was repeated by a computerized voice (male US) and accompanied by captioned text video projected on the cyclorama. In a few sentences, he told the story of his distance from his mother and of his best friend Kirsten who had multiple sclerosis, with whom he liked to drink, but who was taken away in an ambulance, in which she died, when she had had too much to drink, and that she had red hair. The paucity of information in these sentences and the emotional weight they contained testified to the limited window of opportunity for Burrows to communicate with his iPad.

In a kind of sympathetic response to Burrows, Morris then presented a monologue in which he talked about poppies and played with the kind that are sold in remembrance on Anzac Day in New Zealand. A live-feed camera was projected in the background that showed close-ups of his face, his hands, his eyes, his nose, and his forehead as a visual counterpoint to shifts in focus in his narrative. He spoke of losing his job making remembrance poppies when the work was taken away from a disability organization and outsourced overseas, of his fear of having an operation on his nose, and of his shame at being upbraided outside church for texts sent to a young female. He related how this made him want to bang his head against a concrete pole and walk out in the middle of the road into oncoming traffic and started banging the table at which he was sitting. Burrows and Tait came onstage approached him and gently touched him to offer support. Although each solo sequence had been devised individually, when they were put together, possibilities emerged of one responding to another. After Tait and Burrows arrived, Tait's solo sequence spoke of touching, of the sharing of breath that is the Māori *hongi* or greeting, of reaching out beyond individual concerns, and of how still lives might touch.

After the unsure and unsteady touch between the three performers, the first time that this had occurred in the performance, there followed a fantasy sequence of the three escaping the disabled city that never really offered them a community. The performers gathered on Burrows' wheelchair in the same formation as in the video projected behind them. The background of this was the Christchurch Civil Defence video showing the extent of the quake damage, a combination of street level and drone footage of badly

Figure 4.2 *Still Lives* in performance at the Ludus Festival, Riley Smith Hall, University of Leeds, 28–30 July, 2012. Performers: left to right – Ben Morris, Isaac Tait, and Glen Burrows. Image: Stuart Lloyd-Harris for Different Light Theatre.

damaged buildings, overturned cars, the Catholic Cathedral in ruins, a car half submerged in liquefaction and silt. Superimposed over this landscape the three performers appeared to fly on the back of Burrows' wheelchair, swooping down to street level, flying up to inspect an upper room in the Cathedral that had been exposed by the collapsed walls. They flew forwards and then in reverse over the city before appearing to fly off into a panorama that showed the entire city on the plain and the snow-covered Southern Alps in the distance. This video sequence was accompanied by a voice-over that described what they were flying over and 'escaping': the inequities that remained and had become more exposed after the quakes, the issues with access and inclusion that each of them individually and collectively faced, the specific people referred to in *Still Lives*, Kirsten with red hair, the bullies, the sex texters, and their unresolved desires. In an act of imagination, an act of intermedial theatre, they appeared to float free, and to choose freedom:

BEN: And where are we heading to?
ISAAC: Glen?
GLEN: Dunno.
BEN: Dunno.
ISAAC: Dunno.

BEN: But somewhere we choose.
ISAAC: Choice.
BEN: Sweet.
GLEN: Fuck yeah.

The performance at the SDS conference in San Jose not only featured captioning that was integrated into the performance itself and the reiteration of lines of text by computerized voiceovers, but was also live captioned, and signed by two different American Sign Language (ASL) signers. To transport the performers to this performance required extensive fundraising efforts and logistical support. To support Burrows' participation both Kim TePairi Garrett, assistant director and stage manager, and Stuart Lloyd-Harris, designer, operator, and technician took on the roles of full-time caregivers on long-haul flights and supporting Burrows' living needs, administering his regime of medications. Burrows was able to experience the access provisions of the hotel, which included a swimming pool hoist, and the ease of access to San Jose's public transit system. This contrasted sharply with the situation back in quake-damaged Christchurch. The performers were also able to attend other workshops and activities at the conference, including the SDS ball. The experience of the three performers was significant in the development of the potential outreach and international sharing of the praxis of Different Light Theatre. This was, however, an opportunity that was only available to a few members of the group. On returning to Christchurch, the immediate imperative was to re-engage the other members of the company, attempted in two different performances.

The Earthquake in Chile

The first of these performances was a collaboration with Free Theatre Christchurch and Richard Gough of the Centre for Performance Research, Aberystwyth, on *The Earthquake in Chile*. This was a site-specific, immersive performance, that included food shared with the audience prepared by New Zealand TV celebrity chef, Richard Till. It was loosely based on Heinrich von Kleist's novella and staged in and around St Mary's Church in Addington, a wooden structure that was one of the few churches in the city at that time that had escaped quake damage. The devised performance suggested parallels between the Kleist novella and Christchurch in the immediate aftermath of the quakes when what was termed a 'new normal' seemed to establish itself and the potential for a more egalitarian social order seemed briefly to emerge as people shared food and shelter. The performance was intended as a celebration of the impromptu and improvised community that sprang up in the immediate aftermath of the quake. It also gave a warning of the dangers of grassroots initiatives, such as Gap Filler and Greening the Rubble, being co-opted by the government into the disaster capitalism of the 'recovery'.

The project seemed a good opportunity for the performers to collaborate with other non-disabled actors and artists and to participate in very different ideas of performance and engagement with an audience than those to which they had been accustomed. Whilst a valuable experience, particularly coming so soon after the quake, as the city was still shaking from aftershocks, the Different Light performers rehearsed separately, only occasionally checking in with the rest of the team. As guides between the main performance locations, their involvement in the performance and with the audience was somewhat peripheral.

On arrival for the performance, the audience were ushered into the church for the first part of the performance which included hymns and a homily in a pastiche of the Roman Catholic liturgy and the introduction of the narrative elements of the lovers from the Kleist novella. This narrative was then interrupted by a soundscape played through speakers and subwoofers that appeared to shake the church in a manner highly familiar to Christchurch audiences at that time. The audience were then directed to leave the building and when outside they were greeted by the Different Light Theatre members as guides of San Precario, who arrived pushing an old minibus with no engine. They then ushered the audience to five outside stations, a night market, a tented village of sideshow, a belltower dispensing food, and a tent with a long table where people were directed to sit face to face and encouraged to share memories of the quake and to feed spoonsful of jelly to the person sitting opposite. Finally, they were directed back into the church for a communion of wine and biscuits, the presentation of the gifts by members of Different Light Theatre, and then to witness the climax of the von Kleist novella: the recognition of the two illicit lovers by the congregation. They and their illegitimate baby are killed by the righteous mob and the order of the previous oppressive regime is restored, just as, the production implied, was currently happening in the disaster capitalism of the Christchurch 'recovery'.

The members of Different Light acted as guides to this peripatetic performance, but they were precarious guides, the guides of San Precario, and appeared in the production as a kind of separate sect in the quasi-religious atmosphere of the performance. Whereas the Free Theatre performers appeared dressed in the robes and long pointed hats of Hispanic penitents, the Different Light performers wore fluorescent road cones on their heads and high-visibility jackets. This was an ironic positioning of the disabled performers, the cones suggesting dunces' caps, aping the penitents' headgear, and the high-visibility clothing mocking the livery of authority in Christchurch at that time, the marker of exceptionality that allowed access to the Red Zone of the central city and other restricted areas denied to the rest of the population.

San Precario is the 'patron saint of precarious lives and precarious workers' (Tari and Vanni 2005), a figure created for the Euro Mayday in Milan in 2004 whose iconography is that of a fast-food worker. Isaac Tait, a part-time worker at a local McDonalds, instantly identified with this figure and brought in copies of the image of San Precario he had downloaded. He carried this icon in the performance and on the back of the image he inscribed his own text, 'I love you. You know who you are'. He took turns displaying the image of the saint and his own text as he guided the audience. Others in the group made their own versions of Catholic prayer cards, saintly icons, and prayers were replaced with images that meant something to them and their own written texts. Glen Burrows had a support worker write out for him on cards his own contribution to the prayers:

> San Precario please help me to look for a female/She have blond hair and she must be tall and sexy/I will work to pay our bills

Towards the end of the performance, when all performers and audience were back inside the church, the Different Light performers were required to participate in the presentation of the gifts, modeled on the Catholic liturgy which involved carrying food items down the central aisle and presenting them to an actor playing a priest. On one occasion, Isaac Tait, who had previously moved through the church to present gifts of food unremarkably, suddenly decided in one performance to enact a caricature of intellectual disability as he carried a pumpkin down the aisle. On another night, John Lambie gently, elegantly, but forcefully, decided that he should be the last performer to leave the altar space, rather than the actors presenting von Kleist's lovers, and thus re-arranged his exit and the closing moments of the performance.

These interventions in the performance were perhaps a reaction to the noticeably different treatment of the performers in the rehearsal process compared to the non-disabled performers. Uncertainty over the positioning and function of the Different Light performers in the whole project was evident in a contemporary review of the production where the only mention of the Different Light performers was: 'and then mentally and physically handicapped people from the Addington community walked up the aisle' (Phillips 2011). The reviewer did not seem to connect the performers in the church (who had by then shed their high-visibility clothing) with the guides of San Precario outside, who were so clearly marked both in their clothing and their disability. The learning disabled performers were perceived as both highly visible and, in a way, invisible; as performers, and yet not performers. The reviewer assumed that the people he saw in the church must have been 'playing themselves', even though he got it wrong about who they were playing. Interestingly he saw in the people *he thought he saw* the guarantee that this performance was local and indicative of community. The assumption was that 'mentally and physically handicapped people' could only have been there as some guarantee of authenticity of local provenance and community involvement, rather than as performers in their own right.

Still Lives Christchurch

Still Lives Christchurch was a 40-minute performance presented at the Ignition Festival in the NASDA Theatre at the end of November 2011. The second 20 minutes of this performance was a presentation of the version of *Still Lives* that had been staged in San Jose. The first 20 minutes involved the whole company of 15 performers. This section opened with the performers placing 15 chairs onstage and coming on one by one to take their seats. In total, 14 actors arrived and duly took their seats on stage and then Glen Burrows arrived. There followed a three-minute sequence in which Burrows tried to join the group and find a place to sit amongst them. The rest of the group continued to smile at the audience and remained oblivious of his struggles. Eventually, giving up on being included, Burrows went downstage of the main group. He then spoke in his own voice, echoed by a computerized voice, the following words about his father: 'I'm thinking of my Dad. My Dad's dead. I remember. We used to fight a lot. Why? Because of how I am. How I am. How. I. Am'. The rest of the group then came forward surrounding his chair and reached out their arms slowly to Burrows touching, caressing, and tickling him, causing him to laugh.

This was followed by a sequence in which individual performers stood on chairs and gave their own brief accounts of where they were, what they were doing, and their immediate reactions to the 6.3 earthquake at 12.51 pm on Tuesday, 22 February. This then developed into a black comic sequence in which the seating was re-arranged to suggest an aircraft interior and the voice of Kim TePairi Garrett welcomed everybody on board an Air Precario flight from Christchurch to Christchurch. The flight rapidly ran into difficulty but in the emergency procedures, instead of oxygen masks, tiny orange road cones, like those so ubiquitous on the streets of Christchurch at that time, dropped down to the passengers' seats. Instead of life jackets, orange hi-vis vests were contained within these cones. Garrett's voice that had previously encouraged passengers to consume duty-free goods, but then suddenly became panic-stricken, denied the airline's responsibility for injury or death and signed off with an exhortation to pray to a higher power of each individual's choice. At this point, individual actors stood on their chairs to deliver their prayers, some sincere, some humorous, as the stage filled with haze.

The year 2011 signaled changes in the membership of the group. Shawn O' Rourke and Stuart Craig, participants since 2004, ceased their involvement due to changing circumstances in their employment and accommodation in the aftermath of the quakes. Performers newer to the group, Alan Barnes, Peter Rees, Josie Noble, and Rebecca Flint joined Different Light from the Saturday Mixed Ability Theatre class. *The Earthquake in Chile* and *Still Lives Christchurch* were attempts to keep the larger group together, to provide some regular and reliable contact in disruptive times. It marked a shift in the operation of the company from an emphasis on the importance of performance 'outcomes' and maintaining a public performance profile to an acknowledgement of the importance of collegiality, care, and support. These concerns had always been a part of how the company functioned, but the experience of the quakes brought the practice of care and conviviality into focus. The ostensible reason for the meeting was to make theatre, but meanings of what constituted theatrical performance were shifting and the importance of caring for each other became increasingly apparent.

Still Lives Leeds

The final iteration of the *Still Lives* project was an expanded 40-minute version of what had been performed in San Jose presented in the Ludus Festival in Leeds alongside Performance Studies international #16 at the University of Leeds. Creative New Zealand granted funding for the group to travel for the first time under the category 'creative excellence' rather than 'community performance'. This venture involved a considerable amount of organization and support to transport the three performers on two long-haul flights and to factor in accommodation, acclimatization, and rehearsal processes. The support personnel were the same as for the visit to San Jose: Kim Te Pairi Garrett, Stuart Lloyd-Harris, and I, but with substantially increased responsibilities of care.

The following extracts from a Radio New Zealand interview undertaken just prior to the trip discuss the performers' attitudes to the company's working process, relationship to audience, and to touring overseas. It again presents the tension between the enjoyment of performance and the anxiety of the discipline I was trying to inculcate:

COMPUTERIZED VOICE (US ACCENT): Ben is intellectually disabled. But only sometimes. This makes him feel guilty and tense.
BEN MORRIS: Once upon a time in a land far far away there was a handsome prince called Ben. Even though he appeared tense inside he was laughing. Laughing at things he had done in the past. It was a lovely laugh. (he laughs nervously)
KATY GOSSETT: Ben Morris has been involved with A Different Light for about eight years ... and in a week's time they leave for Leeds ... and the Ludus Festival
BEN MORRIS: This is further and a lot more longer than San Jose so, but I mean it will be it will be sort of a good thing and you sort of get to sort of meet people not-not just sort of well when I say the sort of everyday people but you sort of also get to meet the maybe say like the head honcho people who sort of run companies but this is not just a sort of sort of disability festival this is more of a mainstream festival so we're going to be sort of seeing a whole lot more (laughing) ... mainstream scenes.

KATY GOSSETT: Ben says the theatre company and its productions are aimed at encouraging greater individual freedom for those with a disability.

BEN MORRIS: I think probably in one way it try – in some ways – I don't know what that is – it sort of stimulates sort of people sort of getting out out and about whether or not they have an intellectual or a physical disability. One ehm – as Isaac was saying – ehm we did a performance on *Poor Dears* and that was like looking at the spectrum of people who ... who are ... generally ... sort of pitied you know like because they they may have a physical disability they're sort of looked upon as you know ah you must stay inside and you know be inside inside the four walls or be put ehm or be put put in a box and so therefore like ehhh well our company looks at the the outer limits and not try and divide people and put them into boxes We don't want people sort of to be in a box looking out we want them out of the box and and ehm and exploring ... chances you know so that they have more freedom and not sort of less freedom where ehm where it's all sort of dark in in in one perspective.

KATY GOSSETT: How important do you think that some of the productions you've done and the kind of messages you're putting out there have been in changing people's ideas? I mean does it feel good to stand up here and say and describe some of the things that have happened in your life?

BEN MORRIS: Ehm I think ehm I think it does cos you're always gonna get a – well I mean you're gonna get a different reaction from people or they may just sort of go away and think about it but whether they (laughing) actually do it is a whole nother perspective erm yeah

KATY GOSSETT: And Ben and Isaac say they're prepared to do what's needed.

BEN MORRIS: I can actually do a whole lot better and I know that for for ehm for myself and ehm yeah cos ehm we we sort of rehearsed ehm that play ehm sort of leading up ehm to for San Jose ehm and so ehm so we're sort of so instead of going straight into sort of *Still Lives* ehm because we we kind of sort of did that in America we're sort of like looking at maybe like adding on or putting stuff in between that or whatever, so the experience will be huge, so, yeah.

ISAAC TAIT: I think you just have to man up (Ben Morris laughs in the background) and just get on with your lives. Really just, you know – be a man about it. Yeah. You have to don't think about it really. And go home and learn your lines and come back and still get punished (laughing) but ehm yeah we make it work somehow. I think it's really a new experience for me ehm because when we were in California last year it's just disability and ehm in Leeds now it's gonna be like alternative people where like more really alternative than Christchurch. I'm really overwhelmed that we have another opportunity to be going to Leeds and performing over there in a Festival, yeah.

BEN MORRIS: When we went to San Jose we well it was more Glen than anything because ehm it wouldn't be as fun for him as you know just watching us you know all swim you know and he couldn't ehm and stuff so what we did is we had a well it wasn't just our pool but it was the hotel's pool ehm and so and so we got him out of the chair ehm confines and stuff and so we got him like into the pool ehm and so we've got these photos and so Stuart and Kim sort of like holding him you know sort of like above – well he was kind of like on the water you know and he just I think for him that is just like a a whole you know – it's a really exciting experience ehm for for him. Ehm you know because I mean he can't just go oh bother the wheelchair I'm off for a swim you know like he's not and you know he's a really great character, yeah. (Gosset 2012).

The version of *Still Lives* that was presented in Leeds opened with a sequence in which the performers were pre-set on stage whilst behind them images of previous Different Light productions involving the whole company were projected and underscored with a soundtrack of looping and swirling acoustic guitar. As the audience came in the performers sat in their row of three and spoke to the audience welcoming them in English and Te Reo Māori and improvising some 'greeting strategies,' talking about the weather and their journey over, amongst other subjects that they improvised. This had been intended to encourage the performers to relax faced with the anxieties they felt performing to an audience many miles from home. There was also a question-and-answer forum after the performance. Emma Willis in her review of the performance for ADSA (Australasian Association for Theatre, Drama, and Performance Studies) Journal remarked on the 'theme of intimacy' in the performance: 'The actors' sensitive and skilled performances built a strong sense of affinity and *communitas* something strongly evident in the Q and A that followed both performances I saw' (84). It was important to try to establish such a relationship with the audience because the expanded version of *Still Lives* presented intimate material: it referred to masturbation, crying, self-recrimination, and frustration. Willis' review recognized that the performance was 'underpinned by the ethos of giving voice to those not usually heard within public discourse asking Whose voices are heard? Who speaks for whom?' and the strategy of the production was to employ a 'polyphony of voices' (83). The question and processes of 'giving voice' to the voices of the performers was, however, highly complex and did not in any way resolve clearly. Derrida's questioning resonated throughout *Still Lives*: 'Who will decide whether this voice was lent, returned, or given? And to whom?' In adapting the 20 minute piece into 40 minutes the intention had been to afford the three performers more opportunity to find different voices and to experiment with them.

I had assumed that in devising and developing *Still Lives* for Leeds the performers would be able to draw on characters and themes already established from the previous version and use these as a basis to develop existing and create new material. To a certain extent this did occur, but it was also evident that the previous characters and themes had become somewhat over-determining and impeded the devising of what I had assumed would be 'new' or 'deeper' material. One example of this was the emergence of Binky, Bonky, and Glonky. These were a ludicrous development of the repeated reference in the San Jose version by Ben, Glen, and Isaac to themselves in the third person 'Ben', 'Glen', and 'Isaac' and to the othering of themselves, or taking of their voices, in creating these persona that were at once them, not them and not not them (Schechner). Binky, Bonky, and Glonky were versions of the three performers that might appear in an absurd children's television programme version of *Still Lives*. The conscious adoption of goo goo gaa gaa baby language, at once absurd and obscene, flipped the script on the infantilization and de-sexualization of the three as learning disabled young men. This sequence also embodied the whole performance's troubling of master voices, its 'master-baiting'. The exposure of the young men's playing with themselves, their socially constructed 'selves' also teased out the self-consciousness of both performers and audience. Ben Morris spoke in childish babble of toileting accidents and incidents of bullying, exclusion, and thwarted desire that had been less explicitly referred to in *Still Lives,* San Jose. At the same time, he and Glen Burrows acted them out like a manic children's TV presenters whilst Isaac Tait sat aloof at a table holding up naïve, child-like drawings to a camera placed in front of him that projected these images on the cyclorama. The three performers then sat downstage as a female voiceover described the act of masturbation in the same cloying child-like babble until Burrows shouted out a climactic 'Don't fucking infantilize me!'

The performers had become aware that the production had in fact created certain versions of themselves, certain performance personae, and this was part of their reaction or resistance to being made theatre. In another self-reflexive sequence Morris on video berated himself onstage angrily with the voices of the 'cops in his head':

> What do we mean by the term 'socially inept?' Do you want that girl's father to know that you think of her in that way? Are you a horrible, horrible, jumped-up fuckwit?

This video played whilst Morris attempted to learn from a script the soliloquy 'O! What a rogue and peasant slave am I!' from *Hamlet*. He would make some progress with learning the soliloquy until the recorded voice would again interrupt and discomfit him. This was followed by Isaac Tait's version in which a headshot video of Tait either remained silent or uncertainly repeated the questions:

> Where is Isaac? Where is Isaac in performance? Where is his identity and where is his intensity? Why can't you hardly hear it?

as onstage he read from Hamlet's speech 'I have of late – but wherefore I know not – lost all my mirth, foregone all custom of exercises …' until Tait's projected talking head started to tear up and bow his head. As with the Binky, Bonky, and Glonky scene, both performers adopted a character or persona to present the negative voices around them and within them. In this case, they adopted the persona of Prince Hamlet. They interwove the text of *Hamlet* with their own personal texts of self-doubt, the self-abuse, and self-harm, aligning with Shakespeare's agonizing, self-dramatizing prince.

This challenging of how the self is presented in performance was explored in the next sequence: 'Glen's Song'. This consisted of a combination of the soundtrack of a song Burrows had written and projected video with Burrows zooming around onstage. The video intercut footage of Burrows playing his guitar with that of Guns n Roses arriving on stage and Triple H from WWE entering the ring. Captions of the lyrics Burrows had written appeared dynamically out of a black background:

> To the ring I need to go. When I look into your eyes. We'll get into the ring. Help me get on the stage. (Chorus repeated) Fight Gear. Fight Gear. Fight Gear. Fuck Yeah.

Burrows sang and chanted these words to the heavy metal accompaniment of guitars, bass, and drums as he moved his chair at speed around the stage rocking back and forth in it. His physical commitment to this sequence was always intense. He had written the lyrics and worked with Stuart Lloyd-Harris and Demarnia Lloyd on the music. It was a kind of performance in front of a bedroom mirror that we transposed to the stage. We threw a lot of stage technology at it: video projection, dynamic captioning, a vibrant soundtrack mix, and a lighting chase sequence, but it did not capture the energies of Burrows as we experienced them offstage: his sudden bursts of speed and daredevil wheelchair manoeuvring with which he would surprise the group when we were out in the street together. In terms of self-presentation through movement, Burrows was again ultimately left to his own devices, his body constrained to movements in the chair and the movement of the chair itself. His physical commitment in this sequence generally left him exhausted. In this instance, as non-disabled facilitators, I now think we did him a disservice. In our attempts to please him, we had created a 'high-energy' environment that did not best serve his capabilities for performance.

The final sequence of the production was presented by the three performers centre stage as they gave an update on their still lives: 'Ben is still not working making poppies' 'Isaac is still working part-time in McDonalds' 'Glen is still in a wheelchair; he still has cerebral palsy'. The performers then started to move backwards and forwards up and down stage in limited movements as they expanded upon the IN OUT theme and movement dynamic that had been established earlier in the piece. They described what had been brought into their lives and taken out of it in the aftermath of the quakes and the exclusions and inaccessibility of the recovery. They described how the aftershocks were not for them the 'new normal' but akin to what already constituted their normal: epileptic spasms, sudden physical and emotional jolts due to the periodic recalibration of medication, and the heartache and the thousand natural shocks of access hostility that disabled people are heir to. The piece ended with a final twist on the title intimating that their lives, whilst subject to impairment and disabling, were still lives, still worthy of life.

As well as the opportunity to develop experience in performing, the Ludus Festival and PSi conference allowed the performers the opportunity to participate in Salamanda Tandem's immersive and sensory performance experience *The Living Room*. This had a long-lasting effect on the performers with its gentle approach to the interaction of (disabled) people and a fluid environment in which video projection, lighting, and sound could be altered and reconfigured by the participants to create a space and time of play and experimentation.

The Lonely and the Lovely: the soap opera of the earthquake recovery

On arrival back in Christchurch the city and the group were still trying to come to terms with the quakes and the recovery. In response to this, we decided to develop a Different Light version of a soap opera. This was intended to incorporate the heroes and villains of the recovery, the cliff-hangers, and dramatic twists and turns. The genre seemed appropriate to the performers, inhabitants of the city who did not know what was coming next in their lives or when they might be 'written out' of the ongoing (melo)drama. More importantly, soap opera was a format that was chosen by the performers, many of whom were very familiar with daytime television soaps such as New Zealand's long-running *Shortland Street*. The format allowed for an interesting interplay between character, persona, and actor. Devising a soap opera also meant that the performers themselves could choose character and narrative arcs within the conventions of the genre, as well as the option of contributing hidden reveals, shocks, and surprises. At that time the composition of the group suited such a format as, after the quakes, newer members were joining the company. *The Lonely and the Lovely* was like all soaps about relationships, friendships, families, accidents, a popular culture version of the peripeteia and anagnorisis of Greek Tragedy. The genre establishes a contract with the audience that allows for the unbelievable or scarcely credible to co-exist with the dramas of everyday life. As part of research for the project, we showed the ensemble episodes of *Downistie*, a Dutch web series, a parody of *Dynasty*, in which all the characters were played by actors with Down's Syndrome.

The ensemble at this period consisted of some 15–20 regular participants, some of whom were couples, such as Andrew Dever and Caroline Quick, Ben Morris and Rebecca Flint, Michael Stanley and Natalie Walton, and performers who had emerged from the Saturday group such as Alan Barnes, Peter Rees, and Josie Noble. *The Lonely and the Lovely* became the overarching framework for a project that incorporated training and performance and fluctuating numbers of participants. People could develop their own characters and relationships within the world of the soap and extracts from the project could be presented in performance. In addition, video recording allowed the performers to explore understandings of their characters, the world of the soap, and performance itself in a series of 'making of' videos that became part of the archive of Different Light Theatre.

The first iteration of *The Lonely and the Lovely* occurred as a plenary presentation 'Rebuilding Christchurch: A Different Soap Opera' that the group was invited to present at the Arts Activated 2012 Conference, 'Desire and Destination' at the Concourse, Chatswood, Sydney 30th–31st October, 2012. This presentation consisted of two parts: a parodic PowerPoint on the Christchurch Recovery and a staged extract from the work in progress of *The Lonely and the Lovely*.

The PowerPoint was presented by all seven performers who travelled to Sydney with Kim TePairi Garrett and me: Peter Rees, Ben Morris, Matthew Phelan, Caroline Quick, Andrew Dever, Josie Noble, and Rebecca Flint. The presentation parodied the linearity of the PowerPoint format itself. It gave an ironic account of the 'recovery' as a lost opportunity to rebuild the heavily damaged city from the ground up as a city accessible to all. At that time in the city there was a plethora of PowerPoint presentations by organizations set up by Central Government and others that had emerged at a more grass-roots level: Gap Filler, Life in Vacant Spaces, and Greening the Rubble. In addition, students of architecture and urban planning were visiting the city to contribute to, and study, the rebuild. Not many organizations, however, were considering the expectations, rights, and hopes of disabled people. 'Rebuilding the City' was based on the group's discussions and conversations during 2012 researching *The Lonely and The Lovely*. The performers were, of course, living amongst the city in its state of emergency as others discussed and planned their future.

The PowerPoint, intended for an Australian audience, opened with basic information about the country and the city intertwined with a version of a Māori *pepeha* or introduction. At a certain point in this introduction, the performers referred to the country they were from, New Zealand or Aotearoa, as 'sometimes' bicultural, and called out 'Hi' to Kim TePairi Garrett, of the iwi Ngāi Tūhoe, who then came onstage to say 'Kia ora' and went off again. At this point, a PowerPoint slide read by a performer stated 'See? We're bicultural'. The presentation also introduced the audience to Bob Parker, explaining that he used to host *This is Your Life* on New Zealand TV and that this caused him to become Mayor of Christchurch.

Josie Noble chose to present a slide of what had become Parker's signature garment: a designer jacket with orange hi-vis like features and she added the comment: 'He wore an orange jacket called Bob's Parka'.

The presentation was used to mock the linearity, reductiveness, and oversimplification of the presentation of information and opinion in the media concerning the quakes and the recovery.

We drew on Josie Noble's increasingly confident contributions in the devising process: 'There are no women leading the recovery in Christchurch because it is man's work, and you need hard hats'. This was a reference to the regular press and media appearances of John Key, Prime Minister, Bob Parker, Mayor, Gerry Brownlee, Minister in Charge of the Recovery and Roger Sutton, of CERA (Canterbury Earthquake Recovery Authority) all males sporting hard hats.

For the most part I acted as a scribe for the group's discussions of the Soap Opera and the rebuild that formed the basis of this presentation. As with *Still Lives,* the dramaturgical strategy was to generate a polyphony or polylogue of voices. Amongst this polyphony, the voices of the artists themselves were interwoven with the ironically presented voices of authority and common sense and the voices of fantasies and desires.

The Lonely and the Lovely: the characters/the actors

The second half of the conference presentation consisted of semi-staged extracts from *The Lonely and the Lovely*. Ben Morris had chosen the character of Dave Knobbs, a self-employed builder, one of those likely to benefit from the rebuild of the city, but who had alcohol, money, and relationship problems. Creating this character's backstory and motivations allowed Morris to explore the sense of guilt he often referred to in improvisations, particularly in terms of communicating with young women and going into parts of the city that were deemed Red Zone and out of bounds. He spoke of his confusion between what was his freedom of expression and what constituted behaviour that would cause offence or hurt to others. The character allowed Morris to explore the behaviour of somebody who continually oversteps the mark and then is subsequently remorseful, a remorse and guilt that then fuels his next breach of appropriate behaviour, and so on.

A scene was devised presenting the course of one long, eventful night in the life of Dave Knobbs in which he stumbled drunkenly into the cinema and tried to flirt with a woman (Caroline Quick) who turned out to be the wife of his friend. He then ran out to a bar where he tried to impress another female (Rebecca Flint) by taking off his top and doing a handstand on the bar. He offered her a beer as a romantic gesture but ends up pouring beer all over her. He then found himself outside Dr Kate Hunter's (Josie Noble) flat at 4.00 am shouting out that she is the only woman he has ever loved and asking her to explain why 'my inner life is so different to my social life'.

In a later scene Dr Kate Hunter agreed to offer him some counselling. She asked him why he kept going into the Red Zone. Morris, as Dave, answered:

> Dunno ... cos I want to ...and we're not allowed ... and in the quakes I wanted to help and wasn't allowed to ... and ... cos of what I saw there ....

This referred to Morris' experience on the day of the 6.3 quake when he had offered to help and been dismissed out of hand. This was due to the first responders' triaging different critical situations and clearing people away from urgent rescue efforts and unstable structures. It also alluded to his ongoing sense of injustice that his freedoms and liberties were being arbitrarily and unjustly constrained.

Josie Noble who had recently joined the group from the Saturday class chose the central character of Dr Kate Hunter a high achieving professional aligning with Noble's own experience of being a medal-winning Special Olympic swimmer, part-time laboratory assistant at Plant and Food Research, a swimming instructor, and a dancer and choreographer with Jolt Dance. The character of Dr Hunter emerged as a strong female who, whilst coping with the pressures of life and death decisions was beset with romantic difficulties and harboured a secret buried deep in her past.

Andrew Dever, another performer who had started in the Saturday class and who brought a particularly vibrant persona to the group and to the project, chose the role of Danny Sebastian, an aspiring singer, working as a waiter, who, although married, still led a complicated romantic life. Dever was a member of People First and a participant in a University of Canterbury research project on disability studies in education and, therefore, had experience not only of using his voice for advocacy for learning disabled people, but also, more crucially, of people listening to his voice. He also had particular and distinctive ideas about performance and his own self-presentation. He had developed his own performance skill that he called cry-singing. This involved him launching into a well-known song, a favourite was 'Danny Boy', with gusto then allowing the song to proceed riven with sobs. This, he informed us, left him feeling better afterwards. The effect it had upon an audience was, after an initial period of uncertainty, a liberating kind of laughter. In the time he was with the company Dever became engaged to be married three times, to three different young women.

Peter Rees joined the company from the Saturday Mixed Ability class and brought to the group a keen intelligence and a facility with spoken text unimpeded by a slight tendency to stutter. Rees's interest in history and theatre also included his participation in evening improvisation and Shakespeare classes at the Court Theatre. He chose the character of Ed McCann, a property developer seeking to profit from the rebuild who is revealed to have hidden emotional and familial ties with other characters that cause him to reassess his motivations and actions.

Caroline Quick joined the group at the same time as her then fiancé Andrew Dever and chose the character of Bernadette, the strong-willed wife of Dever's character Danny Sebastian. She was continually trying to deal with his fecklessness by steering him toward more responsible behaviour. Bernadette was a talent agent at a modelling agency and was in Auckland on business at the time of the quake but returned later to discover what her husband had been doing in her absence. Quick was likewise a participant in the University of Canterbury research project on education and vocational training for learning disabled people and was forthcoming and articulate in offering her opinions as an experienced self-advocate. In the improvisations, she brought a keen sense of humour and North of England phlegmatism that acted as a humorous and corrective balance to Dever's flights of fantasy and tendency to passionate outrage.

Rebecca Flint joined the group for the *Still Lives* Christchurch production and in *The Lonely and the Lovely* chose the character of Lisa Goodchild, a secretary to Ed McCann who dreams of writing a novel. Lisa was a strong-minded female who did not tolerate the sexism and misogyny of McCann's business associates or the drunken behaviour of Dave Knobbs. Matthew Phelan who had not participated in *The Earthquake in Chile* rejoined the group and chose the character of Don Fitzgerald, like Ed McCann an old boy of Christ's College. He had gone to Australia, made a fortune in the diamond mines, and now returned to his hometown to profit from the rebuild and the old boys' network. His behaviour to others, particularly women, left a lot to be desired. Glen Burrows chose the character of Jason Hart who worked as a receptionist in Dr Kate Hunter's surgery but who had long harboured feelings for her. He flatted with Isaac Tait's character Joe Flint, a graphic novelist who was also a Green Party activist with their other flatmate Ruby Stein (Louise Payne). Theresa King chose the character of Dave Knobbs' mother, Sandy, who ran a hairdressing business, and John Lambie, who was not able to attend rehearsals very often due to illness, played Knobbs' father, Sir John Knobbs, who had separated from Sandy and headed a construction company in Sydney, and to whom his son, Dave, was a great disappointment. The role of Roxie the waitress, with whom Danny Sebastian has a brief affair during the earthquakes whilst his wife was in Auckland, was developed by Natalie Walton who joined the group for a brief period. Andrew Oswin also participated in the project creating the character of Osgood Anderson, a personal trainer. Anderson and Danny Sebastian were friends. Whilst driving through the city together, Danny tries to unburden himself of his infidelity to his wife but the pair end up in a potent face-to-face confrontation. Danny's attention is distracted by this; he crashes the car, and ends up in a coma in hospital on life support.

At the Arts Access conference in Sydney, the company presented extracts from the story of Dave Knobbs' disastrous night out, and his unsuccessful attempts to borrow money from his mother and from his employer, Ed McCann. It also presented a scene in which Danny Sebastian drove his wife Bernadette from the airport on her return from Auckland. He confessed that in her absence he had had a one-night stand with Roxie, the waitress, who was now pregnant. The two argued and the car swerved leaving Danny in a coma. In the final scene, Danny lay in the ICU of a hospital. Ed McCann entered and stood over his bed. He made an emotional speech at the end of which it was revealed that he was Danny's father, prepared to spare no expense for his son's treatment. Dr Kate Hunter then entered, and it was revealed that she was Danny's mother. She and McCann had met as poor students and had a baby, which they gave up for adoption, both choosing to place their careers before bringing up a child. The semi-staged presentation ended with a voice-over giving a preview of what was to come in future developments of the soap, interspersed with questions about the Christchurch recovery and whether the city would take the chance to be rebuilt as a truly inclusive city. The final exhortation to the audience was to tune in to the next episode to discover the answer to these questions and more.

The Lonely and the Lovely and *Still Lives* (Leeds version) were presented in Christchurch at the NASDA Theatre at the end of November 2012 and *The Lonely and the Lovely Part Two* was performed as a plenary presentation at the Disability Studies in Education conference (the first time the conference had been held outside the United States) at the University of Canterbury, 8th–13th June, 2013. This was an extended version of that which had been presented previously. It was not performed on the stage of the auditorium where the conference was held as the building was wheelchair accessible, but the stage was not. To accommodate Glen Burrows, the performance took place on a carpet in front of the raised stage.

At the end of the performance the actors went amongst the audience, largely composed of academics and teachers, with a questionnaire containing three questions: '1. What is your disability? 2. Who are your support workers? 3. What makes you lonely? What makes you lovely?' This was an attempt to flip the script on the expected research relationships between non-disabled researchers and disabled research subjects. This was followed by a Meet and Greet with the actors to discuss the answers to the research questions.

The Lonely and the Lovely project generated much discussion within the company. These discussions centred on the ethics of the soap opera characters' behaviour and the overlap with the performers' own lives. They also included discussions of what was appropriate to present on stage. There were now self-advocates for learning disabled people in the group and performers in relationships and friendships that were echoed in the fictional narrative.

These questions and tensions were apparent in the video interviews undertaken for this project, extracts from some of which have previously been cited. Although relatively new to the group, Josie Noble, Peter Rees, and Andrew Dever were immediately engaged by the project and the creation of their characters and building backstories based on their own lives. Their interviews indicate that they were well appraised of the romantic entanglements and the plot twists, turns, and reveals of the soap opera format and open to exploring a version of themselves in performance personae:

TONY MCCAFFREY: Tell us about your character, Dr Kate Hunter, please.
JOSIE NOBLE: She's smart, a doctor, a counsellor, very attractive, and somewhat rich from her ex-husband. Dave Knobbs stands outside my flat and shouts that he loves me. About three, four o'clock in the morning …. He later tells me that he's badly affected by the quake. I'm just there to – if he needs a shoulder to cry on.
TONY MCCAFFREY: Is she lonely or lovely?
JOSIE NOBLE: She's lonely living in a flat by herself and wants to make a fresh start in her life.
PETER REES: Well, my character is Ed McCann, CEO of a celebrity magazine company. Well now, that's posh. Right anyway, he has an ex-wife, Dr Kate Hunter and their relationship has been broken off because they got a divorce because Ed McCann has been too busy with money and his ex-wife is, is like helping with people and that is the main problem. My character, Mr McCann has a secret son which is revealed in the soap opera play. His son turns out to be Danny Sebastian, a singing waiter who turns out to be the father of Roxie's child. Well, now the earthquake. A sad business that. Well Ed McCann he was in a very tall building in the centre of town.
ANDREW DEVER: Well Danny Sebastian he started out as a singer … he had a job in Marty's bar. He eventually had an affair with Roxie and he also had a wife, Bernadette. They met at a 21st birthday party. Love was at first sight. Eventually I had this affair with Roxie as I said before five minutes ago, which led to her being pregnant with my child. It happened the day after after after Bernadette had her hair cut then I went to Roxie's house that night, saw Marty, he went out, and then, then, then I climbed into bed with, then we stayed up and had a few drinks and then I then I then I fell asleep in Roxie's bed and ehm we had sex (he laughs, his laughter is prolonged) (The Lonely and the Lovely interviews.

Later in the process Peter Rees insisted on conducting his own interviews with the actors about their characters, backstories, and relationships. These were likewise recorded on video:

PETER REES: Do you have any other family members?
BEN MORRIS: I have a mother and a father.
PETER REES: And what did your mother say when she heard about your misfortune?

BEN MORRIS: Ohhh. I don't think she really minds.
PETER REES: And what about your father?
BEN MORRIS: My my my father he's quite strict on me.
PETER REES: So your father's name what is it?
BEN MORRIS: Dougie. Dougie Knobbs
PETER REES: And your father, what does he do as a full-time job?
BEN MORRIS: He's a businessman.
PETER REES: Right so, has he retired yet?
BEN MORRIS: No.
PETER REES: When your father Skyped, did you tell him what you did while he was away?
BEN MORRIS: Ehm. Not in so much detail (laughter from others in the group in the room)
PETER REES: So what did your father say when you told him?
BEN MORRIS: Ehhm. He got angry. And he took – he took his belt off. (he smiles to himself)
PETER REES: So what have you been doing during the day, Dave?
BEN MORRIS: Ehm I'm-I'm-I'm eh a builder but not any builder I'm a dodgy builder.

Rees also interviewed Josie Noble about Dr Kate Hunter's conversations with the waitress, Roxie, to whom she had confirmed her pregnancy:

JOSIE NOBLE: I explained to her about what her options were ehm and if she wants to keep her baby or not and ehm she wants to keep her baby so it's kind of good in some ways.
PETER REES: So what you're trying to say is ehm Roxie decides that she wants to keep the baby and have a loving – have a loving partner to support her.
JOSIE NOBLE: That's what I was kind of hoping. Ehm her husband should help her raise the baby like his own so Danny doesn't have to been involved in this any more.
PETER REES: Well, funny you should say that. Well I would say that I agree with you on that and I have a message I wish to convey to Danny. D-Danny D-Danny if you want to be a part of the baby's life you have to stick up for your self and for your wife. (to Kate) So-so thank you very much for coming down. We will have an ad break now and have an interview with someone else. (Rees interviews, 2012)

Pecha Kucha in the Pallet Pavilion

In 2013, the group participated in two site-specific performances intended to contribute to the rebuilding of community in the recovery. The first of these was a presentation at a Christchurch Pecha Kucha (a presentation format in which speakers present 20 Powerpoint slides with 20 seconds allocated to speak on each) in the Pallet Pavilion in February 2013. The group was asked to participate in presenting a snapshot of the post-quake city's arts and cultural activity. In the words of the online publicity:

> Nearly all our presenters for PechaKucha Night Christchurch '16 are talking about art or Christchurch-city related topics. We didn't set a theme, we figure it's simply a reflection of what folk here are pouring their energy into at present. PKN_CHCH: taking the city's temperature since 2008'. (Pecha Kucha Christchurch website)

The Pallet Pavilion was a temporary venue built by volunteers as a Gap Filler project. Coralie Winn, one of the co-founders of Gap Filler referred to the intention behind such initiatives in the gaps and empty spaces of the city:

> We speak the language of Performance Studies, which actually is the same language as urban design and architecture – it's how people interact with and move through space, and how space performs and how it causes you to perform. (Macfie 2013, 53)

When Different Light performers arrived to present the Pecha Kucha, we discovered that Glen Burrows in his motorized wheelchair was unable to reach the stage area as, being built out of pallets, it was not accessible. One of the organizers of the event offered to lift Burrows and his motorized wheelchair onto the stage with a forklift. Burrows declined. When the group finally did get to the stage there were difficulties running the microphone to Burrows below us and back to the stage again which ate into some of the 20-second units. Peter Rees' stammer, normally not that noticeable, became much more pronounced in the intense kairos, the time pressure of performance, of Pecha Kucha and used up more seconds, Isaac Tait's tendency to lose focus, and the visible strain and painful self-correction of Ben Morris were exaggerated under the pressure and used up even more. Slides cascaded in new configurations combining with words they were originally not intended to accompany. Mistimings and misfirings proliferated. Pecha Kucha is a virtuoso test of aptitude and skill in performance –or even, the performance principle – one of the other presenters after a 'successful' presentation, left the stage punching the air to admiring shouts from his friends of his having 'nailed it'. The Different Light Pecha Kucha presentation became something else.

Different meanings of community performance and community art came into contact when Different Light presented at Gap Filler's Pallet Pavilion. The Gap Filler response to the earthquakes aligned with Rancière's categorization in *Dissensus* of 'a community art dedicated to restoring the social bond' (200) a vision fitting his description of 'a modest contemporary utopia of the architects of new cities, of designers re-inventing a community on the basis of new urban design or the relational artists introducing an object, an image, or an unusual inscription in the landscapes of difficult suburbs' (146). Different Light's participation in the Pecha Kucha manifested what Rancière has termed 'an art bearing witness to the irremediable catastrophe lying at the very origin of the social bond'. (200)

This binary division would, however, be doing an injustice to both Gap Filler and Different Light and missing Rancière's point. Rancière posits that both community art which seeks to restore the social bond and community art which seeks to expose the catastrophe at the origin of that bond are an 'ethical couple' (200) needing to be considered dialectically and in tension with each other, rather than as two separate and mutually exclusive approaches to socially engaged art or performance. The tension is the point, and the tension produces uneasy places, precarious, ambiguous places where the everyday community might learn from learning disabled people and learning disabled people might learn what it means to be everyday community. The utopian time underlying Gap Filler's project of urban regeneration could only proceed because of the disaster event, and the ongoing mourning of the time of exclusion and the marking as dis-abled of Different Light could only proceed in a time of some hope of a reconfiguration. The Different Light performers were uneasy in how they had been accommodated into the community event, but it was an uneasiness generative of a productive dissensus, exposing tensions within meanings of community.

Canterbury Tales

The second event in which Different Light participated was *Canterbury Tales*, 27 October 2013, a large-scale, day-long, site-specific series of performances and installations, organized by Free Theatre Christchurch as part of FESTA Festival of Transitional Architecture, that featured Pacific Underground, the Christchurch Symphony Orchestra, and a number of other Christchurch artists and organizations. The opening day culminated in an evening procession of giant puppets leading people back into Cathedral Square, the central location of the city that had previously been inaccessible due to earthquake damage. Different Light Theatre's contribution *Tales of Canterbury* took place in the afternoon in front of the damaged Cathedral near a market and food stalls. It consisted of the performers acting as two film crews with cameras and microphones approaching people in Cathedral Square and asking them to take part in an interview about the impact of the earthquakes on their lives. If people agreed to participate, they were taken aside and asked to pick out questions to answer from a bag full of questions on strips of paper. These questions had been formulated by the performers about peoples' experiences of the earthquakes, their experiences of disability, and included some random questions. This was a development of the survey undertaken by the performers at the Disability Studies in Education conference. It was an opportunity to give the actors more experience of approaching an 'audience' in a more direct way in a public space. It was a chance for the performers to listen to the voices of others talking about the earthquakes and to listen to what these participants understood by, and felt about, disability when interviewed by (visibly) disabled researchers. We were later able to debrief and discuss with the whole group the ways in which people sought to avoid the encounter with the camera crews or how they responded to being interviewed by disabled interviewers. We also discussed the difference in responses between those who acknowledged the experience of disability in their lives and those who, for whatever reason, did not.

In preparation, we also filmed the performers' responses to questions that they pulled from the bag:

LOUISE PAYNE: *'A story that you don't understand'*. Ehm with dyslexia I don't understand a lot of stories or I get them wrong and then I tell the people and I've got the whole story wrong but it's my story.

'I remember Christhurch when ...' it was the late 1970s and the Square was hopping and there lots of really interesting people ehm and you could just hang out there for hours and have free entertainment. Ehm Yeah. That's all.

PETER REES: *'If I had enough money I would ...'* I would buy my way to the throne of England.

'A story about Christchurch that everyone needs to know' is Christchurch is a city of opportunity like if you want to look for a job, they have the best jobs here in Christchurch and there's great entertainments.

'A story that you do not understand' Well, I do not understand why my dad broke my old toy light sabre in half. It's just plain cruel.

BEN MORRIS: *'A story that starts "My first love"'* but this is a different take on my one is it didn't exactly sort of go anywhere but it sort of dates back to my primary school days where ehm where I had a girl who was a friend ehm we didn't go out because of our age differences and stuff Ehm but ehm we used to sort of hold hands and sort of go like everywhere round around the school grounds and ehm I don't I think we probably kissed each other but not on the lips or something but we definitely sort of held hands and that so yeah so we're kinda like ehm still still friends but not as boyfriend and girlfriend and I did have many girls as friends. It's kind of hard for me not to get attached to ehm girls. Sometimes I can be cautious and sometimes I can't be cautious because people often give maybe false verbal identities about themselves.

'*What makes me feel lonely*' is when not just through not just through texting or something but I think one of my greatest sort of things is probably not being I'm not sort of excluded from other people's social lives ehm but sort of but also not being included ehm in their social life.

(he takes out several other pieces of paper, reads them, then puts them back in the bag, without response.)

JOSIE NOBLE: (pulls out a strip of paper, reads it) Ooh. '*I feel disabled when …*' (Pause) Ehm. Oh this is a hard one. (Long pause. She does not respond further.) (Canterbury Tales interviews, 2013)

The overall aim of the *Canterbury Tales* performance project was to celebrate community and to create community in performance in the transitional city. The participation of Different Light Theatre was to some extent at the periphery, but the performers were present in a distinctive way and able to explore a different kind of performance than that staged within a theatre. The subsequent development of the group over the next two years was characterized by a turn away from the imperative to present staged performance to a paying public, toward street performance and actions in the changing physical and infrastructural landscape of the city, collaboration with visiting scholars and practitioners, and maintaining online connection with disability arts and culture practice outside Aotearoa/New Zealand. This led to a reconfiguration of the self-definition of the group and what it meant to its members. The next chapter discusses how with each successive development of the company's methodologies and practices the performers themselves changed the goalposts in myriad practical, technical, material, unimagined, and imaginative ways, shifting the paradigms, and sending us, the non-disabled facilitators, back to the drawing board to reconfigure what we collectively understood as theatre and performance and the assemblage that constituted the group.

References

A Child Is Waiting. Directed by John Cassavetes, 1963. Optimum Classic, 2009.
"Arts, Access, Excellence," Arts Activated Conference, Powerhouse Museum Sydney, 25–26 March, 2010.
Bryson, Norman. *Looking at the Overlooked: Four Essays on Still Life Painting*. Reaktion Books, 1990.
Calvert, Dave. "Performance, Learning Disability and the Priority of the Object: A Study of Dialectics, Dynamism and Performativity in the Work of Learning Disabled Artists." Unpublished PhD thesis, University of Warwick, March 2017.
Canterbury Tales. Directed by Peter Falkenberg, Free Theatre Christchurch FESTA Festival of Transitional Architecture, Central city and Cathedral Square, Christchurch 25–28 October, 2013.

"Desire and Destination," Arts Activated Conference, Concourse, Chatswood, Sydney, 30–31 October, 2012.

Different Light Theatre. Wizard of Oz backstage interviews, NASDA theatre, 21 November, 2010, Different Light video archive.

———. Video interviews at the International Buddhist Centre, Christchurch, 20 March, 2011. Different Light video archive.

———. The Lonely and the Lovely interviews, Ara Institute 16 September, 2012. Different Light video archive.

———. Peter Rees interviews, Ara Institute, 20 May, 2012. Different Light video archive.

———. Canterbury Tales interviews, Ara Institute, 10 November, 2013. Different Light video archive.

"Disability Studies in Education conference," Jack Mann Auditorium, University of Canterbury, 7–9 June, 2013.

Downistie (De Wereld Draitt Door). VARA, Nederlands TV3, 2012 and YouTube. https://www.youtube.com/watch?v=B7Ut-BzlfOs. Accessed 8 October, 2021.

Gap Filler website. https://gapfiller.org.nz. Accessed 11 October, 2021.

Gosset, Katy. Radio interview with Isaac Tait, Ben Morris, and Tony McCaffrey. "One in Five." *Radio New Zealand National Radio*, 18 April, 2012.

Green Lab website, formerly Greening the Rubble. https://thegreenlab.co.nz. Accessed 11 October, 2021.

Hurihanganui, Te Aniwa. "Canterbury rivers restored to original Māori names." *Radio New Zealand*. 1 February, 2018. https://www.rnz.co.nz/news/te-manu-korihi/349405/canterbury-rivers-restored-to-original-maori-names. Accessed 8 October, 2021.

Johnstone, Keith. *Impro: Improvisation and the Theatre*. Methuen, 1990.

Kuppers, Petra. *Community Performance: An Introduction*. Routledge, 2019.

———. "Literary disability culture imaginations at work: an afterword." *The Cambridge Companion to Literature and Disability*. Edited by Clare Barker and Stuart Murray. Cambridge University Press, 2018, pp. 227–232.

———. *Theatre and Disability*. Palgrave Macmillan, 2017, pp. 73–78.

———. "Disability Performance in the Streets: Art Actions in Post-Quake Christchurch." *TDR: The Drama Review*, vol. 59, no. 1, 2015, pp. 166–174.

Lehmann, Hans-Thies. *Postdramatic Theatre*. Translated by Karen Jürs-Munby. Routledge, 2006.

"Living Room." Salamanda Tandem. Performance Studies International Conference, PSi#18 University of Leeds, 27 June–1 July, 2012.

Macfie, Rebecca. *Report from Christchurch*. Bridget Williams Books in association with New Zealand Listener, 2013.

Manning, Erin. *For a Pragmatics of the Useless*. Duke University Press, 2020.

———. *The Minor Gesture*. Duke University Press, 2016.

"Our Time." Society for Disability Studies Conference, San Jose, California, 17–20 June, 2009.

Pecha Kucha Night Christchurch. https://www.pechakucha.com/cities/christchurch. Accessed 8 October, 2021.

"Performance: Culture: Industry." Performance Studies International Conference, PSi#18 University of Leeds, 27 June–1 July, 2012.

Phillips, Jock. "The Earthquake in Chile-in Christchurch." *Real New Zealand Festival Insider*, 2011. http://realnzfestival.wordpress.com/2011/10/15/the-earthquake-in-chile-in-christchurch

"Pronunciation of local (North Canterbury) Māori place names & their meaning." https://www.waimakariri.govt.nz/your-council/local-government-and-maori/related-content/pronunciation-of-local-north-canterbury-mori-place-names-and-their-meaning. Accessed 8 October, 2021.

Rancière, Jacques. *Dissensus: On Politics and Aesthetics*. Edited by and Translated by Steven Corcoran. Continuum, 2010.

"*Rebuilding Christchurch: A Different Soap Opera*." Different Light Theatre. Arts, Access, Excellence, Arts Activated Conference, Powerhouse Museum Sydney, 25–26 March, 2010.

Still Lives. Devised by the ensemble. Directed by Tony McCaffrey. Different Light Theatre. Society for Disability Studies 24th Annual Conference, San José, California. 15–18 June 2011. Ludus Festival, Leeds and PSi 18 Riley Smith Hall, University of Leeds. 28–30 July 2012.

Tari, Marcello and Vanni, Ilaria. "On the Life and Deeds of San Precario, Patron Saint of Precarious Workers and Lives." *The Fibreculture Journal*, no. 5, January 2005. https://five.fibreculturejournal.org/fcj-023-on-the-life-and-deeds-of-san-precario-patron-saint-of-precarious-workers-and-lives/

The Earthquake in Chile. Directed by Richard Gough and Peter Falkenberg. St Mary's Church, Addington, Christchurch NZ. Body Festival. 13–16 October, 2011.

The Lonely and The Lovely Parts One and Two. Devised by the ensemble. Directed by Tony McCaffrey. Different Light Theatre. Arts Access Excellence Concourse, Chatswood, Sydney, Australia. 30–31 October, 2012. Disability Studies in Education Conference, Jack Mann Auditorium, University of Canterbury. 7–9 June, 2013.

The Poor Dears. Devised by the ensemble. Directed by Tony McCaffrey. Different Light Theatre. NASDA Theatre, CPIT. Body Festival 1–4 October, 2009.

The Wizard of Oz. Directed by Victor Fleming. Metro-Goldwyn-Mayer, 1939.

The Wizard of Oz. Devised by the ensemble, directed by Tony McCaffrey. Different Light Theatre. NASDA Theatre, CPIT. Ignition Creative Festival, 18–21 November, 2010.

von Kleist, Heinrich. *Selected Prose of Heinrich von Kleist*. Translated by Peter Wortsman. Archipelago Books, 2009.

Willis, Emma. "Still Lives: Reflections on the Disabled City." *Australasian Drama Studies Journal*, vol. 62, April 2013, pp. 79–85.

5 Learning Disabled Performance Research
Ecologies, Histories, Philosophies

First attempts at performance research: dérives and environmental performance

The shift from the pressure and momentum of staging one annual production meant more time to explore what the group understood by performance and by the function of the group. Different Light operated and still operates in the interstices of a tertiary educational institution, the NASDA drama school within Ara Institute. This involves access to spaces in the downtimes of the institution, the opportunity to repurpose the props, costumes, part-built and completed sets, and lighting plots of the drama school, repurposing these experimentally but respecting the health and safety of the Different Light performers and the drama school performers. The absence of an imperative to perform meant that the Different Light performers were able to hold up the techne of conventional dramatic and musical theatre performances to observe them in a different light and to put them to uses they were not intended for in these other productions. In *The Undercommons*, Moten and Harney write of the need to 'sneak into the university and steal what one can. To abuse its hospitality, to spite its mission, to join its refugee colony, its gypsy encampment, to be in but not of ...' (26). This period of the praxis of Different Light was an exercise in undercommons 'study' a speculative practice not necessarily as a means to knowledge and qualification, as Jack Halberstam articulates it: '...a mode of thinking with others separate from the thinking that the institution requires of you' (11). The group was studying in the backstage and rehearsal spaces of theatre without the pressure to produce completed projects or performance to a paying public. Objects from one proposed production would temporarily mingle with the scenography of another to create otherwise possibilities. Different Light performers started making appearances in masks in and around civic artworks in the city. A group of performers in larval masks sat outside and interacted silently with each other at the tables of a cafe abandoned during the quakes. Fifteen learning disabled actors staged walks through the road cones, scaffolding, and fences of the city in transition, adapting their formation to the temporary, often inaccessible, constraints on public space. At times they stood and looked at what had previously been a space occupied by a building that was important to them. These psychogeographic dérives (Debord) would sometimes have an audience, sometimes not.

Visiting scholars and practitioners, some drawn to the city by the research potential of the city in transition, some by interest in disability arts and performance, accompanied the group. Yayoi Mashimo, who was researching access for disabled people to museums and art galleries in the wake of recent disasters in Japan participated in the group's indoor and outdoor performance research. Theodore Hoffman of Grinnell College who was on a fellowship studying adaptive theatre in South Africa, New Zealand, India, and Ghana, participated in the dérives and took a role in the ongoing project, *The Lonely and the Lovely* during his time in Christchurch. Beth Cherne of the University of Wisconsin participated in workshops on scene study and character development that continued after the two performance iterations of *The Lonely and the Lovely*. Tatiana Josz, a visiting researcher and teacher in special education and theatre from Brussels attended workshops and also appeared as another iteration of the character Roxie in *The Lonely and the Lovely* in the presentation at the DSE (Disability Studies in Education) conference at the University of Canterbury. Leading disability and community arts practitioner and theorist Petra Kuppers twice visited Christchurch during this period. Members of Different Light had first encountered her at the SDS conference in San Jose in 2011 during which Glen Burrows, Ben Morris and Isaac Tait had participated in Kuppers' and Neil Marcus' physical performance workshop on visiting the Holocaust Memorial in Berlin. In 2012, the group presented at the Arts Access conference in Sydney at which Kuppers gave the keynote and the connection and friendship continued and strengthened.

During Kuppers' first visit to Christchurch, she participated in the 'undercommons' workshop activities within the drama school, documenting this studio process with a series of photographs under the title Christchurch Masquerade. She also incorporated the Different Light performers into her ongoing Olimpias project, *Salamander,* that included water performance and under-water photography in different locations in different countries. She collaborated with Different Light performers on peripatetic street performance through the Re:Start Mall (a retail mall constructed out of shipping containers) and rubble sites where visual artist Liv Worsnip was planting and cultivating plants and herbs amidst the earthquake damage. In 'Disability performance in the streets: art actions in post-quake Christchurch' (2015) she writes about these collaborations in the wider context of visiting Christchurch on the three-year anniversary of the 2011 quake, locating the work of the company at that time as 'socially engaged art in a minor key' (173). In her relatively brief visit, Petra Kuppers established connections of friendship and collaboration with the group that would prove to be long-lasting and about which she has written more than once (2017, 2018, and 2019). Her comment about the 'minor key' with its implicit reference to the work of Erin Manning (2016) was astute, and represented at the same time an analysis and an encouragement to continue to examine what constituted performance and how certain modalities of form and genre – such as the exploration of performance in the interstices of the drama school and the dérives through the broken city could be uneasily, fugitively, but joyously inhabited by learning disabled artists. The 'minor key' or undercommons approach of Different Light at this time had been immanent in the participation in *The Earthquake in Chile*, *The Canterbury Tales*, and the Pecha Kucha presentation. Different Light Theatre inserted minor interventions into the major structures of these performances intended as celebrations or configuration of community in post-earthquake Christchurch.

A further collaboration with Petra Kuppers took place in December 2015 and was located more marginally and eccentrically from the repurposed containers and plant-life amongst the rubble of the then-city centre. This was an hour's bus drive away at Waikuku beach where Kuppers led the performers in a recitation of Ashinaabe poetry as they walked past the General Store and the Holiday Park of the rural settlement (resident population 156) to the beach where the performers improvised poems from objects they picked up from the surrounding environment. Motorized wheelchair wheels became temporarily lodged in sand and soft mud, people spoke words carried off by the Northwest wind, wavesound, and birdsong: spoonbills, oystercatchers, pied and black stilts. Waikuku in Te Reo Māori means the place of fresh mussels. It is where the braided Ashley/Rakahuri river meets the Pacific Ocean, the largest, least modified estuary in Canterbury. Rakahuri in Te Reo Māori could be translated as 'the sky turned round' (Māori place names website) or, in the words of Te Aniwa Hurihanganui: 'it means kind of entangled and turning, and that's exactly what it does ... It's the most amazingly sinuous river, so it turns in on itself all the time' (2018). The place that we had chosen to centre ourselves eccentrically away from the city turned out to be in Te Ao Māori a place that turned in on itself, a place of self-reflection.

One of the photographs that Petra Kuppers took of the Different Light dérive in the Container Mall that subsequently appeared in the Spring 2015 issue of The Drama Review (TDR) was of Louise Payne (Figure 5.1) with her characteristic red hair, her gaunt but elegant frame in black jacket, t-shirt, and trousers set off by large silver earrings, belt, and studded dog collar, her right arm held out to her side at shoulder height tracing a long line to her bangle covered wrist, her left pulling open her jacket. She is gently smiling and looking to her left. I have another photograph of her taken at the end of March 2015 when the whole Different Light group went to visit Isaac Tait who had been hospitalized with a broken leg from a road accident. It shows Louise Payne and Josie Noble on the bus on the way to the hospital. They are both turning and smiling at the rest of us, framed by the yellow metallic tubes of a luggage rack. It seems as if they have both

Figure 5.1 Louise Payne in the Christchurch Re:Start Mall. Ben Morris reflected in a shop window behind her. Image: Petra Kuppers, TDR The Drama Review, Spring 2015.

just turned and the photograph has caught that moment. Above them the red 'Bus Stopping' sign is illuminated. The bus is in motion and about to come to a stop.

Louise Payne died suddenly on 3rd May, 2015. A long-time smoker, she had been diagnosed with lung cancer only weeks before her death.

On 7th December, 2015, I attended a celebration of John Lambie's 50th year at Hohepa residential community in Christchurch. Lambie had become an infrequent participant in Different Light workshops and activities in the period 2014–15. Within a few months of this celebration, Lambie was moved from Hohepa and the people he had known for 50 years to Rosebank, a dementia centre in Ashburton, a town some hour's drive south from Christchurch. Lambie did not drive. He died on 24th June, 2016. I attended a memorial for John Lambie at Hohepa on 25th July, 2016. On the stage in the Hohepa Hall amongst the photographs on display was one of Lambie's and Helen Clark at the Court Theatre, a photograph he had insisted that I organize, and a photograph of him in white costume holding up the grey scarf that represented the albatross in *Ship of Fools*. These deaths prompted a deeper self-examination of the group by means of performance.

Three Ecologies of Different Light

The next public performance by Different Light was presented at PSi # 22 'Performance Climates' the Performance Studies international annual conference at the University of Melbourne 6th–9th July, 2016. The original intention was to focus on three performers: John Lambie, and his life in the ecologies of institutions, his celebration of 50 years at Hohepa and subsequent transfer to a dementia centre, Glen Burrows and the ecologies of support around him each day and in performance, and Ben Morris a precarious flâneur traversing the city 'as if under water' in his own words. As the group worked to devise the piece, however, Louise Payne died, and the focus shifted to honouring her contribution to the group as one of the three performers, and finally, in the weeks prior to the conference, John Lambie died and the section devoted to him materially altered. The piece then sought to weave together strands of caring, memory, and grief. The performers in the group were introduced to the basic concepts of the ecologies of the social, mental, and environmental. These were already familiar to them in their direct experience of the monetization and institutionalization of care, care-workers, and care structures. Such formations were supposed to aid or facilitate their autonomy or independence but often left them having to prove their 'disability' in order to maintain access to funds and services and also circumscribed the range of activities in which they might engage. They were also aware that the contributions they were making in devising and performing with Different Light were only occasionally remunerated financially.

Learning disabled theatre could be described in Moten and Harney's term as 'fugitive' in that it 'refuses to settle' (11). The learning disabled theatre of Different Light, due to the specific circumstances from which it has emerged, makes a contribution that emphasizes potential, the potential of learning disabled people as creators and performers, as theatre artists. The company is held together by sporadic local and national government funding, explicit and implicit institutional support, and, above all, by the generosity and collegiality of the members of the group. This is not offered as any model of best practice. Other groups choose to work in different ways. The ecology of Different Light is specific to the group.

Three Ecologies of Different Light opened with a version of a Māori *pepeha*, or formal greeting, in which each performer came on stage and spoke of their attachments to family or tribe, their river, and their mountain. When all were assembled they then spoke of the *whakapapa* or genealogy of Different Light, an unscripted account of names of people, places, and performances that informed the group's standing on stage at that moment. It was an attempt to invoke the strength and support of all who had contributed to the group up to then. When the name John Lambie was spoken this was the cue to begin the section of the piece devoted to Lambie's contribution to the ecologies of the group.

The whole group then counted to 50, starting with a whisper and gradually getting louder and more intense. After they had reached 50, there was a pause and Josie Noble repeated what seemed nonsensical rhythmic words: A chicky chick a chicky chicky chang chang'. This was part of a montage based around the song 'Do the Blue Beat' by the New Zealand singer Dinah Lee. The song dated from 1965, the year that Lambie as a seven year old became part of the first intake of children into the Hohepa community in Barrington, Christchurch. A recording of the song played and the performers danced to it in a version of The Twist. The performers then took over from the recording, each singing a verse. Josie Noble also traced out a new, distinctive choreography, Peter Rees spoke a verse as if it were a Shakespearean text, Matthew Phelan performed an Elvis-type version, Andrew Dever 'crysang' a verse, Ben Morris spoke a verse as if it were from a horror film, and Glen Burrows and Isaac Tait spat out a verse as if it were a punk anthem.

The count to 50, which was to be reprised with variations later in the piece, was a way of marking time, playing with the tedium and inexorability of such counting that would have been experienced by audience and performers alike. The transition to the nonsensical chorus of the 50-year-old song and how 'dated' it was musically, lyrically, and in terms of its accompanying dance, suggested another perspective on the passage of time of Lambie's residence in the institution. The individual performer's different versions of the verses was intended to highlight the underlying, overwhelming banality of the lyrics: 'come on and do the bluebeat and you'll never be blue'. The counting to 50 and the 50-year-old song were so obviously inadequate to represent in any way Lambie's 50 years. They represented an absurd commentary on somebody's life spent in an institution, or perhaps the unthinking ease with which a learning disabled person's life might be dis-counted.

The Bluebeat sequence was followed by a video projection of an extract from the 1963 film *A Child is Waiting* (used previously in Different Light's *The Wizard of Oz*). This was a scene involving three characters: a young boy with Down's Syndrome resident at an Institute for learning disabled people, a nurse, and the young boy's elder brother a US soldier, there to see him on family visit day. The scene was then repeated word for word three times by three different members of the ensemble:

NURSE: It's your brother, Eric.
SOLDIER: Hello, Eric. Has he –er been a good boy?
ERIC SMILES: Yeah!
SOLDIER: I've –er been meaning to get here a lot sooner but I just haven't gotten the chance.
NURSE: You can take him out on the grounds if you like.
SOLDIER: Come on, Eric.

The repetition of this banal dialogue was intended to expose the depth of suppressed emotion and family history that underlay the surface benevolence and awkwardness of the exchange. It was intended to suggest repeated separation and segregation punctuated by occasional family visits. This was immediately followed by a sequence in which the performers cited an extract from a poem written by Margaret Hatchett, a Hohepa staff member, about the original intake that specifically referred to Lambie:

On a lovely Tuesday morning children started to arrive
To begin with only nine came. It's a wonder staff survived.
Nicky Roper was our baby and she spent time on the floor
Lynley Valentine soon decided that this school was just a bore
Johnny Lambie kept us lively, specially seated on the throne
Henry St John kept repeating 'That new car, is that your own?' (Moss 53)

In the devising of this sequence the performers grew quite attached to Henry St John's repetition and repeated the phrase, increasing their volume and intensity, whilst moving downstage toward the audience. This was perhaps a reaction to how the writer of the poem's benevolence concealed the resistance to institutionalization of the children and their rhetoric: staying on the floor, expressing boredom, wanting to be in a position of authority, questioning the car as a means of mobility and freedom, and the ownership of the vehicle that was not an option for the residents.

In the next sequence the ensemble switched to slow motion movement to the accompaniment of a recording of their voices counting to 50 manipulated to extend the length of each word and each syllable with a consequent lowering of pitch. This was a count to 50 of some duration, testing further the endurance and tolerance of both performers and audience, suggestive of a long-drawn-out version of children's hide-and-seek. At the end of this sequence, video was projected of Lambie moving gracefully in the albatross sequence of *Ship of Fools* and the ensemble onstage amplified them. This led to the third and final repetition of the 'fifty' sequence in which the ensemble attempted to count backward from 50 to one whilst a computerized voice gave an account of the bare facts and figures of Lambie's life: dates, years, and places. The backward count was difficult to sustain as an ensemble and often resulted in miscounts or retracing of steps, but this suited the uneasiness of attempting to reduce a life to quantifiable terms and the inadequacy of conventional theatrical temporality to intimate in any way 50 years of institutionalization.

In 'Learning Disability, Thought and Theatre' Margaret Ames gives an account of the devising process for *Twenty Years in Hospital* in which she and Cyrff Ystwyth worked with Carwyn Daniel's to produce a type of testimonial to his experience of the trauma contained in the work's title. She refers to moments in the devising process when Daniel seemed incapable of producing anything more than 'um' and 'uh' (8) and gestures that were difficult to read: 'There was no hiding place from ... the unspeakability of the insidious trauma he continues to experience – 20 years and counting as a hospital patient ... he was articulating the ineffable qualities of trauma and identity' (16). Ames ends her account with ambiguity: a validation of the devising and performance process for Carwyn Daniel: 'he had communicated and narrated his personhood' and a kind of negation of its efficacy: 'He told me that he never wanted to feel that way again' (17).

At the end of the John Lambie sequence, Matthew Phelan inserted a characteristically positive and redemptive addition: 'John loved hugs. So now we are offering free hugs from John'. At this point members of the company approached members of the audience. This potentially sentimental moment only worked because of the sincerity of the performers. They had been influenced by similar audience interactions in collaborations such as *The Earthquake in Chile*, *The Canterbury Tales*, and performances at other theatre and performance studies conferences. It was also a reminder to all of us in the company of Lambie's open and haptic approach to engaging with people.

The next section of *Three Ecologies of Different Light* was devoted to Glen Burrows and was taken directly from writing he had undertaken 'in his own time'. His own time involved a great deal of time and effort due to the impaired motor control in his hands. Burrows' text was projected on a screen, at the same time a computerized voice 'spoke' this text, and onstage Burrows reacted with his own vocalizations, gestures, and movements:

> I got 2 mums & dads I am a doctored I am adopted Louise and Steve they had to give me up as a baby I need some help with some writing down things on paper or copy of my birth thing saying who my birth mum and dad are

> My dad died in 2007 then my mum died in 2014 or 2015 but I can't remember those dates and also two of my girlfriends and also Matt I can't handle all of this all this fuckin shit place.

> One time David did keep on hurting me sometimes Debbie did tryed to stopped him to that but he didn't want her to stop him Corin did also tried and mum because he did have a bar at home I grow up with it all of my life hating him but he were not very nice between me.

In consultation with Burrows and with his consent the text was left 'as is', without alteration or correction. This strategy was an attempt to honour the flow and force of Burrows' rhetoric as it emerged in the times he had found to write. The intensity and urgency of his writing was that of somebody who did not know how much time people would spend listening to him, and who likewise did not know when he would next be subject to the sparking of epileptic fits that temporarily debilitated him, or to shifts in mood and stamina due to his regime of medication. There are some begged questions in this strategy of translating Burrows' written text 'as is' to stage. Does the text represent Burrows' voice? There is obviously a danger in fetishizing the errors and imperfections in the text as if they are some proof of authenticity of Burrows' disabled discourse. His whole access to typing and speaking is, however, radically different, and not conducive to achieving normative expectations of fluency.

When the text was concluded each of the other four performers sang a verse from the Guns'n'Roses song 'Sweet Child o' Mine'. The performers sang unaccompanied and according to their own lights, as in or out of tune as they were apt to achieve in any given performance, but with the clear intention of responding to Burrows' account of violence and drinking in his childhood with the gift of a version of his favourite song, a song that often marked his arrival at rehearsals, coming out of his iPad. When the following verse was reached:

> Her hair reminds me of a warm safe place
> Where as a child I'd hide
> And pray for the thunder and the rain

The line 'And pray for the thunder and the rain' was repeated by all the performers increasing their volume and intensity and accompanied by Burrows' increasingly violent banging of his wheelchair's armrest with his arm, a rhetorical strategy that he developed in the devising process. When this rhetorical force was spent by Burrows, a solo voice sang gently 'To quietly pass me by'.

The song at times defied the tempo, rhythm, and melody of the Guns'n'Roses original. but suggested the bourbon'n'cola soaked memories that Burrows held onto, the mix of frustrated love and violence 'between' him and his adoptive father. At the end of this song sequence, Isaac Tait offered the audience another opportunity for interaction in the manner of the offer of hugs in memory of John Lambie. Tait offered kisses from Burrows and that all who took advantage of this offer would have their hand stamped with the phrase 'Intellectually kissabled' Tait re-used some of the ink stamps that had been made for those who agreed to be interviewed in *Canterbury Tales*. Tait's offer concluded with the assurance: 'Don't worry. It washes off'. His comment teased and made light of any audience member's reluctance to kiss the visibly disabled Burrows. In the performances in both Melbourne and Christchurch no such reluctance was in evidence.

The third section of *Three Ecologies of Different Light* was devoted to Louise Payne and opened with a video of Payne being interviewed as part of the research for *The Sunnyside Project*. The audio of the video was replaced by gentle music. The performers onstage whispered a slowed-down version of the chorus from *Do the Blue Beat*: 'A chicky chick a chicky chicky chang chang' whilst the video played. Individual performers then each presented a tribute in performance to Payne. Matthew Phelan acknowledged her taking him to Green Party demonstrations in an Elvis jumpsuit and offered his Elvis poem from *The Poor Dears* as a tribute, Andrew Dever offered his rendition of 'Danny Boy' that Payne had once mentioned that she liked, and switched to 'crysinging' part way through, Peter Rees offered a display of stage combat sword fighting as Payne had 'encouraged him to be strong'. Ben Morris attempted to recreate an improvisation that Payne had undertaken with him to encourage him to talk to somebody he liked 'to open up something of himself', Isaac Tait improvised a poem. Josie Noble shared a memory of sitting next to Louise on a bus going to the hospital to see Tait, and of how Payne helped and comforted her at the hospital when being there prompted flashbacks to her open-heart surgery.

Glen Burrows had written out some of his memories of her:

> After class when we were raining so raining it was sunday she had a mate who put my wheelchair on the back of his truck we did not get a fucking taxi ride for me it was a red one my other older chair it were a bit more very hard to get it on to the back of it with some wood they did ask the taxi was it on its way or not book it Sunday a long time back they had problems her mate had put it on there but she died from lung cancer and she did die my hair black and the two of us went to an upstairs bar in Lyttelton we went to a school thing but I don't know which school and I did stay with Alan and her. Louise Payne.

Burrows referred to the perennial problems with the availability of wheelchair taxis, his chair being transported on the back of a truck by an impromptu arrangement of planks of wood, Payne's dyeing of his hair, her efforts to afford him a social life, and her death.

The final section of the piece was an attempt to weave together elements of all three sections to suggest how Lambie, Payne, and Burrows contributed to the three ecologies of Different Light. This centred on certain keywords that emerged in improvisation: 'earth', the earth beneath which Lambie and Payne lay with the earth over which Burrows rolled, 'apart' the apartness of Lambie and Payne who were still part of us and 'light' light and air we breathed and that constitute a part of the stuff of which we are composed. The last word of the piece was 'tender': to suggest gentleness and care but also the vulnerability and fragility of the performers' relationships within and with the planet.

The focus on words in the final sequence was a way of acknowledging the word play that the performers had become accustomed to, and fond of, in their own different ways, in the devising process. Matthew Phelan was very adept at punning, Ben Morris at creating fast-moving verbal pyrotechnics, Isaac Tait at inserting odd, eclectic phrases from his immersion in quirky films, animations, and YouTube trawls in search of the gonzo avant-garde, Josie Noble at terms of warmth and affection, Peter Rees drew on his interest in historical and fantasy narrative, Andrew Dever on his fascination with Kiwiana and nostalgia, and Glen Burrows would add his distinctive contributions in his own time.

The group devising process followed a set pattern, it would start with certain points of focus – a memory of a person, place, or thing, for example – that would then be explored initially in three ways: through gesture and movement, through sound and movement, and finally through words and movement. When it came to the words these often emerged through brainstorming or generating text or ideas. This method tends to produce offers and choices by individual participants that are influenced by the choices of the rest of the group: based on rhyming, or phonemic, morphological, and semantic similarities and patterns. For example, in devising the ending sequence of *Three Ecologies of Different Light* starting with a point of focus on the connections of the group with Louise Payne, John Lambie, and Glen Burrows the following sequences emerged:

> apart, a part of, to part, parting is such sweet sorrow, part ways, part of the time, particles, particles of light, different light, breathing light, sunlight, solar power, sun and earth, under the earth, on the earth, touching the earth, the earth is touching, tender.

Elements from these sequences were then included in the conclusion of the piece but with a particular ear to patterns of sound so that the learning of the words was more akin to learning a song and the movement to gestural choreography.

The group's experience of travelling to Melbourne and attending the PSi conference generated shared experiences that were then almost immediately incorporated into the developed and expanded version of *Three Ecologies of Different Light* at the University of Canterbury presented at the end of September 2016. These included attending a plenary session led by Back to Back Theatre's Bruce Gladwin, Alice Nash, and performer Scott Price in which an attendee had posed the question of whether there were any philosophers or thinkers with Down's Syndrome. Price answered this question by stating that there were people with Down's Syndrome from Different Light in the room. The performers attended other workshop sessions, one presented by a group from New York on the ecology of beavers that involved experiencing different smells in the room and another presenting work in progress on a new play. Elements of the performers' experience of both were incorporated into the September performance. There were also short scenes devised by the performers about travelling around and eating out in Melbourne and the almost inevitable adventures in access involving Glen Burrows. One of these occurred whilst Isaac Tait and I were assisting Burrows in the shower at the University of Melbourne accommodation. A warning on the tannoy was given to evacuate the building immediately. This meant transporting Burrows in the manual shower wheelchair wrapped in a towel dressing gown and as many towels as possible as it would not have been possible to take the time needed to dress him and to heed the alarm. We all assembled outside as requested but became increasingly worried about Burrows' exposure to the cold air. Eventually the fire brigade allowed us to take him into a part of the building that was deemed safe. This happened to be in a room in which academic paraphernalia was stored for ceremonial purposes. The only possibility of warming Burrows up and keeping him warm, until we were given the all-clear, was to wrap him up in academic gowns and to keep rubbing his arms and legs. The final scene that was added to the September performance was a brief account of how on arrival back in New Zealand after presenting a performance at an international academic conference several of the performers received a letter from the Ministry of Social Development telling them that as they had not informed MSD of their departure from New Zealand before they left, their disability benefit payments had been suspended.

Figure 5.2 Different Light in movement rehearsal. Left to right: Peter Rees, Matthew Phelan, and Andrew Dever. Image: Paul McCaffrey for Different Light Theatre.

I Belong in the Past and the Future and the Very Now

The next performance by the group was devised to be staged at the Australasian Association for Theatre Drama and Performance Studies (ADSA) conference: 'Performing Belonging in the Twenty First Century' 27th–30th June 2017 at Auckland University of Technology. This was a 20-minute performance based on the understandings of belonging inperformance of the seven learning disabled performers. We intended to explore what love, home, friendship, and work meant to them and how these might be presented in performance. Isaac Tait had given the piece its title. The implications of this title included consideration of the *very now*, the kairos, or heightened sense of presence and temporal intensity, the pressure and momentum of being on stage. The intention was to incorporate the group's devising and rehearsal processes into the performance *as performance*. These processes included continued work on the disciplinary formations of theatre: line-learning, choreography, character, and narrative development: activities which were increasingly being approached by the group with ambivalence. The past of the title encompassed the whakapapa, or performance and personnel genealogy, of the group and the lived experience that supposedly informed the devised material of performance. It also included the work of the studio and the rehearsal room that in conventional theatre constitutes a past both preparatory for, and preliminary to, the main event of performance. The group's praxis was, however, becoming more self-reflexive and uneasy about this division between the process and performance output, seeking to find ways to value the discoveries of process in performance. The future referred to the unknown efficacy of making theatre for a time and space of inclusion that was always yet to come. Paying attention to the processes of the group also meant giving some account of friendships and relationships within the group that were integral to its continuing existence, function, and efficacy. It also meant exploring the longing in belonging and the desire to belong that might be an unattainable object.

The piece opened with what appeared to be a simple question about theatrical performance: how do they remember all those lines? The question was intended to resonate differently within a learning disabled performance, to challenge audience assumptions about the cognitive (dis)abilities of the performers. The sequence that followed presented a kind of parody of the discipline of line learning in which Peter Rees as an educator-cum-sergeant major drilled the rest of the ensemble in learning a text taken from the New Zealand Ministry of Education National Transition Guidelines (Guidelines for transitioning students with additional learning needs from school to adult life):

> A Transition is a process, not a one off event. During transition an individual student receives support, through planning, to identify and achieve – or move closer – to their career and lifestyle aspirations. (Ministry of Education website)

Transition is the 'stage' within which all the Different Light performers were, and still are, situated. For most learning disabled people in New Zealand, Transition is a continuing cycle of supported activities from which pathways or staircases to meaningful careers and lifestyles do not tend to emerge. Rees used a number of strategies of his choosing – word by word repetition, peremptory instructions to be louder, faster, or funnier, to drill the ensemble through this exercise in line learning. He joyfully modelled these strategies on my cruder attempts at direction.

This sequence was followed by the presentation of a different form of disciplinary formation: Josie Noble led the group in movement improvisation exercises. Matthew Phelan and Andrew Dever took part in a version of Boal's mirror exercise (1992), Ben Morris explored The Container exercise (Wangh), Peter Rees free-formed diagonal and cross-body movements, Glen Burrows and Isaac Tait explored wheelchair-biped contact improvisation. Throughout this sequence, Noble provided verbal side-coaching, a mixture of encouragement, suggestion, and instruction in the terms she was used to as a choreographer and movement instructor with Jolt Dance. Although the discipline in this sequence was gentler it was still premised upon challenging the performers to improve themselves and work on themselves. Both sequences left Rees and Noble 'in charge' in the performance with the exact content and duration of each decided by them.

The next sequence was based on a verbal improvisation by Ben Morris in which he expressed his frustration at being housed in a half-way house with other learning disabled people whom he regarded as less lively and socially-minded than him. His frustration was crystallized in his image of one of the residents on a Saturday night sitting and watching a single sock going around the cycles of a washing machine. This was developed into a movement sequence in which Morris stood on the back of Glen Burrows' wheelchair slowly repeating 'One sock goes round the cycle of the washing machine. A resident is watching'. Burrows followed a repeated movement pattern or orbit as Morris played around with slowing and speeding up the tempo of his delivery of the repeated line, both creating their own version of a cycle until the rest of the ensemble passed a woolen sock around the group, throwing it in the air. The sock was then revealed to be scarf length and then longer and longer, an impossible length for a sock, as it was thrown in the air, held up in the air. This elongated woolen object was then placed around Isaac Tait as he tried to break free from it. The whole ensemble then gradually assembled for a Tait-inspired surreal fantasy montage sequence that included his questioning of where the 'drama' was whilst being tied, held back, and trying to escape the group. This led him to echo the word drama with trauma, the idea of drama being haunted by trauma, silent screaming, ice cream, the diabetes for which Tait injects himself each day, interspersed with the rest of the company sharing in-jokes about haunting, favourite ice-cream flavours, and some of their earliest memories. Although the sequence was scripted, the order in which performers made contributions was not rigid. The whole sequence was an attempt to honour Tait's communicative style, the group making offers that represented their support of him.

The next scene followed a much more conventional narrative structure to allow Andrew Dever to tell stories of his growing up and of his family. The scene was an attempt to make theatre from Dever's own sense of belonging in which there was a heavy emphasis on family and a nostalgia for the artefacts, sights, sounds, smells, and tastes of his 'Kiwi' upbringing. It was a theatrical version of showing family or holiday snaps or memories, artefacts that carry a great deal of meaning to the person presenting but that may not be as interesting to an audience. Tait and Dever's sequences were presented as far as possible according to their instructions as to what they wanted from the scenes. At this stage in the company's development these were exercises in gauging what the performers meant by, and wanted from, performance and what response or engagement these ideas of performance might provoke in an audience.

Tait's sequence presented the learning disabled artist as conscious of being an artist, influenced by techniques and persona from live art and visual art. Dever's sequence was a kind of personal testimonial as performance, reminiscent of grass roots learning disabled performance. Both were presented as two sides of the same coin of questioning what is meant by self-presentation in learning disabled theatre. Both were presented within the context of the whole piece's questioning of how learning disabled performers could belong in performance. Was belonging to be found by submitting to the disciplinary formations of theatre, by learning and 'owning' lines and movements through self-discipline? Or was belonging to be found by the performers merely putting their 'stories' or 'putting themselves' on stage according to their own devices? The performance left these questions open.

The next sequence involving Ben Morris presenting 'The Book of Ben' a quasi-religious text that seemed intent on diminishing Morris' capacity to act and move in the city. It contained a series of commandments including a prohibition on sending texts to young women. His punishment for breaking this commandment would be never achieving or moving closer to his career and lifestyle aspirations (echoing Transition) and being condemned to watch a single sock in a washing machine. In response to Morris' account of his texting behaviour in which he admitted he continued to ask a young woman out despite her repeated refusals, Josie Noble was able to offer a gentle 'No means no, Ben'. Morris' scene finished with his expressing his fear that now the audience would hate him.

There was a section devoted to Glen Burrows. This had as a point of focus Burrows in the shower, drawing on our experience in Melbourne, and his experience of 'sparking' or having mild epileptic fits in the shower. These were becoming more common for him and starting to have an impact on his comfort and confidence participating in the group. The other performers wanted to encourage Burrows' participation in the group by encouraging him to experience happy memories: sparks of happiness. These included the waitress in the Johnny Rockets diner in San Jose who had given him some ketchup formed into a smiley face, and with whom he had his photo taken. They included his sisters, Debbie and Corin and a collection of nieces who lived in Melbourne who had come to see him perform. They also wanted to offer some consolation for his sparks of sadness. These included memories of Kirsten and Louise and of a recent rehearsal during which he had started sparking and crying out in pain and we had called an ambulance, in Josie Noble's words, 'Real life drama at Different Light drama'. The performance concluded with Peter Rees stating that Burrows was not a piece of theatre but like a computer game, a game that you needed to experience 'over months, or years, or possibly your whole life'.

In addition to the presentation of the performance at the conference, the Different Light performers attended other paper presentations and the final plenary. One of those presentations 'Being Emily' by Tiffany Knight was about the issues of inhabiting the role of a friend, Emily Steel, who had written an autobiographical performance staged in a swimming pool that included reference to a 19-week abortion due to the fact the baby was likely to be born with Down's Syndrome (Fuss 2018). This discussion around a woman's right to choose resonated interestingly in a room in which actors with Down's Syndrome were present. At the final plenary, Peter Rees responded from the floor to one of the questions posed by the moderators of the session, and Isaac Tait made the final contribution to the whole conference with a quote from *Hamlet*. This willingness to participate aligned with newly acquired confidence in the group's right to perform and to be present and participate in wider discussions of performance by practitioners and students of theatre. The group's performance praxis was shifting from a model in which I and other non-disabled facilitators supplied a narrative, dramaturgical and choreographic framework for the ensemble to one in which the performers developed strategies to provide onstage care and support for each other in response to the challenges of both the normative imperative to 'give an account of themselves' (Butler 2005) and the disciplinary formations of theatre.

The History of Different Light

When the group was invited to perform at the Christchurch Arts Festival in 2019 this was an opportunity to present some account of what the group had been doing for the past 15 years to an audience in the performers' home city. The intention of *The History of Different Light* was for the performers to give their own histories of 15 years of working together. When this was explained to the group at the outset of the devising process Isaac Tait's immediate response was a focus on 'people who were missing'. This observation took account of the fluctuating numbers of the company, actors who had joined in and moved on, artists and academics who had come down to Christchurch to work with the company, those whose family or living circumstances had changed preventing them from continuing with the group, as well as John Lambie and Louise Payne who had died. This idea of disappearance then began to permeate the process and the performance, ultimately in a way that could not be anticipated. It led the performers to question what appears and disappears in a 'history' as a series of events, what appears and disappears in memory and in performance, and what disappears only at some stage later to reappear unprompted. In *The History of Different Light* the performers were encouraged to revisit scenes, memories, characters, lines of text and objects from previous productions, at times connecting with videos of their younger selves in rehearsal or in performance and exploring what had been gained and what had been lost in 15 years of working together. It was an invitation for the company to examine the life of the company by means of self-reflexive performance.

The audience arrived to recordings of radio interviews that the performers had given to Radio New Zealand followed by an opening sequence described by Erin Harrington in her review in *Theatreview*:

> ... the piece's wonderfully tongue-in-cheek opening, in which the performers 'evolve' to the sound of Aaron Copeland's epic 'Fanfare for the Common Man'. Five of the actors wiggle like amoeba, flop like

Figure 5.3 Different Light Theatre in rehearsal for *The History of Different Light* (2019). Left to right: Ben Morris, Glen Burrows, Peter Rees, Isaac Tait, and Matthew Phelan.

fish, groom each other like apes and then wander about as distracted, device-wielding contemporary humans, lit dramatically by a powerful torch held by ... Glen, who cruises around the stage in his hi-tech wheelchair in God mode. (2019)

The group was conscious that they had not performed to a Christchurch public in a theatre for a number of years and wanted to present a humorous take on the development and evolution of the group. It was not the ambition of the group to develop in a conventional arc of progression. There had been periods during which the group had retreated from public performance and found different ways of holding on together and to each other. The commitment was as much to care and conviviality within the group as to public performance and profile. Venturing into online and academic spaces was a way of tracing the wandering lines or lines of flight of learning disabled theatre as it was emerging with groups such as Theater HORA, Per.Arts, and Teatr 21, groups for whom performance research or research by means of performance was as important as commercial, public performance. Different Light had 'evolved' since the previous public performance in Christchurch but in a manner that was not easy to identify nor to promote nor even to hope to articulate in a 45 minute performance in the Arts Festival.

This sequence was then followed by the group's introduction of itself. This time it was not as fictional characters, nor the persona of Not the Poor Dears, nor the *pepeha* and *whakapapa* of Māoritanga, it was a bald statement of identity: 'We are Different Light'. The statement was then qualified in a number of different ways: 'You may not know about us. We are a Christchurch secret'. Theatre itself often feels like a clandestine, cult practice in the city. Different Light performs its secret ministry in the interstices of a drama school within a polytechnic in a city in which the University had disestablished the Theatre and Film Studies Programme that had fostered the emergence of Different Light, Gap Filler, Greening the Rubble and Christchurch's Free Theatre.

Tait's idea of people disappearing was presented early in the performance: the ensemble whispered the names of some of those who had disappeared as the screen on the cyclorama showed earlier images of the company: rehearsing, backstage, and on tea breaks in the Hohepa Hall, in Auckland, Sydney, Melbourne, San Jose, and Leeds: moments of conviviality not normally visible in conventional performance. The first member of the company to be introduced was Glen Burrows who had recently been appearing and disappearing. His 'sparking' or spasming had increased in frequency and intensity and he was in fear of this happening in front of the others in rehearsal or of an audience in performance. During the season of *The History of Different Light* it was a struggle for him to deal with this performance anxiety each night and he was given a lot of support by Sofie Martinsdottir, a NASDA student stage managing the production who had also trained as a nurse, and with whom Burrows had established a relationship of trust. We were in continuous conversations with him and with the support workers of the Trust in the house where he lived as to his continuing participation in the group's processes and performances. It became a delicate balance to tread between supporting and encouraging him and giving him the leeway not to attend when he did not feel up to participating. In those periods of his participation, he had let us know that his actual name was Benjamin and not his adoptive name of Glen, although his support workers continued to call him Glen. This was a source of some confusion to the ensemble in terms of distinguishing Glen/Benjamin from Ben/Benjamin (Morris) and this confusion made its way into the performance.

In rehearsal discussions and improvisations, it had become apparent that the actors had very different memories of the past productions. There were, however, some scenes, objects, or moments that were held in collective memory, that constituted the archive of the company for the performers. Matthew Phelan who was constantly seeking to obtain copies of recordings of each performance, was a kind of living archive as he had a remarkable memory of his own participation, characters, lines of text, movements, and the specifics of performance, down to dates and durations, but yet was extremely reticent to speak about process. Isaac Tait and Ben Morris had memories of specific experiences of touring and travel outside of the performance, many of them quite forgotten by other members of the ensemble.

In the rough and tumble structure of the performance that emerged through the devising process, Matthew Phelan became a kind of go to person to introduce specific performances and dates, Peter Rees represented a voice of some authority but always tending toward the ambivalent, the ironic, and the humorous. Tait, Morris, and Burrows were the keepers of the affective archive of shared experiences outside of the theatre. Josie Noble held knowledge, memories, and practices of movement in improvisation and performance, in warm-up and other exercises, that she could call upon to gather and galvanize the group. The performers had also got to know each other enough to want to showcase the capabilities of each: Josie Noble's work at Plant and Food Research was acknowledged in a scene in which she discussed the properties of different kinds of light, and her experience in choreography was acknowledged in a half-serious half-comic movement sequence in which she moved the others as a corps de ballet around Glen Burrows' version of a dying swan from *Swan Lake*. She led the others in a focussed movement theatre warm-up exercise to represent the training practice she as a Special Olympic swimmer brought to the group. Peter Rees supported Matthew Phelan's desire to perform Shakespeare by participating in an extract from *Romeo and Juliet* playing Tybalt to his Romeo. These sequences were placed early in the performance to subvert the audience's expectations of Festival performance – part of a canon of high cultural capital – and of disabled performance as endlessly recycling narratives of overcoming difficulties and shining as notable exceptions.

Learning Disabled Performance Research 171

The whole project was an attempt to present something of an 'anarchive' of Different Light Theatre as outlined in Erin Manning's *For a Pragmatics of the Useless*. She describes the praxis of SenseLab that was set up to register in some way the (performance) 'event's anarchic share' (84): 'Our concern was always about the way capture for archival purposes registers a mode of valuation (76). ... Our work, as regards the anarchive, was to devise techniques that could make the unrealized as real felt' (80). The anarchive of Different Light would include the anarchic share that comprised the company's experiences on the way to performance, the different memories we kept with us individually and collectively and the 'extra-theatrical' forms of being together and being untogether together that the group was becoming. It would include what the performers felt was gained and what was lost in our time together, of what had been given voice and what possibilities of other voicing had been taken away in making the choice to select what was spoken and what was performed. What had been overlooked or left behind in the rush to make meaning, to make characters, to show and to tell?

The scenes from previous performances shown in *The History of Different Light* were not presented as a series of 'greatest hits' but spoke of where the group was in the present through the performers' examination of their past. They were self-reflexive presentations allowing the previous performances to speak back to the performers before an audience. They did not necessarily represent a record of progress. For some of the performers, lack of access or ability to participate meaningfully in a social life obdurately remained the same or had become worse from when they had first performed to the present. This was certainly the case for Glen Burrows and his deteriorating physical health. Each of the performers brought their own perspective to the revisiting of past performance. Matthew Phelan collected experiences as he did DVDs of film and performance, so that they became capable of being replayed and enjoyed again at any time, in the manner of the old actor's store of anecdotes. Glen/Benjamin Burrows did not want the history of his involvement with the company to become the totality or last word on his contribution: he wanted a present and a future. Ben Morris' ambivalent attitude to revisiting past performances was apparent in a sequence in *The History of Different Light* in which a video was shown of Morris performing the shower scene from *Ship of Fools* at the Awakenings Festival in 2007.

In the performance he introduced the video with: 'I remember performing that show to a schools audience in Australia. One interesting scene in that show was the shower scene'. He stayed on stage and watched his younger self on video. His body responded ever so slightly to moments in the scene and the loud and appreciative audience reactions. The audience for *The History of Different Light* may or may not have noticed these microreactions and the ambivalence of these in the context of his more general disengagement in the act of observing. His ambivalence was akin to Ben

Ellenbroek's ambivalence over his engagement in performance (Chapter 2), akin perhaps in some way to Carwyn Daniel's comments to Margaret Ames (2019) at the end of her account of *Twenty Years in Hospital* in 'Learning Disability, Thought, and Theatre' Certain practices of learning disabled theatre draw so much on the persona of the performer, on the blurring and shifting lines between character, persona, and perceived self of the actor. Performance prompts a questioning of how the self is informed by the experiences that inhabit us or that we inhabit. Do we expect the coherence of 'an ongoing accountable self' (Ridout and Woods 2020–21), like a character in a naturalistic drama? An alternative perspective to this ongoing accountable self is provided by Lisbeth Lipari in 'Ethics, Kairos, and Akroasis':

> Our minds are a tangle of braided melodies, rhythms, recapitulations, and syncopations of memory and anticipation, sparkling with occasional echoes of the present moment. (97)

Morris was supposedly doubly present in observing himself perform on video from the stage, but he was also doubly absent. He seemed caught wanting to believe in the power of representation, that in some way still triggered muted physical reactions when he observed himself but was also prone to disbelief in the efficacy of past theatrical performance to endure or to have meaning in the present. The learning disabled theatre of Different Light and other companies relies heavily on the self-presentation of learning disabled actors. This is a particularly potent mix of illusion and disillusion, belief and disbelief, in which the actors are cast as both the subject of theatre and subjected to theatre.

The History of Different Light asked what the history of the company's performances meant to the learning disabled performers. The answer was not clear. Perhaps it lay in Morris' word *interesting*. 'Interesting' is a word often used to deflect from expressing a judgment on whether a particular piece of theatre or film or artwork engaged or affected a spectator. Was it good? Did you like it? It was ... *interesting*. Different Light Theatre's 15 years of history had not led to commercial reward, nor to the establishment of an institution providing pathways of employment or education for learning disabled people. What the company had achieved remained something interesting, or curious, and, above all, elusive, as much based upon disappearance as appearance, upon the ephemerality of theatre as much as the potential for theatre to change lives. At the end of her review of *The History of Different Light* Erin Harrington referred to the company as a 'taonga' the Māori word for an object or natural resource that is highly prized. In the South Island a taonga might well be a pounamu, a piece of greenstone picked out of a river, carved, touched by hands, worn next to the skin, and bearing the powerful secret history of the mantle of the earth condensed into stone.

Video extracts of past performances that were also presented in *The History of Different Light* included Matthew Phelan's Elvis poem, Isaac Tait's play, and Glen/Benjamin Burrows playing electric guitar. These extracts were never more than two minutes, intended to be just long enough to gain the attention of an audience and to allow for whatever brief initial interaction might occur between the performers themselves 'live' in 2019 and their previous performance selves: Phelan speaking or mouthing along to his recorded self, Tait distanced but curious, Burrows rocking in his wheelchair, all of them visibly changed over ten years, all of them having aged.

There was also a section running together sequences involving and devoted to Glen/Benjamin Burrows. Running together these sequences was done in part so that we could more effectively and expediently accommodate his increasingly diminished ability to contribute.

Running together also hints at the urgency and intensity with which we all approached Burrows' contributions to the company at this stage. We were aware both of his great desire and longstanding commitment to participate, and of his struggles, his overriding fear of 'sparking' in front of the others and an audience. These fears we attempted to allay by a ritual wheeling and walking around the building with Sofie Martinsdottir before each performance, and by assurances that we would be there for him whatever happened, as he was more important to us than the performance. He never once experienced sparking in performance but his fear of it needed support and reassurance. We presented his writing about his adoptive father's violence and the response in song of the other members of the ensemble, his writing about Louise Payne, from *Three Ecologies of Different Light* the sequence in the shower from *I Belong in the Past and the Future and the Very Now*. These sequences represented the group's attempts to date to give Burrows voice. They were deeply problematic. Burrows' continued participation in the group was difficult, pushing him, his support network, and us, to the edge of questioning whether it should continue. We explained to him that he was welcome to participate in whatever way he felt comfortable, that we could find ways of working around him, that he should not hesitate to tell us if at any point he felt uncomfortable about continuing and wanted to stop, that he was always welcome in the group. We extended to him the bonds of hospitality. By doing so, did we implicate him in an irredeemable obligation, the fulfillment of which might ultimately contribute to the detriment of his health? We continue to monitor the terms of his participation in the group, to stay in touch with him, to visit him, to communicate as best we can through video on Zoom and Messenger when this suits him better. By doing so, do we really commit ourselves to the bonds of hospitality? These questions continue to confront us.

The final section of *The History of Different Light* took its shape in the light of events that occurred during the rehearsal period for the performance. In the course of these events and their aftermath the group, Christchurch, and Aotearoa/New Zealand were confronted with very different meanings of *them* and *us*, and of hospitality and hostility. On March 15th at 1.32 p.m. an Australian white supremacist terrorist, who had recently been living in Dunedin, emailed his manifesto entitled 'The Great Replacement' to New Zealand Prime Minister Jacinda Ardern and 70 other politicians and media outlets. A few minutes later, he started to livestream his journey by car to Al Noor Mosque. At 1.40 p.m. he entered the mosque and opened fire. He used five guns: two semi-automatic weapons, two shotguns and a lever-action firearm. There were more than two hundred people answering one of the Friday calls to prayer. According to eye-witness accounts, he spent about six seconds shooting people in the women's hall, then turned his attention to the men's hall. He then went to his car to get another weapon and returned after about two minutes. He next spent two minutes firing shots into bodies already on the floor. At 1.48 p.m. he got back into his car, some nine minutes since he had first started shooting. He drove through town to the Linwood Mosque, where eighty people were praying, and continued shooting. It took him about seven minutes to drive the three miles between the two mosques. Christchurch is a small place.

The shooter was greeted at the door of the mosque by Haji Mohammed Daoud Nabi, a 71-year-old man from Afghanistan, whose words have been variously reported as 'Hello, Brother, welcome' or 'Welcome, brother'. He was the first to be shot dead by Tarrant. He died with the words of hospitality on his lips. He himself was a refugee who had sought and gained asylum in New Zealand in 1977. Other accounts say that his act of hospitality on greeting the shooter saved another, younger man's life. Haji Mohammed Daoud Nabi was the cousin of the grandmother of a former student at the drama school where I teach. Christchurch is a small place.

On the day of the shooting, I had attended the School Strike for Climate Change in Cathedral Square. I took a photo tagged at 1.21 pm. I arrived back at Ara Institute between 1.30 and 1.40 pm. Shortly after that the institution was put in lockdown as the Armed Offenders Squad made their way across the campus. Where I teach and where Different Light rehearses are only a few streets away from Al Noor Mosque. Christchurch is a small place.

Haji Mohammed Daoud Nabi's practice of a selfless act of hospitality to a heavily armed gunman was grounded in Islamic codes of hospitality that have been described by Rustom Bharucha (2014) as the 'radical antithesis' to the 'paranoid nationalism' (177) of John Howard and other Australian politicians that helped fuel 'The Great Replacement' ideology and actions of the shooter. In the wake of the shooting certain reactions stood out. One of these was the slogan sprayed on walls and festooned on Facebook posts 'They are Us' meaning the 'they' of Christchurch's Moslem community, the only victims of the shooter, were part of the 'Us' of the wider community:

a slogan that seeks to elide and gloss over the distinction already epistemically embedded in 'them' and 'us'. Another ubiquitous slogan was 'This is not Us' meaning the shooter did not represent the supposedly multicultural community of Christchurch. In fact, as Dame Anne Salmond (2019) has pointed out, Christchurch has a long, dishonourable history of racism and discrimination in the context of which, the shooter could not easily be dismissed as some foreign imported aberration.

The Christchurch Arts Festival went ahead some six months after the massacres as a celebration of community. Within the Festival we were invited to repair to the Commons, land appropriated for common use after the earthquakes, for a *hangi* on a huge scale. The major artists of the festival were Māori and Pacific. There was yet no place in the Festival for artists and performers from the Muslim population of Christchurch. This was not because of out-and-out hostility. This was not because of inhospitality. Perhaps we as Christchurch did not yet know how to be hospitable, we did not know how to align different codes and different obligations of hospitality. Perhaps we do not yet know how to accept the bonds of the absolute and unconditional forgiveness that was expressed so unbearably and so movingly by the relatives of those killed in the massacres. Just as Haji Mohammed Daoud Nabi practised unconditional hospitality at the entrance to Al Noor Mosque, Farid Ahmed practised unconditional forgiveness. His wife was killed by the shooter as she was trying to save others, yet his words of forgiveness echoed in the aftermath of the massacres: 'I have forgiven him and I am sure if my wife was alive, she would have done the same thing …. I hold no grudge' (Leask 2019). These examples of giving hospitality and forgiveness feel in some ways unbearable, unattainable, unfathomable. Such behaviour, such practice renders the formulas of hospitality and forgiveness, through the flames of deep suffering and sacrifice, to their profoundest meaning and efficacy.

At the end of *The History of Different Light* the performers addressed the audience in their own words that we all knew would be inadequate. Isaac Tait expressed a desire for identification: 'Al Noor is the Arabic word for light. A different word for light. A different light'. Ben Morris aligned his own anxiety with the ethical anxiety and ambiguity of many in the city: 'We are not the Muslim population of Christchurch. It's not our place to speak for them. But maybe it is our place as well'. Matthew Phelan's response spoke of his firm Christian faith and patriotism: 'In the bonds of love we meet' lines from the New Zealand national anthem – but perhaps these words resonated further than Irishman Thomas Bracken's hymn to the new colony (1876). Perhaps they speak back to us, of the obligations of love, and of hospitality, and of *manaakitanga,* the Māori concept of hospitality based on acknowledging the mana of the guest, that are in their fullest implications unbearable, but toward which we might move in how we live, think, and make theatre together.

Figure 5.4 Different Light performer Josie Noble in rehearsal, promotional image for *The History of Different Light*, Christchurch Arts Festival, 1st–3rd August, 2019. Image: Paul McCaffrey for Different Light Theatre.

References

A Child Is Waiting. Directed by John Cassavetes, 1963. Optimum Classic, 2009.
Ames, Margaret. "Learning Disability, Thought, and Theatre." *Contemporary Theatre Review*, vol. 29, no. 3, 2019, pp. 290–304.
"Back to Back Theatre in Conversation." "Performance Climates" Performance Studies international conference. PSi#22. University of Melbourne, 8 July, 2016.
Benjamin, Walter. "Theses in the Philosophy of History." In *Illuminations*. Translated by H. Zorn. Pimlico, 1999.
Bharucha, Rustom. *Terror and Performance*. Routledge, 2014.
Boal, Augusto. *Games for Actors and Non-Actors*. Translated by Adrian Jackson. Routledge, 1992.
Bracken, Thomas. *God Defend New Zealand*. Queen's Theatre, Dunedin, 25 December, 1876.
Butler, Judith. *Giving an Account of Oneself*. Fordham University Press, 2005.
Canterbury Tales. Directed by Peter Falkenberg, Free Theatre Christchurch FESTA Festival of Transitional Architecture, Central city and Cathedral Square, Christchurch 25–28 October 2013.
Fuss, Eloise. "Australian play *19 Weeks* breaks the silence around abortion." *ABC News*. 23 March, 2018.
Guattari, Félix. *The Three Ecologies*. Translated by Ian Pindar. Continuum, 2005.

Harrington, Erin. "Probes the complexity and beauty of the human condition." *Theatreview*. Online. 2 August, 2019.
I belong in the past and the future and the very now .... Devised by the ensemble. Directed by Tony McCaffrey. ADSA Conference, Auckland University of Technology. 27–30 June, 2017.
Leask, Anna. "Christchurch Mosque Shootings: 'I Forgive Him' – Survivor's Message to Gunman Who Killed His Wife." *New Zealand Herald*. 18 March, 2019.
Lipari, Lisbeth. "Ethics, kairos, and akroasis: an essay on time and relation.' In *Philosophy of Ethics, Alterity and the Other*. Edited by Ronald C. Arnett and Patricia Arneson. Fairleigh Dickinson University Press, 2014, pp. 87–106.
Manning, Erin. *For a Pragmatics of the Useless*. Duke University Press, 2020.
Manning, Erin. *The Minor Gesture*. Duke University Press, 2016.
McCaffrey, Tony. "Polyfest postponed: performing 'us' in Christchurch in 2019?" *Australasian Drama Studies, Australasian Association for Theatre, Drama and Performance Studies Online Journal*, vol. 76, April 2020, pp. 87–122.
McCaffrey, Tony, McCaffrey, Paul and Parker, George, Garrett, Kim TePairi. *The Sunnyside Project*. Devised performance funded by Creative New Zealand. Developed 2007–2010. Intended for Christchurch Arts Festival 2010, cancelled due to earthquakes, 2010–2011.
Ministry of Education. Te Tāhuhu o te Mātauranga. National Transition Guidelines. https://www.education.govt.nz/school/student-support/special-education/national-transition-guidelines-for-students-with-additional-learning-needs/national-transition-guidelines/. Accessed 9 October, 2021.
Moss, Maryann. *Learning to Live: A History of Hohepa Homes 1956-2006*. Hohepa Homes Trust Board, 2010.
Moten, Fred and Harney, Stefano. *The Undercommons: Fugitive Planning and Black Study*. Minor Compositions, 2013.
———. *All Incomplete*. Minor Compositions, 2020.
"Performance Climates," Performance Studies International Conference. PSi#22. University of Melbourne, 5–9 July, 2016.
"Performing Belonging in the Twenty First Century," Australasian Association for Theatre Drama and Performance Studies (ADSA) conference. Auckland University of Technology: 27–30 June, 2017.
Ridout, Nicholas and Woods, Orlagh. *Performance, Possession and Automation*. https://possessionautomation.co.uk Online research project and collaboration, 2020–2021.
Salmond, Anne. "Christchurch shootings: The doctrine of white superiority is alive and well in NZ." *Dominion Post*. 19 March, 2019.
Ship of Fools. Devised by the ensemble. Directed by Tony McCaffrey. Different Light Theatre. Awakenings Festival, Horsham, Victoria, Australia, 13–15 October, 2007.
The Earthquake in Chile. Directed by Peter Falkenberg and Richard Gough. St Mary's Church, Addington, Christchurch NZ. Body Festival. 13–16 October, 2011.
The History of Different Light. Devised by Different Light Theatre. Directed by Tony McCaffrey, Christchurch Arts Festival, NASDA Theatre, Christchurch, 1–3 August, 2019.

The Wizard of Oz. Devised by the ensemble. Directed by Tony McCaffrey. Different Light Theatre. NASDA Theatre, CPIT. Ignition Creative Festival, 18–21 November, 2010.

Wangh, Stephen. *An Acrobat of the Heart: A Physical Approach to Acting Inspired by the Work of Jerzy Grotowski*. Vintage Books, 2000.

6 From the Theatre to the After Party

The after party

On the last night of the performance of *The History of Different Light*, the Different Light performers were given artists' passes by the Christchurch Arts Festival organizers and told to present them as invitations to the Festival After Party. This was a dance party with food and drink held within an industrial venue near where Different Light had performed. After the last performance, we all walked and wheeled from the theatre to the party. The Different Light group was earlier to arrive than any of the other artists or partygoers. We went into a room away from the dance floor waiting for others to arrive and, due to unforeseen circumstances, ended up locked in a room that contained a small supply of drinks and a cake. Matthew Phelan launched into cutting and eating the cake saying, 'This is the life'. Due to a hole in the wall, we were able to observe other partygoers arrive onto the dance floor. Eventually, we were freed. The dance floor had filled up. People kept to their groups. Outside the building, a parent of one of the performers waited in the cold for their offspring to choose to leave the party. That person knew their parent was waiting. Central Christchurch late at night does not constitute a hospitable environment for a visibly learning disabled person. In due course, after a short time on the dance floor that performer and the rest of us went home. The After Party that had been so anticipated by the performers did not live up to the expectations that had been raised by the artists' passes and invitations. It struck me that inclusion needs to be about more than merely being invited to an event. It means accommodation and access intimacy. Inclusion may well be a journey, but for many disabled people, it is a journey with many false starts, a circular journey from exclusion to the promise of inclusion and back. Going from the Theatre to the After Party proved to be a disappointing transition. Transition is a process not an event. It may not always be possible to identify and achieve – or move closer – to one's career and lifestyle aspirations.

The History of Different Light was the last performance in which Ben Morris participated. Morris had been with the group since the early workshops in 2004. His contribution to the work of the company had

DOI: 10.4324/9781003083658-7

been substantial. His living or accommodation situation had often been fraught with difficulties. A semi-documentary film that had been made at SkillWise, an organization for some 300 learning disabled people of which he was also a member, included recurring scenes in which Morris attempted to seek flat-sharing accommodation. He was seeking such an arrangement rather than staying in the halfway house about which he had contributed the 'one sock in a washing machine' sequence in *Three Ecologies of Different Light*. After *The History of Different Light*, he decided to focus on working with Many Hats Theatre Company, a company operating out of SkillWise.

Having seen *The History of Different Light*, two performers with Down Syndrome, who also worked with Josie Noble at Jolt Dance, then joined the company. Biddy Steffens quickly established herself as an integral member of the group with a strong work ethos, commitment to equal opportunities for women, and advocacy for the environment of Aotearoa/New Zealand. Matthew Swaffield also joined the group. He is a part-time volunteer firefighter at a rural fire station on the outskirts of Christchurch.

The journeying of Māui

In Mātauranga Māori, there are various accounts of the journeys of Māui: Māui, the traveller, Māui the trickster. Hargrave in *Theatres of Learning Disability* devotes the concluding section to a chapter on stereotypes of learning disability to the learning disabled performer as 'trickster' (132–7). If Māui's journey begins with his birth, then it is a precarious genesis. Born well before his time, with a frail body, nobody thought he could survive, and because of this, his mother decided to throw her child into the ocean. In other accounts, his mother threw her premature infant into the sea wrapped in a tress of hair from her topknot or 'tikitiki'. In the next phases of the evolution of Different Light the story and the journeyings of Māui became intertwined with that of the group. In the first instance, I wished to consult the group on their experiences and thoughts on travel for a proposed chapter for a book on 'How Disability Performance Travels' by members of the Performance and Disability Working Group of the International Federation for Theatre Research. The journeyings of Māui were familiar to the members of the group as they had been taught about it in school. Māui's adventures included his discovery of his family, the slowing of the sun, the fishing up of Aotearoa/New Zealand's North Island or in Te Reo Māori Te-Ika-a-Māui: the fish of Māui, and his bringing fire to the world. In the myth of origins, the attempted rejection of Māui at his premature birth was due to perceived disability. His mother tempered this rejection by throwing him into the sea with the support of her hair. I am grateful to Hemi Hoskins, Director of Māori Achievement at Ara Institute, for introducing me to the idea that the journey of Maui is also the journey of research. The researcher feels as if they are thrown into a hostile environment on their own, but the journey can only take place not as an individual, but with the support of others around them, and of others who came before them, in other words with the support of *whanau*. This applies equally to the journey of research and performance of Different Light. This journey has included geographical travel: touring overseas and within New Zealand, with all the issues of (lack of) access that involved. It has included the journeys of the actors in and around the quake-damaged and rebuilt city, and the journeying through theatrical forms: community theatre, dramatic theatre, site-specific, intermediality and intertextuality, collaborations, derives, and street performance, Pecha Kucha, conference presentations, online interactions, social media, performance research, and philosophy. This journeying has also included how the work of the company has 'travelled' or reached out to wider audiences than the public performances through analysis and documentation within academic books, chapters, articles, and courses. Different Light, the group, like Māui, had been thrown into the world in a rushed and imperfect state, but along the way had acquired some of the strategies of Māui the trickster. The group could only exist with the support of funders, institutions, families and caregivers, fellow artists, and practitioners as collaborators.

At the start of 2020, we were preparing to travel to the International Federation for Theatre Research conference at the National University of Ireland in Galway in July 2020 and subsequently to the Performance Philosophy Problems conference at the University of the Arts in Helsinki in June 2021when the COVID-19 pandemic put a stop to all plans to travel geographically. The Government of Aotearoa/New Zealand declared a State of National Emergency and the whole country went into a strict Level 4 lockdown on 25th March, 2020.

As with many other groups and organizations, Different Light Theatre continued to meet and have some form of contact through Zoom meetings, that started on 26 April 2020. As the country went up and down alert levels during the year the company only met in person in Alert Level One due to the compromised immunity and pre-existing conditions of members of the company. The regular meetings on Zoom were a way of maintaining regularity of contact and of adapting working methodologies to an online connection. It was important to allow for 'how are you travelling, how are you doing' conversations with individuals and with the whole group. It was also important to vary the methods of communication as much as Zoom would allow: sharing images, video extracts, participating on 'in the moment' writing' on a shared whiteboard and through the chat function. Sessions were reduced from three hours to one hour and tasks and discussions to a 20-minute maximum duration. Between sessions script extracts, mood board type images, and other materials were circulated prior to the brief meetings, with contingencies in place for those who might experience difficulties of whatever kind with accessing email.

Different Light floating in space and time imagining the future

Communicating with each other through Zoom boxes whilst separated in space, the initial devised material explored imagining Different Light in the future. This was heavily informed by the actors' familiarity with popular culture science fiction and outer space-based narratives. Some members of the group had extensive knowledge of the universes, tropes, paraphernalia, characters, and narrative conventions of this genre.

The spaceship sci-fi format allowed the performers to build character biographies, histories, relationships, secrets, and secret missions with which they were familiar from the soap opera world of *The Lonely and The Lovely* but translated to the crew of the 'Different Light', a spaceship on an 'intellectually disabled intelligence mission' to discover new worlds.

During 2020 and 2021, Different Light continued to meet and make theatre that might or might not be possible. This included a children's story based on a girl who was a wheelchair user and escaped from the isolation in the lockdown into fantasy, and the Englefield House Mysteries – a projected hybrid of animation and live performance based on imagining the history of an earthquake-abandoned building, a former orphanage, near Glen/Benjamin Burrows' new house. When the lockdowns were lifted we held meetings at his house when he was not well enough to attend, as was increasingly the case. Different Light Theatre continued to try to hold onto the practice of some form of live or hybrid theatre that was so materially threatened by the COVID pandemic. We attempted to keep alight the flame of live theatre online. We attempted to stay in touchless touch with each other.

The following are my field notes of the content of one of our online sessions together:

Travelling together, talking about travelling together overseas and locally, travel as research into moving through an ableist world, caring for each other when ill or not up to attending or fully participating in rehearsal, Zooming or video messaging, sharing refreshment breaks and meals, shopping for things with which to celebrate birthdays and anniversaries, doing trivia quizzes, inventing personal and group trivia quizzes, reminiscing on the history of the group, planning impossible performances, dipping in to different narrative genres, planning impossible journeys, in-jokes, disciplining each other and ourselves to act our age, learning about other learning disabled artists, performers and activists, word association, singing freely, unashamedly, badly, writing new lyrics, checking in with what people are doing, how people are doing, being bored, trying out different kinds of rhetoric, planning for future presentations and performances, reading and discussing easy-read material for other productions, playing with words, variations on a theme of in-jokes, thinking we are serious and working seriously, talking about the hobbyhorses of Transition the carousel of hobby courses that process people with intellectual disabilities in New Zealand after they leave High School in their 20s, unplanned humorous intervention by Peter Rees: Peter repeating, Peter the repeater, Peter petering out ....

The learning disabled artists are present online

In the lockdowns and isolation of the pandemic many people were going from the theatre to the after-party, from the energy of social gathering and interaction to uncertainty and fear of sharing the same space and air that seems so integral to the experience of theatre. The 'human pause' of the pandemic also called into question the environmental costs of existing habits of travel between countries, travel to and from the theatre, and of trying to revert to the pre-pandemic 'normal'. Online participation in theatre offered both the opportunity for increased access to people whose mobility was limited but also presented difficulties for those not wealthy enough to have internet access or for whom engaging with an online world was still fraught with sensory or processing difficulties. Disabled people with compromised immunities in those countries where lockdowns occurred said 'Welcome to our world' but in the rush to re-establish the in-person contact and free movement of consumers across borders pandemic restrictions continue to be lifted even in the face of new variants and increasing case and death numbers.

Theatre attempted in various ways to incorporate an online dimension. Initiatives to move learning disabled theatre online included the Crossing the Line Festival, which had been scheduled for an in-person iteration in Galway in 2020, but which in September 2021 took place entirely online. This version of the festival was a partnership between six European learning disabled theatre companies: Theater Babel, Rotterdam, Netherlands, Blue Teapot Theatre, Galway, Eire, Mind the Gap, Bradford, UK, Moomsteatern, Malmö, Sweden, Théâtre de l'Oiseau Mouche, Roubaix, France and Teatr 21, Warsaw, Poland. The festival was streamed online and free on selected dates over a period from 16th September to 19th November, 2021. The online events of the festival consisted of videos of performance, documentaries, and discussions on the 'accessibility of artistic education' for learning disabled artists in each country.

The paths of development that emerged in the discussions aligned very closely with that of Different Light Theatre. To take one example, Moomsteatern of Malmö, Sweden, was founded in 1987 and set out to include learning disabled artists in 'mainstream artistic education and theatrical life' without conventional educational or therapeutic goals. The company emerged out of an adult education institution and was connected, through non-disabled personnel to Swedish universities which gave the company prestige and access to resources and funding in the pursuit of research. The company adopts a different methodology and practice to Different Light in that they espouse a 'professional model of theatre'. They have a clear methodology and ethos that the practice of theatre is not an idealized democracy but operates from a hierarchical model of inclusion in which the final decisions are made by the (non-disabled) artistic director as that is their profession, just as the learning disabled actors' profession is to collaborate but primarily to work as actors.

Different Light Theatre were also able to participate in such discussion having been invited to participate in an online panel 'Include Art: a dialogue on theatre-making involving people with intellectual disabilities' organized by Vocational Training Centre Margarita, Athens (established in 1979) under the auspices of the Greek Ministry of Culture and Sports. This took place on 17th December, 2021 and the learning disabled artists involved were Josie Noble, Peter Rees, and Isaac Tait of Different Light Theatre, Lawrie Morris of Blue Apple Theatre, Winchester, UK, Guillaume Paps of Créahm, Brussels, Belgium, Justin Mellhuish of Hijinx Theatre, Cardiff, Wales. Also participating were the non-disabled artistic directors of these companies, Richard Conlon of Blue Apple, Ben Pettitt-Wade of Hijinx, Stephan Stock of Theater HORA of Zurich, Switzerland and Vassias Tsokopoulos, Eleana Papachristou and other representatives from VTC Margarita, Athens.

The learning disabled performers were able to participate via panel discussions or the presentation of videos of performance and interviews. It became clear that performers from each company appeared in alignment with each company's choice of methodologies, aesthetics and paths of development, whether these were toward Shakespearean performance, avant-garde experimentation, performance art, movement-based theatre and mask work, or a more heterogeneous, irreverent, Antipodean mix of performance styles. It was, however, also interesting to observe how the kairos and pressures to perform on the online panel are not always congenial or amicable to learning disabled performers. In addition, the 'voices' of the learning disabled performers were to some extent influenced by the presence of non-disabled facilitators more at ease in such a format and whose verbal fluency and articulacy highlighted educational and experiential epistemic injustice. 'Dialogue' on learning disabled theatre seems to be still subject to certain inequities or to require an ability to listen to the polyvocal mix in such a way as to listen into speech the participation of the learning disabled artists. In this respect, Per.Arts in Serbia have implemented some interesting initiatives with their annual Dis_Festival that has taken place both online and in-person and with a series of conversations with disability culture artists, both disabled and non-disabled. Learning disabled artists and creators Natalija Vladislevic and Dalibor Sandor of Per.Arts have taken a prominent role in these online discussions in which they comment on their artistic processes and define the terms of their participation.

Care, collaboration, and conviviality

In 2020, Different Light was invited to contribute to a Key Group presentation for the Performance Philosophy Problems Conference due to take place at the University of the Arts Helsinki. The invitation was to give a 90-minute presentation with Dave Calvert, speaking on conviviality (see 2020) and Kate Maguire-Rosier (see Czymoch et al) and Janet Gibson (2020) conducting a dialogue on care in disability dance and dementia performance. Different Light were scheduled to present on collaboration. The conference was postponed due to the COVID pandemic, eventually taking place as a hybrid in-person and online event in June 2022. By this time, Angie Douglas, a strong female presence and another motorized wheelchair user like Glen/Benjamin Burrows, had joined the group. None of us were able to travel to Helsinki so the group devised a ten-minute video to be presented at the opening of the conference and I drafted a paper attempting to weave the words of the group into a kind of performative academic paper on our collaboration. In addition, two members of the group, Josie Noble and Peter Rees were present on Zoom during the entire 90-minute presentation, included 30 minutes devoted to questions. The text the performers devised and that was presented, captioned, at the conference was as follows:

In the NASDA theatre, a black box theatre.
JOSIE NOBLE AND BIDDY STEFFENS (smiling): Hello, Helsinki!
ANGIE DOUGLAS (arriving on stage in her wheelchair and approaching the camera): Hello, Helsinki.
JOSIE NOBLE and BIDDY STEFFENS (running onstage to join her): Hello, Helsinki!
MATTHEW PHELAN (running onstage to join them): Tahi, Rua, Toru, Wha!
ISAAC TAIT, DAMIAN BUMMAN and MATTHEW SWAFFIELD run on stage.
ALL (waving, looking at the camera): Hello, Helsinki! Hei, Helsinki!
DAMIAN BUMMAN (coming right up to the camera): How can we get to Helsinki?
How can we do that?
BIDDY STEFFENS (smiling): We can communicate with you via Zoom
PETER REES (his face is on a laptop in the theatre as he is isolating at home due to the pandemic): Welcome to Performance Philosophy Problems.
ALL: Welcome!
MATTHEW SWAFFIELD: Haere mai Haere mai
ALL: Haere mai.
MATTHEW PHELAN: What are Performance Philosophy Problems?
JOSIE NOBLE: We are Performance Philosophy Problems.
PETER REES: No, you are!
ALL (to each other and the camera): You are! You are!
BIDDY STEFFENS (interrupting the shouting): Guys! Please stay focused.
MATTHEW PHELAN: We are Different Light Theatre, a theatre group from Christchurch, New Zealand.
PETER REES: We've been through earthquakes-
ANGIE DOUGLAS: floods and massacres-
MATTHEW SWAFFIELD: fires-

JOSIE NOBLE: viruses, a global pandemic-
ANGIE DOUGLAS: lockdowns and isolations-
BIDDY STEFFENS: anti-mandate protests-
ISAAC TAIT: and war on Ukraine.
DAMIAN BUMMAN (coming right up to the camera): And now Isaac's poem.
ISAAC TAIT: So much depends on our support workers
   So much depends on vaccinations
   So much depends on police
   So much depends on our lives matter
   So much depends on thinking
MATTHEW PHELAN: Now we are going to ask you some questions-
BIDDY STEFFENS: For our research.
JOSIE NOBLE: Please answer them to the best of your ability
PETER REES: Number one. What is your disability?
ISAAC TAIT: Number two. Who are your caregivers?
ANGIE DOUGLAS: Number three. How do you get in and out of bed?
MATTHEW PHELAN: Unfortunately we don't have any time for your answers.
JOSIE NOBLE: You will need to take your answers away with you.
ANGIE DOUGLAS: I try to talk to people all the time but they walk away from me. By the way I use a hoist to get in and out of bed.
PETER REES: Question four. Why did the person in a motorized wheelchair cross the road?
MATTHEW PHELAN: *How* can the person in the motorized wheelchair cross the road?
BIDDY STEFFENS: Hei, Esa Kirkkopelto!
ALL: Hei, Esa!
PETER REES: Esa Kirkkopelto told us that we need to do something like a performance but we can rehearse it.
BIDDY STEFFENS: He looks like ... he looks like he is a professional, he's been doing this for a while.
MATTHEW PHELAN: I've been doing theatre for a while.
ALL: I have too! Same here! Me too! Me too! Me too!
JOSIE NOBLE: The last public performance we did was *The History of Different Light* in the Christchurch Arts Festival in 2019.
ISAAC TAIT: And since then we had to rethink what we mean by performance.
MATTHEW SWAFFIELD: We can make theatre together.
ISAAC TAIT: And thinking.
ANGIE DOUGLAS: Right now-
JOSIE NOBLE: we are in an Omicron surge here in Christchurch.
MATTHEW PHELAN: To protect ourselves and others we need to meet on Zoom.
PETER REES: On Zoom you can talk to your mates-
ANGIE DOUGLAS: we can laugh with them-
BIDDY STEFFENS: we can share filters or share screens with them.
JOSIE NOBLE: On Zoom you can't be with them in person-

From the Theatre to the After Party   187

MATTHEW PHELAN: you can't hug them-
JOSIE NOBLE: you can't drink coffee with them or share a meal with them.
MATTHEW PHELAN: The question is – can you do theatre on Zoom?
ISAAC TAIT: The question is – can you do thinking on Zoom?

This intervention by learning disabled artists in an international academic conference was followed by my paper presentation. The beginning of this was a pepeha or formal greeting in Te Reo Māori, given with the proviso that we are Tangata Tiriti, people of the treaty (of Waitangi), and that in the land on which we stand and whence we speak (our turangawaewae) we are uneasy guests, uneasier hosts. Drawing from the presentation by the learning disabled artists I asked the questions 'How can I get to the learning disabled artists?' and 'How can Different Light get to learning disabled theatre?' We started from my assumption that we were getting to know theatre and each other: that *We can communicate via theatre*. Community theatre. Theatre can help us find what we have and hold in common. *We can make theatre together*. Performers and audience. Disabled and non-disabled. *We did something like performance, and we rehearsed it*. At times we needed to freeze or stop or slow down what we meant as process and performance. In my understanding of theatre *so much depended on* resonant voices, *so much depended on* engaged and articulate bodies, *so much depended on* 'scarce half made up' ideas, and on words, words, words. This one particular understanding of theatre then came into contact with the learning disabled artists. It has taken me 18 years to listen, if only a little, to them, to try to attend and attune to them. In the theatre resulting from this encounter the learning disabled artists are uneasy guests, uneasier hosts. Learning disabled artists make for uneasy guests, uneasier hosts in the academy, at the conference, at the symposium. The symposium as drinking and eating, a convivial discussion after a banquet: an after party. *On Zoom you can't drink coffee with them or share a meal with them.*

Every week ten of us, two in motorized wheelchairs, follow our customary lines to take a break from devising and rehearsal. To get to the café we cross a six-lane road with two sets of traffic lights. They are on timers. Green man. Red man flashing. Beepbeepbeepbeep. Traffic revving. Red man. Zoom. They're off. There is never enough time. Why would a person in a motorized wheelchair want to cross the road? On Zoom we talk over each other, miss turns, look at ourselves, cannot feel the non-verbal cues of the person responding, the slight delay, the freeze, the microphone disabled. What of the zoomtime of necrocapitalism and the Socio-Ecological Disaster, can we do theatre, can we do thinking, in this zoomtime?

At the conference, in response to the Different Light presentation, Laura Cull Ó Maoilearca questioned how we, meaning the academic members of the conference, could be together in the conference (Zoom) space and in academia with the performers of Different Light. She referred to the well-known tenet of disability justice 'Nothing about us without us'. She asked how the presentation from Different Light makes an academic paper look and feel in this space? How we can be together in conferences in meaningful, inclusive ways? What is aboutness? What is with-us-ness? These are the continuing questions of this book and of the praxis and research of Different Light.

Peter Rees' response to this question was:

> Well, I've been doing theatre for quite a while through my academic years at school up to now with two different drama groups. I've been working towards the conference with my presence and also with my disability which is Down Syndrome and I am so honoured to live a wonderful long life with this disability and I do have some help and support from my parents and my sisters as well as my extended family including my grandparents who sadly have passed away and I miss them and it's just brought out the inner hero in me.

Rees acknowledged the support on the journey of research and theatre of, precisely, *whanau*: family both living and ancestral.

A few days later, Different Light were able to have some sort of presence in the meetings of the Performance and Disability Working Group of the International Federation for Theatre Research conference at the University of Iceland in Helsinki and online. This took the form of a video postcard sent by the performers greeting the people they knew who would be attending the conference in person and addressing in their own ways the theme of the conference, shifting centres (in the middle of nowhere):

MATTHEW PHELAN: The centre of Different Light is Ōtautahi, Aotearoa.
JOSIE NOBLE: The centre of Different Light is everyone here – in a cold theatre.
ISAAC TAIT: It's thinking.
ANGIE DOUGLAS: It's Glen and Angie.
JOSIE NOBLE: The centre of Different Light is acting.
GLEN BURROWS: We are.
MATTHEW PHELAN: Performance.
BIDDY STEFFENS: We do scriptwriting.
GLEN BURROWS: Yeah.
ANGIE DOUGLAS: We do fun things.
ISAAC TAIT: Dancing also. Yeah.
JOSIE NOBLE: And also the centre is everyone here and devising scripts.
ISAAC TAIT: People's birthdays (laughter)
GLEN BURROWS: Yeah. Yeah.

Glen Burrows had been too ill to participate in the video sent to Helsinki but had recovered sufficiently to be able to be present for the video to

Reykjavik. As with the Helsinki conference, I presented a paper online that tried to weave around the brief contributions of the learning disabled artists and to place this in the context of the time at which the conference was held. This coincided with the start of Matariki, the Māori New Year which was celebrated on 24th June, 2022 by the whole country as a public holiday, the first such holiday celebrated in Aotearoa/New Zealand based in indigenous culture. Disability-led dance company Touch Compass first presented InMotion Matariki parade in 2019. The company interestingly claims a disability provenance for the constellation of stars that gives the Matariki Festival its name. Matariki is an abbreviation for 'Ngā Mata o te Ariki Tāwhirimātea' – the eyes of the god Tāwhirimātea.

> It refers to a cluster of stars in Europe known as the Pleiades. According to Māori tradition, Tāwhirimātea, the god of the wind was so angry when his siblings separated their parents, Ranginui the sky father and Papatuanuku, the earth mother, that he tore out his eyes and threw them into the heavens.

At the time of writing Different Light Theatre is scheduled to present a live performance at the ADSA Conference at the University of Auckland, 6th–9th December, 2022. *The Journeyings of Different Light* devised by the performers is intended to address the conference theme of 'Travelling Together' It is also my intention to accompany this performance with an academic paper. Isaac Tait has made an intervention into this intention by producing his own academic paper which will be part of Different Light's participation:

<u>Burn before and don't <u>consider</u> <u>reading</u></u>
A Academic paper by Isaac tait
Disability, Theatre, Philosophy.
Hi, I am Isaac and I have a disability.
Think of it more like this. Hi, I am Isaac, and I have a label.
How can I identify
Give me your twitch, your phones, your huddled masses yearning to breathe free! Oh, academic papers … there are lots of barriers for people with disabilities to become academic. It is too hard to get help with a disability. So, academic papers … a real time waste for us.
People with disabilities are seen as people that only operate on the level of an eighth grader, and are treated on the same level as eighth graders. Academic studies show that. Stanford.
I was walking in a park one day and this guy was talking to me, while he shaved his beard, an inconsistent rambler, he thought he knew me. He was living in his car. Labelling people is not helpful in the long run. Everybody should be allowed to have the choice of what they call themselves. I don't know what I would call myself. An artist.

Watching the sun go down as I write about labels on Father's Day, the sunset golden like a painting by Turner and I walk home. I tell myself stop thinking about the guy in his car with his girlfriend, him and his behaviour that was very obscure, you couldn't see what was going on because it was dark. Stop thinking about the guy in his car with his girlfriend. Positive vibes. Stop thinking.

Where is Isaac's intensity? Maybe somewhere in the future.

There should be more scholars in philosophers with Down syndrome what is normal is it different?

Read more scholars and phosphors in this room with what is philosophy?

Franz Kafka was a German-speaking Bohemian novelist and short-story writer, widely regarded as one of the major figures of 20th-century literature. The philosophy of the absurd. Witch takes me to the ideas of imagination but I am not to have one for I have a disability or mental illnesses. Or autism Franz Kafka would like The modern day. The absurd way of life. Or he might not. We may never know.

Be happily trade war for peace wounded.

Bleeding thou the gift shop.

Gun's germ's and Ukraine.

Something in the way. Year my disability. Philosophers like Sigmund Freud Aristotle Socrates should be able to have Academics with disability or mental illnesses. Labels from all walks of life.

Your motion to dismiss is denied

'Hell is—other people!' jean-Paul sartre

Sound's like autism in the way that autistic people don't like to be touched have and are more sense The sensors. Touch, sounds

Holistic health were you have to to think about Emotional, mental, physical, Spiritual health.

We could all read Friedrich Nietzsche or burn books. You don't see philosophers with any disability or Academic Writing that would be helpful in today and traveling to future. We're is intensity in my philosophy....

Every week ten of us, two in motorized wheelchairs, follow the footpath to take a break from devising and rehearsal. The footpath still buckles awkwardly in places, the traces of the 2010–11 earthquakes, evidence beneath our feet and wheels of tectonic shifts, of a geological time that stretches back two to four billion years. What is the centre of Different Light? Isaac Tait responds 'Birthdays'. Everybody laughs. We mark these times. We mark our time. Over the 18 years, two key performers, John Lambie and Louise Payne, have died. In the words of Māori playwright Briar Grace Smith in *Purapurawhetu*: 'When someone special dies, their spirit joins the others in a wild tango in the night sky'. As a learning disabled theatre company, we need to pay attention to modes of knowing that go beyond the rational, the normate, and the neurotypical, we need to weave into our mix of togetherness and untogetherness the knowledge of tangata whenua, and we need

Figure 6.1 Different Light Theatre on a break, Christchurch, 2011. Left to right and clockwise around the tables: Michael Stanley, Peter Rees, Louise Payne, Theresa King, Paul McCaffrey, John Lambie, Tony McCaffrey, Josie Noble, Andrew Dever, Shawn O'Rourke, Julia Guthrey, Isaac Tait, Ben Morris, and Glen Burrows. Image: Stuart Lloyd-Harris for Different Light Theatre.

to heed the cries of the planet. We continue to walk and wheel down the pavements of Otautahi, Christchurch: we grow old together. Below us Papatuanuku, the earth mother, for the moment, is still, supportive. If we look up, we will see, or we will feel, the stars of Matariki. The stars of Matariki are weaving in our ageing, vulnerable, precarious, precious bodies. They are dancing within us.

References

Blue Apple Theatre. https://blueappletheatre.com. Accessed 10 January, 2022.
Calvert, Dave. "Care and debility in collaborations between non-disabled and learning disabled theatre makers." In *Performing Care: New Perspectives on Socially Engaged Performance*. Edited by Amanda Stuart Fisher and James Thompson. Manchester University Press, 2020, pp. 85–102.
"Care, Collaboration and Conviviality," *Key Group presentation at* Performance Philosophy Problems: How does Performance Philosophy Collaborate? *Fifth Biennial conference of Performance Philosophy network*. University of the Arts, Helsinki, Finland, Online. 16 June, 2022.
Créahm. https://creahm.be. Accessed 10 January, 2022.
Crossing the Line Festival. https://www.crossingtheline-festival.com. Accessed 4 October, 2022.

Czymoch, C., Maguire-Rosier, K. and Schmidt, Y. "International percolations of disability aesthetics in dance and theatre." In *Theatre and Internationalization: Perspectives from Australia, Germany, and Beyond.* Edited by Ulrike Garde and John R. Severn. Routledge, 2021, pp. 232–249

Dis_Festival, https://kalendar.novisad2022.rs/en/events/per-art-festival-3/

Gibson, Janet. *Dementia, Narrative, and Performance: Staging Reality, Reimagining Identities.* Palgrave Macmillan, 2020.

Hijinx Theatre Company. https://www.hijinx.org.uk. Accessed 07 December, 2022.

Margarita Vocational Training Centre. https://www.eeamargarita.gr/en/home. Accessed 07 December, 2022.

Sandor, Dalibor. "In Conversation with Learning Disabled Artist Dalibor Sandor." https://www.facebook.com/europebeyondaccess/videos/312829623073176/. Accessed 07 December, 2022.

Theater HORA. https://hora.ch/en/hora. Accessed 07 December, 2022.

The History of Different Light, Devised by Different Light Theatre. Directed by Tony, McCaffrey, Christchurch Arts Festival, NASDA Theatre, Christchurch, 1–3 August, 2019.

Vladislavljevic, Natalija, "Dance, Politics, Disability, and the Body." https://www.disabilityartsinternational.org/resources/europe-beyond-access-dance-politics-disability-the-body/. Accessed 07 December, 2022.

———. "Inside Natalija Vladislavljevic's Notebook." https://www.facebook.com/europebeyondaccess/videos/334593454722948/ Accessed 07 December 2022.

Appendix: Chronology of Different Light Theatre Performances, Presentations, and Participants

2004 *A Different Light.* Southern Ballet Theatre, Christchurch.

Stuart Craig, Ben Ellenbroek, Michael Krammer, John Lambie, Ben Morris, Shawn O'Rourke, Matthew Phelan, and Michael Stanley. Support: Cloe Anngow, Janette Dovey, Amiria Grenell, Paul McCaffrey, Kim TePairi Garrett, and Carrie Wilson.

2006 *The Birds.* Southern Ballet Theatre, Christchurch.

Stuart Craig, Ben Ellenbroek, John Lambie, Ben Morris, Shawn O'Rourke, Matthew Phelan, and Michael Stanley. Support: Julia Guthrie, Kim TePairi Garrett, Paul McCaffrey, and Catriona Toop.

2006 *Dante.*

Stuart Craig, Ben Ellenbroek, John Lambie, David Macnamara, Ben Morris, Shawn O'Rourke, Matthew Phelan, and Michael Stanley. Support: Meli Bach, Merrin Cavell, Kyle Chuen, Amiria Grenell, Julia Guthrie, Paul McCaffrey, Tola Newberry, Kim TePairi Garrett, and Catriona Toop.

2007 *Ship of Fools.* Southern Ballet Theatre, Christchurch and Awakenings Festival, Horsham, Victoria, Australia.

Stuart Craig, Ben Ellenbroek, John Lambie, Ben Morris, Shawn O'Rourke, Matthew Phelan, and Michael Stanley. Support: Meli Bach, Julia Guthrey, Roslen Langton, Paul McCaffrey, Tola Newberry, and Kim TePairi Garrett.

2008 *Frankenstein's Children.* NASDA Theatre and Christchurch Town Hall.

Damian Bumman, Glen Burrows, Verity Carter, Stuart Craig, Ben Ellenbroek, John Lambie, Shawn O'Rourke, Matthew Phelan, Michael Stanley, and Isaac Tait. Support: Chris Reddington and Kim TePairi Garrett.

2009 *The Poor Dears.* NASDA Theatre and Southern Ballet Theatre.

Damian Bumman, Glen Burrows, Stuart Craig, Ben Ellenbroek, Theresa King, John Lambie, Drew McLean, Shawn O'Rourke, Louise Payne, Matthew Phelan, Michael Stanley, and Isaac Tait. Support: Demarnia Lloyd, Stuart Lloyd Harris, and Kim TePairi Garrett.

2010 *Is it Normal, Any Different?* Powerhouse Museum Sydney. Video and Question and Answer.

Damian Bumman, Glen Burrows, Theresa King, John Lambie, Ben Morris, Matthew Phelan, Michael Stanley, and Isaac Tait.

2010 *The Wizard of Oz.* NASDA Theatre, Christchurch.

Damian Bumman, Glen Burrows, Ben Ellenbroek, Theresa King, John Lambie, Drew McLean, Shawn O'Rourke, Andrew Oswin, Louise Payne, Matthew Phelan, Michael Stanley, and Isaac Tait. Support: Stuart Lloyd-Harris and Kim TePairi Garrett.

2011 *The Earthquake in Chile.* Site-specific collaboration with Free Theatre Christchurch and Richard Gough.

St Mary's Church, Addington, Christchurch. Different Light participants: Alan Barnes, Glen Burrows, Andrew Dever, Theresa King, John Lambie, Josie Noble, Andrew Oswin, Louise Payne, and Isaac Tait. Support: Kim TePairi Garrett.

2011 *Still Lives.* 20-minute version. Society for Disability Studies Conference, San Jose, California, USA.

Glen Burrows, Ben Morris, and Isaac Tait. Support: Stuart Lloyd-Harris and Kim TePairi Garrett.

2012 *Still Lives.* 40-minute version. Ludus Festival and Performance Studies international conference, University of Leeds, UK.

Glen Burrows, Ben Morris, and Isaac Tait. Support: Stuart Lloyd-Harris and Kim TePairi Garrett.

2012 *Still Lives, Christchurch.* NASDA Theatre Christchurch.

Alan Barnes, Damian Bumman, Glen Burrows, Andrew Dever, Rebecca Flint, Theresa King, John Lambie, Ben Morris, Andrew Oswin, Louise Payne, Matthew Phelan, Peter Rees, Michael Stanley, Isaac Tait, and Natalie Walton. Support: Toni Jones, Stuart Lloyd-Harris, and Kim TePairi Garrett.

2012 *Rebuilding Christchurch: A Different Soap Opera.* The Concourse, Chatswood, Sydney, Australia.

Andrew Dever, Rebecca Flint, Ben Morris, Josie Noble, Matthew Phelan, and Caroline Quick, Peter Rees. Support: Kim TePairi Garrett.

2013 *The Lonely and the Lovely.*

Damian Bumman, Glen Burrows, Andrew Dever, Rebecca Flint, Ben Morris, Josie Noble, Andrew Oswin, Matthew Phelan, Caroline Quick, Peter Rees, Isaac Tait, and Natalie Walton. Support: Theodore Grenell, Tatiana Josz, and Kim TePairi Garrett.

2013 *Canterbury Tales.* Site-specific performance in collaboration with FESTA and Free Theatre, Christchurch.

Damian Bumman, Glen Burrows Rebecca Flint, Ben Morris, Josie Noble, Louise Payne, Matthew Phelan Peter Rees, and Isaac Tait. Support: Kim TePairi Garrett.

2014 Petra Kuppers' *Masquerade, Olimpias* and other performance research projects.

Damian Bumman, Glen Burrows Rebecca Flint, Ben Morris, Josie Noble, Louise Payne, Matthew Phelan Peter Rees, and Isaac Tait.

2015 *Waikuku Beach.* Petra Kuppers.

Glen Burrows, Andrew Dever, Ben Morris, and Peter Rees. Support: Kim TePairi Garrett.

2016 *The Three Ecologies of Different Light.* University of Melbourne.

Glen Burrows, Andrew Dever, Ben Morris, Josie Noble, Matthew Phelan, Peter Rees, and Isaac Tait.

2017 *I Belong in the Past and the Future and the Very Now.* ADSA Conference, Auckland University of Technology.

Glen Burrows, Andrew Dever, Ben Morris, Josie Noble, Matthew Phelan, Peter Rees, and Isaac Tait.

2018 Performance research.

Glen Burrows, Andrew Dever, Ben Morris, Josie Noble, Matthew Phelan, Peter Rees, and Isaac Tait.

2019 *The History of Different Light.* Arts Festival Christchurch, NASDA Theatre.

Glen Burrows, Ben Morris, Josie Noble, Matthew Phelan, Peter Rees, and Isaac Tait. Support: Sofie Martinsdotter.

2020–2021 Zoom workshops.

Damian Bumman, Glen Burrows, Josie Noble, Matthew Phelan, Peter Rees, Biddy Steffens, Matthew Swaffield, and Isaac Tait.

2021 Online panel organized by VTC Margarita, Athens, Greece.

Josie Noble, Peter Rees, and Isaac Tait.

2022 Contribution to 'Care, Collaboration, and Conviviality' Performance Philosophy Problems conference, University of the Arts, Helsinki, Finland and online.

Video contribution: Damian Bumman, Angelia Douglas, Josie Noble, Matthew Phelan, Peter Rees, Biddy Steffens, Matthew Swaffield, and Isaac Tait. Zoom participation: Josie Noble and Peter Rees.

2022 Contribution to IFTR Performance and Disability Working Group, IFTR Conference, University of Iceland, Reykjavik and online.

Damian Bumman, Glen Burrows, Angelia Douglas, Josie Noble, Matthew Phelan, Peter Rees, Biddy Steffens, Matthew Swaffield, and Isaac Tait.

2022 *The Journeyings of Different Light.* ADSA Conference, University of Auckland.

Damian Bumman, Glen Burrows, Angelia Douglas, Josie Noble, Matthew Phelan, Peter Rees, Biddy Steffens, Matthew Swaffield, and Isaac Tait.

Index

Note: *Italicized* pages refer to figures.

ableism 12, 15, 21, 26, 51, 86
ablenationalism 29
abuse 9, 54, 89, 101
access 3, 6, 10, 16, 26, 29–32, 35, 51, 53–54, 64–65, 69, 84, 90, 92, 95, 114, 124–130, 138–139, 142–143, 146–147, 152–153, 156, 160, 162, 171, 179, 181, 183
Access All Areas 26–27
access intimacy 179
'after party' 179–180
Agamben, Giorgio 11
agency 1, 15–16, 18, 21, 23, 62–63, 142
agora 49
akroasis 4, 84
All Incomplete 30, 48
Al Noor Mosque 174–175
Ames, Margaret 21–22, 158–159, 172
anarchic anti-archive 9
Aotearoa 80, 103, 139, 149, 174, 180–181, 188–189
archive 8–9, 64, 67, 73, 93–96, 111, 116, 139, 170
Atlantic slave trade 15–16
Australasian Association for Theatre, Drama and Performance Studies (ADSA) 35
'authentic' voice 1, 12, 14
autism 8, 49, 190
autistic 4, 7, 9, 27, 31, 62, 106, 190
autonomy 1, 10, 16, 18, 21, 23, 34, 111, 156

Back to Back Theatre 4, 26, 30, 32, 77, 162; *see also The Shadow Whose Prey the Hunter Becomes*

Bairstow, Liam 27
Barnes, Alan 132, 139
'beformance' 75
being together or being-with in performance event 5
Bel, Jérôme 17, 20–21, 26
Bleeker, Maaike 21
Blue Apple Theatre 27, 184
Blue Teapot Theatre 26
Boal, Augusto 33, 58
Boone, Christopher 27
bourgeois 'self' 15
Bracken, Thomas 175
Burrows, Glen 77, 85, 90–91, *91*, 92–95, 97, 99, 101–102, 110, 114–115, 119, 121, 124–129, 131–132, 136–137, 142–143, 146, 153, 156–157, 159–163, 165–171, 173, 182, 185, 188, *191*

call to order 5
Calvert, Dave 5, 19–22, 125, 185
Canterbury Tales 35, 94, 104, 147–149, 159–160
captions 35, 45, 99, 137
care 1–3, 5, 9, 18–20, 49, 54, 57, 59–60, 81, 87, 92, 107, 115, 133, 156, 161, 167, 169, 185
Carriageworks 42
Carter, Verity 95
cerebral palsy 8, 9, 90, 101, 125, 137
Chan, Michael 49
Christchurch Arts Festival 35, 167, 175, *176*, 179
clinamen 56–57
co-creating learning disabled theatre 6

198 Index

collaboration 1, 9, 14, 17–19, 22, 26, 35, 47, 49–50, 55, 61, 129, 149, 153–154, 159, 181, 184–185
collage of voices 7
company ethos 33, 55, 58–59, 61
conscious neologism 75
consumer capitalism 29
Contained 19
conviviality 5, 9, 20, 50, 125, 133, 169, 185
COVID-19 pandemic 29, 181–182, 185
Craig, Stuart 78, 82, 87, 91, 99, 132
creative enabler 18
crip time 4, 10, 19, 31, 84, 116
Crossing the Line Festival 26, 183
Cyrff Ystwyth 21
Cull Ó Maoilearca, Laura 187

deconstruction 11
Deligny, Fernand 7
dérives 35, 152–154, 181
Derrida, Jacques 11–12, 24–25, 25, 53–54; aporia 55; paradox of hospitality and hostility 33, 52–54
Dever, Andrew 95, 144, 157, 161–162, 163, 165–166, *191*
devising process 6, 8, 21, 24–25, 30, 33, 42, 45, 47, 57–59, 61, 63, 66, 74, 78, 81, 87, 90, 92, 96, 98, 100, 103, 105, 107–108, 111, 116, 118, 120–123, 135–136, 138, 140, 158–162, 167, 170, 187
différance in voice 11, 45
A Different Light 56, 58–61; characters and identities 62; first public performance 59; group sequences 61; self-devising/improvisation 61, 66, 69, 73–74, 77; voices of performers 61–81
Different Light Theatre 2–3, 5, 7–8, 23, 32, 36, *191*; anarchive of 9; archiving or transcribing communications 63; *The Birds* 56, 75, 77, 81; collaboration 185; community of performers and audience 56–57; *Dante* 56, 74, 77–78, 81; *A Different Light* 56, 58–61; as dramatic theatre 84–85; exploration and training 55; female voices in 95–97; first performance 8; *Frankenstein's Children* 85, 90–91; future 182–183; *The History of Different Light* 167–175, 179; *I Belong in the Past and the Future and the Very Now* 164–167; *The Lonely and The Lovely* 35, 80, 96, 105, 114, 138–147; membership 8; narrative framework 57–58; *The Poor Dears* 34, 62, 71, 85, 100–102, 106–112, 114; *Ship of Fools* 85–89; theatre company ethos 55, 61; *Three Ecologies of Different Light* 156–163; use of assistive devices 92–95; voices of performers 61–81, 102–106; workshops 33, 54–56
Disabled Theater 17, 20–21
disciplinary formations 3, 12, 34, 112, 164, 166–167
Dis_Lecture 26
Dis_Sylphide learning disabled artists 22
Dolar, Mladen 11
Douglas, Angie 95, 188
Downistie 138
Down's Syndrome 8, 27–29, 62, 68, 90, 98, 105, 108, 115, 138, 157, 162, 167
Drag Syndrome 28
drama school model 33, 35, 55–56, 59–60, 123, 152–154, 169
dramatic theatre 18, 34, 81, 84–112, 125, 181
dramaturgy 12, 17, 20–21, 46, 69–70, 77, 87, 100, 109, 111–112
Dynavox speech 92, 94
dysfluency 43

earthquake 34–35, 63, 72, 76, 79, 93, 96, 102–103, 105, 110, 114, 116–118, 120, 124–125, 129, 132, 138, 140, 142, 144, 146–148, 153–154, 159, 175, 182, 185, 190
The Earthquake in Chile 35, 129–131, 159; interventions in performance 131; presentation of gifts 131
ecologies 6, 9, 35, 93, 95, 156, 159–162, 173, 180
Ellenbroek, Ben 73–75, 87
entitled self 15
Entr'Actes 27
epistemic injustice 3, 10, 32, 85, 184
Esposito's concept of 'community' 22
'exceptional' learning disabled people 29

facilitated communication 63, 108, 111
feminist ethics 4
Flint, Rebecca 95–96, 132
Fluency Machines 15, 52
forgiveness 53–54
Foucault, Michel 87, 107
Frankenstein's Children 34, 85, 90–91; improvisations and devising process 90; 'Mapping the Human Genome' 90; production and characters 97–100
Free Theatre Christchurch 129
fugitivity 5–7

Gap Filler 35, 129, 139, 146–147, 169
Garland, Judy 121–123
Garrett, Kim TePairi 8, 133
Geertz, Clifford 3
'giving' itself 51
Gladwin, Bruce 3
Gordy, Sarah 27
Gosset, Katy 23–24, 133–134
Gottsagen, Zack 27–28
Gough, Richard 129
Graeae Theatre 18
Greek philosophy and theatre 47
Green Party 142, 161
Greening the Rubble 35, 129
Guthrey, Julia 87

Halberstam, Jack 152
hangi 175
Hargrave, Matt 17
Harney, Stefano 1, 5, 15, 22, 28, 48, 152
Harrington, Erin 172
Harrop, Lauren 27
Hartman, Saidiya 15
Häusermann, Julia 20
Hayden, Robert 2
Hexentanz 22–23
Hijinx Theatre 184
Hoffman, Theodore 153
Hohepa Canterbury 64, 93, 95
Hohepa residential community 33, 54, 56–57, 60, 64–65, 81, 96, 155–158, 169
hospitality 51–56, 175; in *Acts of Religion* 53
hostility 52–56

identity politics 44, 49
immersive performance 26, 35, 129
improvisation 33, 45, 55–57, 60, 66, 69, 73–75, 81, 86, 89–90, 95–96, 101, 104, 106, 116, 118, 120–121, 123, 126, 140–142, 161, 165, 170
improvisational community 57
inclusion 3, 9, 16, 22, 28–29, 31, 36, 52–53, 61, 64, 69, 85–86, 92, 95, 101, 125–126, 128, 164, 179, 183
inoperative community 56
institution 19, 28–29, 54–57, 59, 61–62, 64, 81, 87–88, 93, 95, 101, 108–109, 120, 122–123, 152, 156–158, 172, 174, 181, 183
intellectual or cognitive disability 31
intermediality 121–124, 181
interviews 12–14
Is it Normal? Any different? 107, 114

Jessop, Tommy 27
Johnstone, Keith 33
Josz, Tatiana 153
journeyings of Māui 180–181

kairos 4–5, 19, 84
kairos as *akroasis* 4–5, 84
kairotic space 4
King, Theresa 95–96
Kittay, Eva Feder 10
Kontakthof 22–23
Kuppers, Petra 7, 35

Lacan, Jacques 46
Laherty, Simon 44
Lambie, John 52, 52, 57–58, 58, 62–66, 71, 87–88, 93, 95, 98–100, 108–111, 115, 119, 122, 131, 142, 155–162, 168, 190, *191*
Laurie, Daniel 27
learning disabled, definition 31–32
learning disabled artists 1, 31; choreographic and aesthetic possibilities 21; inclusion of 16, 36; online participation 183–184; perception as *others* 11; presence and voice of 1, 3; professional acting 85; in television and film 27–28; times and spaces 6
learning disabled experience 3
learning disabled theatre 16; care and rigour principles 2–3; conviviality in 5; critical discussion and analysis 17–23; distinction between *demos* and *idiotai* 49; inter-relationships and interdependence 51; tension in relation 2

200 Index

learning disabled thought 21
Lecoq, Jacques 33, 58–59, 65, 109
legal fiction of self 16
LGBTQ/gender-variant artists 27
liberalism 10
Life in Vacant Spaces 35
lines of flight 169
Lipari, Lisbeth 4
listening 4–6, 9–10; active and passive 5; others to speech 4–5
Lloyd-Harris, Stuart 8, 90, 133
lockdowns 33, 42, 49, 174, 181–183, 186
The Lonely and The Lovely 35, 80, 96, 105, 114, 138–147, 153; characters and actors 140; participants 139; presentation at Christchurch Pecha Kucha 145–147

Mainwaring, Sarah 45–46
major keys 11
mana of learning disabled artists 33
Manning, Erin 9, 11, 16, 49; *Minor Gesture* 11; volitional intentionality agency triad 15
Māoritanga 169
Marlowe's *Dr Faustus* 57
Martinsdottir, Sofie 169
Mashimo, Yayoi 153
Matariki Festival 189
McCaffrey, Paul 8, 12, 100
McCaffrey, Tony 97, 102–104, 144
McLean, Drew 110
Messenger 8, 173
metaphysics of presence 11
mimetic theatre 11, 19, 30, 75, 118
Mind the Gap Theatre 19, 26–27, 29
minor 49
Minor Gesture 11
minor keys 11, 153–154
mixed ability theatre 86, 100–101, 114, 123, 132
Mixed Blood Theatre Company 27
modern agential self 16
Monolingualism of the Other 11, 24
Moomsteatern 26, 183
mosque 174–175
Morris, Ben 70–73, 95, 110, 133–135, 144–145, 153, 161, 175
Moten, Fred 5, 15–16, 22, 31, 48, 152, 156

Nancy, Jean Luc 56
NASDA 8, 35, 60, 90, 101, 114, 116, 132, 143, 152, 169, 185
neoliberalism 55
neoliberal self 15
neurodiverse 31
neurotypical 15, 17, 73, 89, 190
New Zealand male phenomenon 55
New Zealand secondary school system 55
Noble, Josie 95, 132, 144–145, 154, 176, 188
normative self 15

ontology 32, 47, 57
Open Circle Theatre Company 27
O'Rourke, Shawn 76–78, 87, 132
Oswin, Andrew 106
Ōtautahi 188
otherwiseness 32
Outside Voices Theatre Company 27

pandemic 9, 15, 29, 33, 36, 42, 49, 54, 103–104, 181–183, 185–186
Payne, Louise 76, 85, 88, 94–95, 97, 101–102, 106–108, 119, 122, 142, 148, 154–155, 155, 156, 160–162, 168, 173, 190, *191*
Pecha Kucha 145–147, 154, 181
pepeha 139, 156, 169, 187
Per.Arts 4, 22, 26, 30
Performance, Possession, and Automation project 15
Performance Philosophy Problems conference 5, 181, 184–185
performance research 152–155
Phamaly Theatre Company 27
Phelan, Matthew 13, 66–71, 76, 78–79, 86–87, 90, 97–98, 101, 108, 111, 117–119, 122, 139, 142, 157, 159, 161, *163*, 165, 170–171, 173, 179, 185–188
physical theatre 58–60, 81
politics of communication: giving and taking of voice 10–12, 52; interaction with disabled voices 10; process of listening 9–10
polylogues 7, 35, 140
polyphony 35, 135, 140
The Poor Dears 34, 62, 71, 85, 100–102, 106–112; devising methodologies 107–108; dramaturgical strategies 111; narrative framework 107; rehearsal

and production process 111;
  workshop sessions 114
positionality 2
Powerpoint 35, 64, 139, 145
presence in learning disabled theatre
  1, 3
Presley, Elvis 70, 108
Price, Scott 45, 48
Project Eugene 90
prosthesis 18
proximity 3

queer 31
Quick, Caroline 95–97

Rancière, Jacques 15, 146–147
'recovery' 34–35, 116, 125, 129–130,
  138–140, 143, 145
Rees, Peter 13, 117–118, 132, 139,
  141, 144–146, 148, 157, 161, *163*,
  164–165, 167, 170, 183–186, 188,
  191
rehearsal processes 6, 8, 19, 22–24, 59,
  61, 66–67, 73–74, 78, 90, 92–93,
  103, 105, 108, 111, 116–117, 121,
  124, 131, 133, 152, 164, 167–170,
  173, 182, 187, 187, 190
rigour 2–3
Rosebank 155

Saint Pierre, Joshua 10, 15, 43
Salamander 153
Salmond, Dame Anne 175
San Precario 130–131
#*saytheword* movement 31
Scenes of Subjection 51
Schmidt, Yvonne 18–19
self-devising/improvisation 10, 33,
  45, 55, 60–61, 66, 69, 73–75, 77,
  81, 86, 89, 96, 101, 106, 116, 118,
  120–121, 123, 126, 141, 161–162,
  165, 170
self-possession 15–17
*The Shadow Whose Prey the Hunter
  Becomes* 33; allocation of voice
  of authority 43–44; audience 49;
  captions 45–46; identification and
  disclosure of disability 44; identity
  of community 42–43; narrative of
  48; non-specific 'public meeting' 49;
  origin story of 47–48; processes of
  collaboration 47; self and knowledge
  47; subject and object 46; *theatron*
  and *agora* 49; voices 49–50

Ship of Fools 34, 85–89, 112;
  appearance of non-disabled
  performers 88; devising and
  performance methodologies 87, 89;
  narrative and dramaturgy 87
slavery 47–49
Siri 43–45, 49
site-specific performance 26, 35, 94,
  129, 145, 147, 181
soap opera 35, 60, 80, 96, 103, 105,
  138–140, 143–144, 182
Society for Disability Studies 34–35,
  100, 124
'The Socioecological Disaster' 1, 15,
  48
Sophocles' *Oedipus the King* 47
Sound Theatre Company 27
Southern Ballet Theatre 56
speculative practices 6–7
Stanley, Michael 78–81, 87, 95, 109
Steffens, Biddy 95
Steiner, Rudolf 56
Still Lives project 23–25, 34–35, 105,
  128; in Leeds 133–138; opening 125;
  Still Lives Christchurch 132–133;
  stillness 124–125; voices 125–129
study of learning disabled theatre 5–7,
  30
subaltern 17, 51
subjectivity, production of 44
The Sunnyside Project 89, 100–101
support 1–2, 14, 18–19, 31, 58, 60, 78,
  81, 88, 92, 98–99, 107–108, 115,
  121, 127, 129, 131, 133, 142–143,
  156, 164, 166–167, 169–170, 173,
  180–181, 188
Sydney Ballet Company 115

Tait, Isaac 23–25, 85, 94, 101–104,
  107, 111, 118–119, 121, 124–127,
  128, 130–131, 134, 136, 153–154,
  157, 160–162, 164–167, 170, 173,
  175, 184–190, *191*
Tangata Tiriti 187
tangata whenua 190
taonga 172
Teatr 21 26
temporality 5, 10, 81, 84–85, 158
Te Reo Māori 65, 69, 135, 154, 180,
  187
Theater Babbel 26
Theater HORA 4, 17–19, 26, 32
Theatre and Performance Studies 15
Theatre Terrific 27

theatron 49
Three Ecologies of Different Light 95
Till, Richard 129
touring a production overseas 34
transcription 14, 62, 64, 72, 89, 102
Transforming Leadership programme 27
The Triumph of Religion 46
truth-telling 52
turangawaewae 187

The Undercommons 5–6, 22, 30, 152
un-together 9

visibility of learning disabled artists 29
Vladisljević, Natalija 23
voice in language 11
voices of learning disabled artists 1, 3–4, 7, 10–11, 14, 35; female voices in 95–97; polylogues 7; use of assistive devices 92–95
volitional intentionality agency triad 15

Waikuku beach 154
Walton, Natalie 80, 95–96

wandering lines 169
Ward, Charli 19–20
Webster, George 27
Western mimetic theatre 11
whakapapa 65, 156, 164, 169
Whatley, Sarah 2
wheelchair 24, 77, 90, 92, 101, 110, 114–115, 119, 121, 125, 127–128, 135, 137, 143, 146, 154, 160–162, 165, 169, 173, 182, 185–187, 190
Wheeler, Tim 29
Williams, Moira 32
The Wizard of Oz 34, 104–105, 114, 115; devising and performance processes 116, 118–121; intermediality and intertextuality 121–124; negotiation of character, persona, and person 121; rehearsal process 121; theatrical techniques 119–120

Yergeau, M. Remi 4, 45, 47

Zoom 173, 181–182, 185–187